To: _____

From: _____

Date: _____

journey

DAY BY DAY

A Woman's Devotional *from* Walk Thru the Bible

LIVING LIFE WELL

Susan Nelson and Pamela Nixon, *editors*

B&H
PUBLISHING GROUP

www.BHPublishingGroup.com

NASHVILLE, TENNESSEE

978-1-4336-7901-8

Published by B&H Publishing Group
Nashville, Tennessee

Dewey Decimal: 242.643
Subject Heading: WOMEN \ DEVOTIONAL
LITERATURE \ SPIRITUAL LIFE

1 2 3 4 5 6 7 • 17 16 15 14 13

To our dear friend Jill Milligan,
whose extraordinary gifts and dedication
to excellence made an immeasurable impact
at Walk Thru the Bible for twenty-seven years.

Introduction

Everyone loves a good story. Some of your fondest childhood memories may be of a parent or grandparent reading you your favorite bedtime story. During your school years, you may have read books by authors like Beverly Cleary, Louisa May Alcott, Jane Austen, or Charles Dickens.

When you pick up your Bible and read the Gospels, you learn that Jesus was a skillful storyteller. People followed Him and longed for a compassionate glance, a healing touch, or an answer to their desperate need. When crowds gathered around Him, He didn't teach like the Pharisees, dispensing long lists of rules to follow. Instead, Jesus gave them the truth in the form of parables. People loved good stories then, and they love them now.

But as appealing as it is to sit down with a good book, women today may feel they don't have as much time as they would like. In spite of all the modern conveniences we have, we are busier than ever. Many women work, attend Bible studies, contribute to their communities, and care for their families. And in the midst of living our lives, sometimes we deal with issues our mothers and grandmothers never dreamed of.

So for today's busy women, we have compiled 365 one-page devotionals that are written in story form in *Journey: Day by Day*. Rather than the expository style of writing that you may find in your Sunday school lesson, these devotionals are real stories written by women, for women. They realistically address the problems and challenges we face while offering the hope and encouragement found only in the person of Jesus Christ through cultivating a deep, abiding relationship with Him.

I pray that as you take a few minutes to read each devotional and meditate on each verse, You will allow the Lord to speak to your heart. And dear sisters, I pray as you read this book, He will help you grow closer to Him. Because "He who started a good work in you will carry it on to completion until the day of Christ Jesus" (Phil. 1:6).

Susan Nelson

New and Renewed

His mercies never end.
They are new every morning. (Lam. 3:22–23)

"Do you ever get discouraged in your walk with God?" I asked my good friend Kristin. "Do you ever just get stuck and feel like you're struggling with the same old things?"

"Sure, I know what you mean. For example, when I got married, I realized how selfish I could be about doing things my way. Now, even after having three kids, I still struggle with being selfish and wanting to put my desires first."

"It just seems like the more I try to grow, the more I see my sin and the real condition of my heart. It's disappointing to me."

"But at the same time," Kristin said, "the fact that you see your sin more clearly shows that you're growing. It shows that the Holy Spirit is at work in you. And we're supposed to keep running the race, keep our eyes on the prize. We're not going to be perfect this side of heaven, but we can be encouraged that Jesus defeated sin for us, and we are made new because of what He did for us. God sees us as spotless and blameless, white as snow, and He is making us holy."

When we become Christians, we are new creations in Jesus. However, our struggle with sin does not end. We continue to struggle with our sinful desires and with the darkness that surrounds us. But we can live in the security God gives us through Christ, knowing that we are no longer slaves to sin—and that when we do sin, His mercy and compassion still cover us. We will experience growing pains as we see the grip of sinful desires on our hearts, minds, bodies, and relationships; but we can rest in the victory of Jesus, who has made us new and brought us into His kingdom forever.

Everyone's Doing It

Do not be conformed to this age, but be transformed by the renewing of your mind. (Rom. 12:2)

When you hear about unmarried couples living together, you probably picture a young man and woman who have never been married. But now when I hear about couples living together, I think about my granddaughter's other grandma. She divorced her husband last year and now lives with her new boyfriend.

A generation ago most Americans would consider this scandalous. But few people even blink at it today.

My daughter and her husband, for example, don't think it's enough of an issue to forbid their five-year-old daughter Emma from having sleepovers at Grandma Diane and "Grandpa" Craig's house. Diane and Craig also take trips together, and this summer they will be taking my granddaughter with them to Florida for a "family vacation."

Because of the slippery slope on which our society now finds itself, I pray for wisdom for myself, as well as for my daughter and her husband. I pray that in holding fast to a righteous standard, I will still show others God's love, mercy, and grace. But I also pray that He will protect my sweet, innocent granddaughter from adopting beliefs and values that are not consistent with His Word.

Some argue that living together is a good way to "test drive" a couple's compatibility in marriage. But the latest research shows that couples who cohabit before marriage have a much higher divorce rate than those who don't. These couples have higher rates of domestic violence and are more likely to be involved in sexual affairs, since the element of commitment and covenant is so obviously missing. The best advice is still to trust God's wisdom and obey His Word. "Be holy," He says, "because I am holy" (1 Pet. 1:16).

The Confession

Your sins have been forgiven because of Jesus' name. (1 John 2:12)

When my sister Lynn told me she had a confession to make, I thought she'd bring up some minor offense. But when she told me that during her freshman year in college she'd had an affair with a married professor, I was floored. My baby sister, barely eighteen at the time, had slept with a married man who was more than twice her age and who had two teenagers of his own. Lynn began to cry as she told me how she was drawn to his charm and sophistication. Young, naive, and vulnerable, she thought he really cared about her.

Now older and wiser, Lynn knew God had forgiven her, but she hadn't yet forgiven herself. "I just can't believe I was that stupid," she cried. "What was I thinking?"

"Lynn," I said, "we've all done things we regret. God has forgiven you, and He doesn't want you to spend the rest of your life beating yourself up."

"I know, but . . ." Lynn began.

"Do you remember the woman caught in the act of adultery?" I asked. "Jesus told her He didn't condemn her. His forgiveness is so complete, we don't need to add our own to it. All we need to do is just receive His—so fully that we 'go, and sin no more'"(John 8:11 KJV).

Forgiveness can be difficult in any situation. But what about forgiving ourselves? The truth is, if we refuse to experience God's forgiveness by faith, we're actually saying He's not able to cover every sin. Not *this* sin. Not *my* sin. Jesus died for you, and His is the only judgment that matters.

Home Alone

Pity the one who falls without another to lift him up. (Eccl. 4:10)

My husband's employer has transferred us a half a dozen times in sixteen years. When we moved the last time, I was lonely once again. In the mornings David would leave for work, the kids would leave for school, and I was home alone. I'd met a couple of the neighbors, but most of the women worked, and our family hadn't found a new church.

After I unpacked the boxes and organized all the rooms, I began what became a daily routine of sitting down at the computer and joining online chats. But when my friend Connie called long distance to find out how we were settling in, she could sense something wasn't quite right.

"What's going on, Melissa?" she asked.

"Nothing really. We haven't found a church yet, but I'm finally meeting some friends online."

That began a long heart-to-heart conversation, and I told Connie about my struggles with loneliness. She said that while she didn't have anything against appropriate online friendships, I should develop some real relationships. In person.

She was right. It's becoming more common for people to develop relationships through the Internet. And while there's nothing wrong with having friends online (assuming we use caution), God created us for face-to-face interaction. If you or someone you know needs real friendships, limit the time spent online. Get involved with your neighbors, coworkers, and friends at church. Consider volunteering and helping someone else who is lonely. Proverbs 11:25 says, "Whoever refreshes others will be refreshed" (NIV).

Although I still talk to my online friends once in a while, they're not my main source of friendships. I'm glad I took Connie's advice.

I Promised

Rejoice in hope; be patient in affliction;
be persistent in prayer. (Rom. 12:12)

I could hear anxiety in Lisa's voice when I picked up the phone. "Please pray for my mom," she said. "She's having open-heart surgery tomorrow. She's really scared, and even though I know God is in control, I'm scared too. I don't want to lose her." Before I hung up, I promised Lisa I'd pray. But I didn't. I got busy with my own agenda and forgot about Lisa's request.

When I saw her at church on Sunday, I remembered immediately. She ran up and hugged me and said, "Mom is recovering, and the doctor says she's doing well. Thank you so much for praying. It means so much to me."

I felt so guilty. I couldn't bring myself to admit to her that I had forgotten to pray. But when I got home, I *did* pray. I prayed for Lisa, her mother, and her recovery. I asked God to forgive me for taking a request for prayer so lightly. I made up my mind that in the future if someone asked for prayer, I would pray right then and there. I now keep a notebook by the phone, and I check it regularly.

If we had any idea about the power of prayer, we would probably take it a lot more seriously and do a lot more of it. Like Hannah did, and the Lord answered her prayer to have a child (1 Sam. 1). Like Daniel did, and God shut the mouths of lions (Dan. 6:10–24). Like Paul and Silas did—in prison—and God sent an earthquake that opened the doors and loosened their chains (Acts 16:25–34).

You may say, "But I'm just an ordinary person. Can my prayers really make a difference?" Absolutely. James 5:16 says, "The urgent request of a righteous person is very powerful."

The Big Meeting

*Though the LORD is exalted, He takes note of the humble;
but He knows the haughty from a distance. (Ps. 138:6)*

Pamela pulled Rachel aside as everyone exited the staff meeting for lunch. "*You* came up with the idea for the ad Marcus raved about," she whispered. "Why didn't you speak up? That ad was raise material." Rachel shrugged. "If he had asked, I would have said something. But it didn't seem appropriate to draw attention to myself. It was a group project after all."

Rachel recalled the internal battle she'd had during the meeting. Her pride tempted her to take the credit she felt she deserved, especially since she'd done most of the work on the project. But she sensed that God wanted her to let the truth come out in His timing. Before becoming a Christian, she'd have thought nothing of seizing an opportunity for recognition. But God had begun showing her the benefits of humility.

Pamela shook her head. "You're nuts. I wish I were more like you, but I still think you're nuts."

In a competitive world where talent and boldness pay off, it's hard to opt for humility. It can be extra tough in the workplace where those who do the most impressive job get the desired promotions and raises, or at least a lot of pats on the back in the break room. At times we all fight the temptation to promote ourselves and our accomplishments in hopes of gaining more.

Psalm 138:6 says that God "takes note of the humble." Does this mean we should never take due credit or share something God called us to do and equipped us to do well? Not necessarily. His Word shows us repeatedly that the God who knows our hearts and motives simply rewards our willingness to keep quiet when He asks us to.

A Good Deal?

Do not owe anyone anything, except to love one another, for the one who loves another has fulfilled the law. (Rom. 13:8)

Janice listened to Beth talk excitedly about her upcoming trip to the coast and the beautiful condo they'd be staying in. She was a little envious that her friend could still plan such a trip even though Beth and Steve were just as much in debt as Janice and her husband, Tim.

"We probably shouldn't be taking this vacation after we charged so much at Christmas," Beth confessed, "but it's just too good of a deal to pass up!"

"That's exactly what I said every time I pulled out my charge card during the holidays," admitted Janice. "But I'm paying interest on all those 'deals,' and now they don't seem so great."

When Janice and Tim decided to pay off their credit cards, they knew it would require foregoing a summer vacation and cutting back on some other expenses. But she silently thanked God that she and Tim had come up with a budget so they could honor God with their money and enjoy it without guilt.

Many of us ignore our budgets somewhat during Christmas. Little extras like entertaining and decorating can derail our carefully planned holiday budgets and tempt us to pull out the credit card too often. While the Bible doesn't forbid the use of credit cards, it does warn against debt—owing money without a sure and timely way to repay. Credit card debt costs more than just interest fees; it robs us of financial freedom, steals our financial integrity, and restricts our ability to minister to others in need.

If your debts are mounting instead of decreasing, prayerfully consider how God would have you regain control over your finances. Ask Him to help you handle your money with integrity.

Your Mighty Warrior

*The husband is head of the wife as Christ is the head of the church.
He is the Savior of the body. (Eph. 5:23)*

Monica stretched out on the sofa, adjusting the cast that weighed down her injured leg. She heard her husband getting dinner on the table for the rest of the family. Mike encouraged their rambunctious boys to wash their hands and get to the table.

Monica was the one who usually reminded the boys to bow their heads while she prayed before the meal. Because Mike once said he wasn't comfortable praying aloud, she always spoke the prayers at family meals and bedtimes but hoped he would eventually step up and become the spiritual leader in their home. So far Mike hadn't attempted to own that role.

Monica listened more closely to the lively conversation in the dining room. She heard chairs scooting closer to the table and then Mike's firm, steady voice saying, "Boys, let's bow our heads." There was a pause, then, "Father, thank You . . ."

Closing her eyes, Monica breathed a prayer of her own. *Lord, help me get out of the way so Mike has the opportunity to be the spiritual leader. Show me how to encourage him in that role.*

Some women complain that their husbands don't take the spiritual lead in their home. Whether the husband is unsaved, spiritually immature, or seemingly unmotivated, he simply won't (or perhaps can't) lead his family. What can a wife do in such a case?

First, pray for your husband to have an increased desire for the things of God and to know how to lead you graciously. Next, give him opportunities to lead. Treat him like a leader and be willing to follow. And try not to criticize when he does lead.

Marital Status?

If anyone is in Christ, he is a new creation; old things have passed away, and look, new things have come. (2 Cor. 5:17)

"Rhonda, we're just concerned. Your father and I married when we were twenty-two. You're almost thirty." Rhonda felt the familiar tightening in her stomach as she tried to smile politely. She knew her mom meant well, but this conversation always made her feel like there was something wrong with her.

"Mom, I'll get married when God brings the right man, and if that isn't until later—or never—then it will be all right."

"I know, I know. Your father and I think if you just tried harder."

"I don't know, Mom," Rhonda said, growing impatient.

"Because I think I have the perfect guy for you."

After her mother left, Rhonda threw herself on the couch in exasperation. *Lord, am I not married because there is something wrong with me?* she asked. Suddenly, it occurred to her that Jesus was never married. She actually laughed out loud as she thought of how silly it had been to equate her worth with her marital status.

Even well-meaning people can make singles feel like misfits if they aren't dating or engaged. In Mark 12:25, Jesus says that people won't be married in heaven. Paul advises that some people shouldn't marry so they can serve God without distraction. The truth is, God doesn't look at us as an incomplete person if we aren't married. We are loved by Him simply because we are His children, regardless of our marital status. Our relationship to Jesus is what matters, and God sent Jesus to die for the unmarried, the married, the widowed, the divorced . . . for everyone.

Stand against Injustice

A generous person will be blessed, for he shares his food with the poor. (Prov. 22:9)

When I was in college, I had a roommate who sponsored a young African girl, whose smile radiated from her photo despite her obvious poverty. Tara sent money every month that helped pay for food, medical needs, and even an education. She wrote letters to encourage her and tell her about the Lord, and she prayed for her.

I was impressed by Tara's generosity and compassion. But living on ramen noodles and barely able to afford to keep my clothes washed, I didn't see how I could ever give that money every month. Yet it didn't take me long to figure out that God cares deeply about the plight of the less fortunate, and that, despite my ramen noodle dinners, I wasn't the less fortunate one.

Strangely, once I understood God's heart, it wasn't at all difficult to pay the monthly sponsorship fee. In faith I pledged to support a little boy in Brazil, trusting that God could continue to supply all of my needs, as well as little Wellington's. Nine years later I have no doubt that I made the right decision and continue to enjoy my relationship with my Brazilian friend.

God is a champion for the needy and abused in this world. Fifty-six percent of the world's population currently lives on less than two dollars a day. Women and girls in the Congo are being brutalized by men who believe doing so gives them "good magic." Some believers in Thailand aren't allowed to translate the Bible into their language, enduring imprisonment and torture for their faith. As Christ's followers, we can't ignore these and so many other injustices. Pray today about how God wants to use you to make a difference.

Am I a Good Mom?

If any of you lacks wisdom, he should ask God,
who gives to all generously and without criticizing,
and it will be given to him. (James 1:5)

"Misty," I asked my best friend, "do you think I'm a good mom?"

"Of course you are," she replied without hesitation.

"After yesterday I'm beginning to wonder. You know I mentioned that Jonathan has been acting up in school occasionally. Yesterday one of the other mothers told me Jonathan hit her son. I was so embarrassed. When Jonathan got home from school, I didn't even give him a chance to explain. I just ended up yelling at him."

"Sharon, I'm not saying that it's OK to lose your temper, but sometimes it happens. Have you apologized to Jonathan?" Misty asked.

"Yes," I replied, "but it doesn't change the fact that I lost my cool. It seems like a constant battle to get him to listen, but yelling isn't the solution."

"We all make mistakes, but you can't let the enemy trick you into thinking you're a bad mom." Misty gave me a quick hug. We bowed our heads and asked God to give both of us wisdom to be good moms and for me to let go of guilt for past mistakes.

No mother is perfect, but don't ever forget that God chose you specifically to be the mother of your children. He knew ahead of time what specific challenges both you and your children would face. God also gives us loving advice in His Word about how to raise our children. We need to make sure we are setting a good example and disciplining our children in a Christlike manner. Proverbs 2:6 says, "The LORD gives wisdom; from His mouth come knowledge and understanding." And remember, "With God all things are possible" (Matt. 19:26).

Stop and Think

Though the tongue is a small part of the body, it boasts great things. Consider how large a forest a small fire ignites. (James 3:5)

"Kevin," Devendra called as she tossed her husband's clothes into the hamper, "you left your clothes on the floor again! Can't you ever pick them up yourself?"

"What's that, honey?" Kevin called from the couch. The TV was tuned into the football game, and he hadn't heard a word she'd said. Devendra walked into the family room and stood in front of the television, glaring at Kevin.

"I'm not your mother, and I shouldn't have to pick up your clothes," Devendra snapped. "Why don't you pick up after yourself?"

Kevin paused the DVR and looked at his wife apologetically. "I'm sorry. I didn't do it to annoy you." Devendra sighed. She was about to say more when she felt the Holy Spirit prompting her to stop and think before she said something to escalate the situation. She sat down next to Kevin and hugged him. "I'm sorry I get so snippy sometimes. Will you forgive me?" Kevin pulled her close. "Of course. And I'll work on picking up after myself, OK?"

One of the biggest battles we face is controlling the tongue. James 3:8 reminds us that "no man can tame the tongue. It is a restless evil, full of deadly poison." We all have times when we want to speak our mind, but we should pause to seek wisdom for tact and timing. Some things are just better left unsaid. First Peter 3:10 says, "The one who wants to love life and to see good days must keep his tongue from evil and his lips from speaking deceit." When you're tempted to give someone a piece of your mind, stop and think about the consequences first.

Sabbath Keeping

*The LORD made the heavens and the earth,
the sea, and everything in them in six days;
then He rested on the seventh day. (Exod. 20:11)*

One day I woke up with a terrible pain in my chest. I thought I was having a heart attack. My husband was frightened; he bundled me up and took me to the doctor. The diagnosis? Acid reflux, probably stress induced. After instructions from my doctor on stress management, I left her office armed with pills and dietary restrictions.

Having recently returned to work full-time, I no longer have much time to relax. At home, chores beckon, laundry duty calls, and empty stomachs wait impatiently for the meals I prepare. And Sundays, the Lord's day, are not much better. My responsibilities at church overwhelm me at times. But this little setback is His reminder that I must rest and "remember the Sabbath day" (Exod. 20:8). God knows that refreshment is necessary, and relaxation is key.

It may be difficult to shift my focus from the tyranny of the urgent. But next Sunday, after worshipping my Creator, I'm going for a walk in the park, noticing the clouds, the ants, the beavers in the pond. Then I'll play with my kids, and later I'll take a nap!

God told the Israelites to honor His day. In Exodus 31:15, He said, "Work may be done for six days, but on the seventh day there must be a Sabbath of complete rest, dedicated to the LORD." They were to do no work on the Sabbath, collect no manna on the Sabbath, light no fire on the Sabbath. Animals and slaves rested too.

Refreshment is life and health, prescribed by our Master Physician. Busyness, stress, and anxiety are killers. So within God's good guidelines, do things to promote life and health on the Sabbath.

Tough Love

The LORD disciplines the one He loves, just as a father,
the son he delights in. (Prov. 3:12)

"Did you hear *The Dr. Matthews' Show* yesterday?" my friend Annie asked. "A mom called in asking how to handle her son's disrespectful attitude, and Dr. Matthews said she should let it go, that it's just a phase her child will grow out of. What do you think about that?"

"God teaches that children should honor their parents," I replied, "and if we parent by His standards, we must teach our children how to be respectful. It's not loving to let your child live in disregard of authority or in disobedience to God's Word."

"So how would you handle that?" Annie asked.

"One way we deal with disobedience at our house is with a privilege chart. When one of the boys disobeys, he loses one of the privileges on the chart—like video games—for the rest of the day. So far that's worked really well for our family."

Children need loving guidance every step of the way, and this requires careful, intentional, biblical parenting. Parents have the God-given responsibility to train and direct children in the way they should go. God trains and disciplines us in love for our well-being and to help us become more like Jesus. That's the biblical model for raising our own children.

As you seek balance and wisdom in discipline, be prayerful. Ask God to show you your child's struggles and how to deal with them effectively and lovingly. We have a tremendous responsibility to raise them in the fear and knowledge of God, a task that can only be achieved by His grace and power. Pray that your child will be given a heart that seeks the Lord and obeys His authority so that he or she might live and love as Jesus did.

Speak Up

Always be ready to give a defense to anyone who asks you for a reason for the hope that is in you. (1 Pet. 3:15)

My sister Elizabeth was diagnosed with celiac disease three years ago. Dr. Patil told her she could no longer eat or even touch foods containing wheat because it would act like poison to her body. But recently during a routine checkup, Dr. Patil said all her tests were clear—the celiac was gone. Overjoyed, Elizabeth said, "God healed me, Dr. Patil! I've been praying that Jesus would take away this illness, and I believe He has."

Dr. Patil looked surprised. "I've heard of Jesus, but I've never heard anyone talk about Him like He's their friend." Dr. Patil explained that he was raised Hindu, but now he only believed in science. Elizabeth wondered aloud if he would like to talk more about Jesus. When he murmured a soft consent, she invited his family to eat dinner with her family. And he actually accepted. Two weeks later Elizabeth and Ron welcomed the Patil family to their home, and a friendship began to grow.

Jesus said, "I am the way, the truth, and the life. No one comes to the Father except through Me" (John 14:6). In a world that believes many roads lead to God, we must hold fast to the truth that every person needs Jesus, and He is the only way to the Father. We can reach out in love to non-Christians, speaking and living the gospel before them. By prayerfully building relationships with them, we can talk about our relationship with God through Christ. A friendship includes dialogue, so we must be willing to listen. Then, as God provides the opportunity, we can share our faith as the Holy Spirit leads us.

Do Not Fear

In God, whose word I praise, in God I trust; I will not fear. (Ps. 56:4)

"Couple Ordered to Stop Holding Bible Study at Home Without Permit," the headlines on the news website said. "The pastor and his wife have been told that they cannot invite friends to their San Diego, California, home for a Bible study—unless they are willing to pay tens of thousands of dollars to San Diego County."

I was shocked, but at the same time I've seen it coming. Ridicule and downright hatred of traditional values and the people who hold them has been growing. Nativity scenes normally displayed during Christmas (now called "Winter Holidays" in some places to be politically correct) are being banned in various locations. The Ten Commandments have been banished from public buildings. Alternative lifestyles and couples living together before marriage have been promoted and accepted. In the media and on the Internet we hear and read stories of increasing violence and sexuality.

The story I read was chilling, and the prospect of further trouble and persecution was frightening. But later that night as I studied my Bible, God reminded me that He is in control.

No matter what is happening in our country and around the world, God wants us to maintain a healthy perspective on what we see and hear. Yes, we need to be informed and keep abreast of issues that are of great importance to people of faith. But over and over again throughout God's Word, we are told not to worry. When we see national and world events appearing to unravel before our eyes, be encouraged. Luke 21:28 says, "When these things begin to take place, stand up and lift up your heads, because your redemption is near!"

Where Will You Serve?

*Based on the gift each one has received, use it to serve others,
as good managers of the varied grace of God. (1 Pet. 4:10)*

When our children were young, my husband and I helped in the nursery at church. Due to a lack of volunteers, all parents who had infants and preschoolers served on a rotational basis. As a stay-at-home mom, I was around kids 24–7, so when it was our turn for nursery duty, I wasn't exactly jumping up and down with excitement. I didn't feel called to serve there full-time, but since we had kids in the nursery, we took our turn, just like everyone else.

As our children grew older, I taught Bible studies and mentored younger women. It was rewarding to help some of them through stressful stages in life that I had already gone through. But now that our children are grown and gone, I miss holding little ones in my lap and cuddling with them in a comfortable rocker. We're blessed with five grandchildren, but most of them live far enough away that we don't see them as often as we'd like.

Since I am feeling the ache of an empty nest, I realized it was time to start serving in the nursery again. The preschool director was delighted to have a volunteer and said she usually has to beg for help. So now for this season in my life, I'll be working with babies and toddlers. God has put this desire in my heart, and I want to be obedient to His call to serve these little ones.

Often it seems like a few people end up doing most of the work in church. But that's not how God wants us to function. He has uniquely gifted each one of us and wants us to use our gifts to serve others in the body of Christ.

For What Purpose?

We know that the whole creation has been groaning together with labor pains until now. (Rom. 8:22)

Suffering was first made real to me when I witnessed my mother struggle with asthma. Watching her fight for breath, seeing her neck strain and her chest heave, I felt helpless when her medication didn't work and the paramedics took too long to arrive. On three occasions it nearly took her life.

But suffocation wasn't her only suffering. When she was fifty-one, her son (my brother) was killed in an auto accident. Mentally and spiritually, she was never the same. She slid into depression and blamed herself for all kinds of things she thought could have changed the outcome of the accident. That summer, I believe, was when she lost her will to live.

Then two years ago her kidneys and liver began to fail, and her life of various sufferings advanced to a whole new level. Slowly her body shut down organ by organ until her breathing became like that of a child, easy and rhythmic, and she passed away in peace. Her suffering was over. I can look at my mom's life and make sense of the suffering. In her final weeks she prayed, "Thank You, Lord, for this situation, for it draws me and my family closer to You."

Suffering impacts everyone, and its purpose, at first glance, may elude explanation. But we know it gives us an opportunity to bring glory to God. It is a tool of holiness, changing us and shaping us into the image of Christ. It helps us empathize with others and comfort them as we have been comforted. It turns our attention toward heaven and Jesus' suffering on the cross, where He paid for our sins so we might know God and have eternal life.

Everyone's Mommy

We must not get tired of doing good, for we will reap at the proper time if we don't give up. (Gal. 6:9)

"I thought mothering would stop when my youngest went off to college," Kacy said. "Yesterday I received three teary calls from Kate about the breakup with her fiancé. Then my mom called in hysterics, thinking she heard someone in her yard. Her prowler turned out to be an overgrown rosebush scraping against the side of the house."

Rachel hugged Kacy and laughed. "Welcome to the Everyone's Mommy Club. Remember what I went through with my dad, while the girls were off at college, one partying instead of studying and the other changing majors every semester?" Kacy nodded. How many times had they prayed together during that year? "I stayed sane by praying constantly, venting when I needed to, and clinging to Jesus. Now I see how He used that stage to teach me patience and to entrust my girls to Him. Look at them now. They're doing great."

Kacy prayed silently, *What do You want to teach me during this stage, Lord? Help me cling to You as Rachel did and to remember it won't last forever.*

Our kids don't stop needing us when they leave home. Many empty nesters barely have time to enjoy extra couple time before calls begin flooding in from adult children. "The wedding is off." "Can I borrow rent money?" For those also caring for aging parents, life can feel crushing. But like the terrible twos and the teen years, each stage is temporary. And God is with us through all of it, carrying us in His strength, teaching us new things, giving us grace to love those who are calling on us for help.

A Mark of Shame

*Restore the joy of Your salvation to me,
and give me a willing spirit. (Ps. 51:12)*

Amy hurried back to her car, holding back the tears that had been welling in her eyes since the doctor first gave her the news. Chlamydia. She quickly got into her car and pulled out the information sheet. Now that tears were pouring down her cheeks, she could barely read the pamphlet.

"Chlamydia . . . a common sexually transmitted disease (STD) . . . can damage a woman's reproductive organs . . . serious complications . . . can occur 'silently' before a woman ever recognizes a problem." Amy looked up, startled, hearing someone knocking on her car window.

Dr. Canfield's nurse, who was also a friend, motioned for Amy to let her in. After seating herself in the car, Leslie assured Amy that the antibiotic prescribed by the doctor should take care of the infection.

"But I'm so ashamed," confessed Amy. "I'm a Christian, and I promised not to have sex outside of marriage."

"Oh, Amy," Leslie replied, "I understand. Could I pray for you right now?"

Amy nodded. As Leslie prayed, Amy began to remember God's grace and feel hopeful.

Many of us live with the painful consequences of past sins, but God can remove the shame attached to that consequence and redeem it for good. Make sure you've confessed and repented of the sin that brings such guilt; but once you have, accept God's gracious gift of forgiveness and refuse to let the enemy shame you again. God doesn't want His children to live in shame and hopelessness.

Rough Patches

I follow close to You; Your right hand holds on to me. (Ps. 63:8)

Dana pulled down the garage door on the storage unit, picked up the box of miscellaneous items she had decided her family might need, and headed to the car where her mother waited for her. The familiar tears threatened to flow again, but she fought them back as she got in the car.

"Dana, honey," her mom said, "I know this is a difficult time for you, but we're more than glad to have you, Jim, and the kids living with us for a while."

"I know, Mom," Dana replied, wiping away a persistent tear. "I'm glad we have family to help us through this foreclosure. I just never thought this would happen to us; and, quite honestly, I'm ashamed. I know Jim is too."

Dana's mom thought a moment before she responded. "Instead of being ashamed, why don't you just look at this as a humbling situation? Shame might push you away from God, but humility will draw you closer to Him."

Most families experience a few crisis situations over the years. Whether you struggle with financial losses, a serious illness, the death of a loved one, the physical destruction of a home, or a horrible crime, your family will undoubtedly experience its share of grief and pain.

When you approach a crisis with attitudes such as bitterness, anger, shame, resentment, and pride, the situation will almost certainly get the best of you. But God tells us that if we respond to trials with submission, faith, humility, and dependence on Him, He will exalt us at the proper time. He'll also work in the situation to produce good results out of what seems to be so terribly bad. How will you respond to the difficult times ahead?

The Date Debate

My son, pay attention to my words;
listen closely to my sayings. (Prov. 4:20)

My fifteen-year-old son stared across the table in shock. After praying about it, my husband and I had decided against traditional dating for Josh. But I guess this was news to him. "You mean I can't go out to dinner with a girl?" demanded Josh.

"We didn't say that," said my husband, "but that kind of dating will probably be the exception, not the norm. We'd like you to get to know a young lady through group outings and by spending time together with your family."

"I have to bring the girl to meet you?" asked Josh.

"Josh, we're simply saying if there is a girl you want to spend time with, we'll want to meet her, and we'd like you to do some of your socializing with her in our home or on outings with us," I explained. "We won't be difficult about this. You can have her over to play games, visit on the back porch, or watch a movie together . . . when one of us is here, of course."

The discussion was difficult, but we got through it. And six months later when Josh asked if he could invite a "friend" over for pizza and games, he seemed eager to comply with our rules.

Ready or not, your children will eventually want to spend time with someone of the opposite sex. Will you allow traditional dating? Do you prefer group outings? Will you require them to introduce their friends to you and to spend time with your family? Before you answer, consider what you want this time in your child's life to accomplish. Pray about your decision, talk with other wise Christian parents, and look for Christian books on the subject. Then discuss your standards with your children and be willing to listen while remaining true to your convictions.

The Choice

Sons are indeed a heritage from the LORD, children, a reward. (Ps. 127:3)

The Chinese couple had a choice to make. They were only allowed one child, and it looked like they were going to have a mentally handicapped son. Their doctors urged them to have an abortion. But their belief in Jesus and in the value of all human lives as God's creation wouldn't let them give in to the temptation to terminate the pregnancy. Though their hopes, like all parents, were for a healthy child, they knew if God was in control, He had a purpose even in this.

Ten years later I had the privilege of teaching that little boy. Not only were the doctors' predictions wrong, but James was also a delight to his classmates and me. Class leader, star of school musicals, gifted pianist, straight-A student, and best of all, a tender and humble heart for Christ. Knowing his story, I took great joy in watching James thrive that year. He was a gift who would have never existed if his parents had listened to fear instead of trusting God.

Unlike James's parents, many girls who get pregnant feel confused and helpless. Maybe they are young and unmarried. Possibly they haven't finished school, or they have career plans. An abortion may be tempting, but the Bible teaches that God is the Author of life and He loves life (Matt. 22:32).

If you or someone you know may be unable to raise an unborn child, people on long waiting lists want to adopt. Women who face an unwanted pregnancy can get help and encouragement at a crisis pregnancy center. Ask the God who loves you and created all life to give courage to women who find themselves in difficult situations so their children can have a chance at a lifetime.

A Little Help

*God in His holy dwelling is a father of the fatherless
and a champion of widows. (Ps. 68:5)*

The image of Ashley and her daughters at the playground after church stayed with me all week. I glanced over and saw her holding baby Bella on her hip, waiting for Ally to come down the slide. "You can do it, honey," she said. "I'm right here." Ally shook her head. "No, Mommy," she said, starting to cry. "It's too high!"

"What if I come beside you and hold your hand while you slide down?" Sniffling, Ally nodded. Ashley walked over, reached up, and took her daughter's hand. She tugged gently, and down the little girl went, squealing all the way. "I did it! I did it!" she cried, beaming.

"I knew you could," Ashley said quietly. "You just needed a little help. Everybody needs help sometimes."

I noticed that Ashley's shoulders were slumped, and she looked tired. I felt a pang in my heart and wondered if, like her Ally, she needed help too. I didn't know her well, but I knew that single mothers have a hard life trying to raise their kids while making enough money to get by. I prayed, *God, what can I do to help Ashley? Please show me.* Soon I had several ideas, including inviting them over for lunch next Sunday.

If you know a single mom, chances are she needs help in some way, whether financially, practically, or emotionally. What can you do to ease her burden, even if just for a little while? You could offer to babysit, help fix things around the house, give coupons or gift cards to stores or kid-friendly restaurants, invite them to Sunday dinner and even holiday gatherings. Listening to and praying for her and her kids can also help lift her burden.

Copyright Laws

"Hey Mom, how come this DVD doesn't have a picture on it?" my eight-year-old son asked. "It's just got the name of the DVD written on it with marker."

I didn't like the fact that my brother-in-law downloaded movies off the Internet. My husband, Joe, had confronted Danny about it during his recent visit, but stealing what Danny considered to be "free" just didn't seem to register with him.

"It doesn't have a picture on it because it was downloaded from the Internet," I admitted. I hated explaining that to my son, but I didn't want to lie to him either. I was angry with my brother-in-law for setting a bad example for my son.

"Oh. How come he doesn't buy the DVD from the store like everyone else?"

"Well," I said, "Uncle Danny told Daddy that he's trying to save money. But the truth is that he's breaking the law. If he gets caught, he would have to pay huge fines and face the possibility of jail time."

"Then why does he do it, Mom? I don't want Uncle Danny to go to jail."

"Neither do I, sweetie."

Our children are always watching us. They see our behavior and want to emulate us. Are your children learning that as Christians they need to "be imitators of God" (Eph. 5:1), or are they learning that things such as downloading movies and songs without paying for them is OK as long as they don't get caught?

God wants us to live our lives in a way that is pleasing to Him. Romans 14:12 says, "Each of us will give an account of himself to God." Our godly examples will bear witness to our children.

Confidence in Your Mate

Just as you want others to do for you,
do the same for them. (Luke 6:31)

"It must be hard having your 'handsome doctor' husband working with all of those women. Do you ever wonder if he'll be unfaithful?" I was a bit taken aback by my neighbor Mary's boldness.

I said, "I did have some jealousy issues when Mark and I first got engaged, but when I prayed about it, God gave me the confidence I needed to admit my insecurities to Mark. It really helped him to see things from my point of view."

Mary said, "I don't know if I would have been able to keep from getting jealous if it was me. But I'm suspicious about a lot of things. That happens when you've been cheated on before. But maybe you two are different." Mary was still bitter after her divorce. Her ex-husband had had an affair with a coworker for two years before Mary discovered it.

"I'm sorry for what you went through," I said. "But Mark and I decided from the beginning that neither one of us would put ourselves in vulnerable positions where we might be tempted. We have certain rules we've agreed on when interacting with the opposite sex—like no confiding about our marriage, avoiding spending time alone together—things like that. We asked God to give us both wisdom and to help us keep our hearts pure."

Marriage is a covenant we make with God and with our spouse—the joining together of two people who follow Him and live according to His laws. It's not easy to trust another person, especially if you've been hurt before. But God can heal your wounds and help you have the kind of healthy relationship that brings glory and honor to Him. Trust Him to meet all of your needs.

Uncertain Future

*Your heart must not be troubled. Believe in God;
believe also in Me. (John 14:1)*

"I'm worried that Peyton might have some kind of learning disability," my friend Kristen said as we walked up the hill. "I just had the midyear parent-teacher conference, and she hasn't been progressing like her classmates."

"What did her teacher say?"

"She said I should consider having Peyton tested. I just called to set up an appointment for later this week. They'll be running tests on her—everything from vision tests to hyper-activity and dyslexia." Kristen shook her head. "I know she's a smart girl. I just wish everyone else saw the potential in her that I see."

I put my hand on Kristen's shoulder and asked if we could pray. We both bowed our heads. "Heavenly Father," I prayed, "please give Peyton's doctors and specialists wisdom about the issues she may be having. Give her confidence and help her excel in school. Father, we thank You for this precious little girl and ask that You bless her. Please give Kristen peace." Although neither one of us knew what the future held, we knew God did, and that He is in control.

He tells us, "Don't worry about tomorrow, because tomorrow will worry about itself. Each day has enough trouble of its own" (Matt. 6:34). God doesn't want us to worry about our children. If they are having problems of any kind, He wants us to pray, trust Him with the results, and leave the situation in His hands.

He reminds us in Isaiah 26:3 that "You will keep the mind that is dependent on You in perfect peace, for it is trusting in You." No matter what you may be going through, God wants you to cast your cares on Him and believe with unwavering faith that He will take care of those needs.

Miracle in a Tree

God, who is like You? (Ps. 71:19)

I was fretting again. My husband has been out of work for a while. God has taken good care of us, but sometimes it's tough to be that dependent. Sometimes our thoughts stray to the "what ifs" of life without a steady income.

Lately I've been worried about a tree, of all things. A pine tree in our backyard keeps dropping bits and pieces of itself onto the grass. I've brought it to my husband's attention, but having the tree cut down isn't in the budget right now. While we ignore it, however, I fear it will drop something on someone's head or fall on the house. That tree has become a symbol of stress for me.

Last night we had a terrific thunderstorm, full of wind, lightning, and lots of rain. When the storm was over, we saw that the tree had come down, snapping off about ten feet above the ground. It had fallen away from the house into a creek that borders our backyard. Since the storm had torrential rains, the creek was rushing, sweeping away a major portion of the tree.

I knew in that moment that I was looking again at the miracle of God's provision, as if He were saying to me, *I still see you. I'm still here. And I'm still taking care of you.* He knocked the tree down safely to a size my husband could now manage, and He even swept half of it away! The tree became another symbol of His love for me.

Our God still works miracles. He still provides. He still takes care of His own. His provision probably won't look the way you think it will, but He can do things we could never dream of. Look for the miraculous in your every day.

Healing Broken Hearts

He heals the brokenhearted and binds up their wounds. (Ps. 147:3)

". . . and then he said he didn't love me anymore." Stella's voice cracked. She began to cry. Rhonda struggled with how to respond. She could hear the pain in Stella's words. Having known Stella and Tom for years, she couldn't conceive of him leaving her. They seemed to have the ideal marriage. Rhonda fumbled for the right words to say, but her mind was blank. "Stella, I'm in shock. I can't imagine this. I wish I knew what to say."

"What can you say?" Stella said. "I just don't understand. I never thought he'd do anything like this."

"Stella, I know how painful this is, and I want you to know I'm here for you. We'll get through this together. God has answers for you, and I promise to help you find them. Let me pray with you."

When a friend's marriage falls apart, we struggle to know what to do. Particularly if we have not successfully worked through a serious marital crisis ourselves, it may look hopeless in our eyes. But when God is brought into the situation, marriages can be restored. God promises that He "heals the brokenhearted and binds up their wounds" (Ps. 147:3). He tells us, "My ways are higher than your ways" (Isa. 55:9). Even a person who feels no love for his spouse may discover months later that those feelings of love have returned when God has a chance to work in both their lives.

If you have a friend in marital crisis, spend time with her, listen to her, give her hope, and encourage her to give it time. Studies show that many people who persevere are able to reconcile and end up with a stronger marriage than before.

Busy

He leads the humble in what is right and teaches them His way. (Ps. 25:9)

Valerie glanced at the clock on the dashboard. *If I can just make it through this traffic, I can pick the kids up at school and get them to soccer practice on time.* Valerie seemed to be busier than most of the women she knew. Although she was a single, working mom, she agreed to provide items for school bake sales whenever she was asked. She drove her children and their friends to sports practice and special events on a regular basis. She was also active in her Sunday school class and hosted a small group in her home on Thursday nights.

Valerie frequently groused about how little sleep she got and how her prayer times were sporadic at best. When her best friend Karen asked her why she didn't cut back on her schedule, Valerie said she couldn't because so many people needed her help.

Karen asked, "Is there maybe a little pride involved in working more, being busier, getting less sleep, and spending more time in the minivan than anyone else?" Valerie was stunned, and for a moment she couldn't think of an answer. "I . . . I don't know. I never thought of it that way before. Maybe you've got a point. I know one thing—I've got to make some changes. I just can't keep up the pace anymore."

Women may get too busy because they want to please everyone or they have a hard time saying no. But sometimes, on an unconscious level, busyness is due to pride and the need to feel important. God doesn't want us to be so busy we're overwhelmed; He just wants us obedient to the things He calls us to do, knowing we are completely accepted and unconditionally loved by Him.

There Is a Season

[God] has made everything appropriate in its time. (Eccl. 3:11)

I don't know how my sweet mother did it. She had two daughters at home: a tween (that would be my sister) and a bratty teenager (that would be me). My sister was the perfect one; I was just learning how to drive (and driving my parents crazy) and not doing very well in trigonometry. Then our grandmother, Nonni—Mom's mom—had a stroke.

Nonni came to live with us. She was still ambulatory, but she did not know danger. She would get up and walk around in the middle of the night; she would turn on the stove and leave it on; she would forget to chew her food. It was almost like having a grown-up two-year-old in a house that wasn't baby proofed.

It was an extremely hard time for my mom. She tried desperately to be the wife, mother, and daughter she felt she had to be. Always on call, my mom became physically, spiritually, and emotionally exhausted.

Years later, when I had my first baby, Mom told me I couldn't be all things to all people. She said there are seasons in a woman's life, like when Nonni lived with us, when we simply cannot do everything and be everything. The demands are just too great. She told me to delegate, to let some things go, and to seek and accept help.

Are you in a challenging season? Perhaps you have a new baby or a teenager at home, or you're going through a season of unemployment or relocation. Some seasons are joyful and full of love and laughter. Other seasons are sad, disappointing, or frightening. Just remember that seasons don't last forever. God will give you the grace you need for each day.

When Pain Won't End

*My heart races, my strength leaves me, and even
the light of my eyes has faded. (Ps. 38:10)*

On Super Bowl Sunday my husband injured his back while shoveling snow. This catapulted him into months of doctor visits, physical therapy, cortisone injections, and other treatments that only took the edge off his pain. Back surgery finally brought relief, but until then the kids and I saw the toll that physical suffering can take on a person's mood and energy level.

I got a taste of physical pain soon afterward when I had both my gallbladder and appendix removed within six weeks of each other. In both cases surgery came as a welcome light at the end of the tunnel. Recovering from incisions felt like nothing compared to the agony of a sick organ.

Once we'd both recovered, I wondered about those who live with pain for years with no relief in sight. Some work, serve in their churches, attend Bible study, and even care for their children while managing a painful illness or the results of an injury. My experiences gave me an extra dose of empathy. How could I be more sensitive? How could I help? How could I offer encouragement? When I see someone now who is obviously hurting physically, I say a quick prayer that God will give them strength and relief.

All of us endure pain on occasion—ailments that zap our energy and seem like they'll last forever—but they eventually end. Perhaps these experiences can prompt us to pray for those who are in pain on a regular basis. Who needs some extra strength today? Who needs to find the right medical treatment to ease his or her suffering? Who needs a healing touch from God and a reminder that He will sustain them until He calls them home?

Respect

The wife is to respect her husband. (Eph. 5:33)

My husband, Brad, sat at the desk in our den paying bills. I was in the kitchen trying to scrape up some crusty remnants that had spilled on the bottom of the oven so I could start dinner. When I heard Brad call me, I heaved a sigh and rolled my eyes. "Now what does he want?" I muttered, not realizing my daughter had just walked into the room. When I saw Emily, my memory verse from the previous week's Bible study flashed in my mind: "May these words of my mouth and this meditation of my heart be pleasing in your sight, LORD, my Rock and my Redeemer" (Ps. 19:14 NIV).

I was convicted. I knew my rolling eyes and heavy sighs were evidence of a bad attitude and didn't teach my daughter a thing about respect. No wonder Emily had the same reaction when I asked her to do something.

I've asked the Lord to take control not only of my words but also of all other signs of disrespect, both verbal and nonverbal. We are commanded in Scripture to teach our children about God's laws and show them how that will look as we walk it out in our lives. How can we expect our children to respect us if we don't give others the same courtesy? Respect should extend to others outside the family circle as well—teachers, police officers, pastors, and yes, even those who hold elected office, whether we voted for them or not.

Romans 13:7 says, "Pay your obligations to everyone: taxes to those you owe taxes, tolls to those you owe tolls, respect to those you owe respect." Ask the Lord to show you if there is someone to whom you need to show more respect.

Looking Good!

A person's pride will humble him,
but a humble spirit will gain honor. (Prov. 29:23)

I stood in the ladies' room at work and looked at myself in the mirror. A twenty-pound weight loss, a new hairdo, and a new outfit. *Looking good,* I said to myself. I checked my lipstick one last time and strutted out to the break room.

I walked over to the coffeemaker and smiled at Greg, our computer guru. "Hi, how's it going?" I asked as I filled my mug. "Mmm, OK," he mumbled as he looked the other way and grabbed the creamer. *What's wrong with him today?* I wondered. I stirred my coffee as my friend Rita walked over to me. She had a smile on her face that resembled a crooked stick.

"Your skirt," Rita hissed. "I'll walk behind you and follow you to the ladies' room." I felt the back of my skirt and realized that part of it was tucked inside my panty hose, partially exposing my backside. I was mortified! Yeah, I was looking good all right.

Later that evening as I nursed my bruised ego, I picked up my Bible and ran across Proverbs 11:2: "When pride comes, disgrace follows, but with humility comes wisdom." *OK, God, I get the point. I was getting a little too puffed up about my appearance when I should have been thanking You for the grace and strength to live a healthier lifestyle.*

Genuine humility is a beautiful thing. We love to see it in others and often think of ourselves as humble. But pride keeps rearing its ugly head, and from time to time we're tempted to think a little too highly of ourselves. But Philippians 2:3 says, "Do nothing out of rivalry or conceit, but in humility consider others as more important than yourselves." Now that's good advice.

Bathing Suit Shopping

I will praise You because I have been remarkably and wonderfully made. Your works are wonderful, and I know this very well.
(Ps. 139:14)

Lacy examined her image in the dressing-room mirror. "Now I remember why I hate shopping for bathing suits. Maybe we should tell our husbands to forget the cruise."

"No way!" Brenda called from the next dressing room. "Let me see."

Lacy hid behind the door as she let her friend in. "No matter how much I diet and exercise, I can't get rid of my enormous thighs. My ballet teacher always nagged me about them."

Brenda adjusted Lacy's shoulder strap. "It's perfect. Why are you always picking your body apart? You're beautiful, and your thighs are not enormous—they're athletic. Stop listening to voices from the past. Listen to your friends and to God."

"That's easy for you to say. You're built like a model."

"Hey, remember what I shared at the retreat last year about the eating disorder I developed in college?" Lacy felt her cheeks grow red. "I'm sorry—I forgot." Brenda was a prime example that tall and slender did not always equal a healthy body image.

"Now," Brenda backed up, "let me see another one. For a cruise we need more than one swimsuit." *Listen to her, Lacy,* God seemed to say. *I made you just the way I want you.*

As difficult as it is to accept, God made each of us just as He wanted us. No matter what the magazines show us, we should take care of the bodies He created for us to live in. When we are caring for them with the right food, exercise, and a healthy image, God has a way of freeing our minds to enjoy what we see in the mirror, knowing He made us, loves us, and sees us as beautiful.

Picture-Perfect Marriage

They are no longer two, but one flesh. Therefore, what God has joined together, man must not separate. (Matt. 19:6)

My friend Stephanie was helping me create a memory book for my parents' fiftieth wedding anniversary. I had collected pictures spanning the years of their life together, and Stephanie was helping me arrange them in a lovely album. "My parents divorced when I was eleven, and being a single parent was really tough for my mom," she said. "How have your parents made it fifty years?"

"I've thought a lot about that lately," I admitted. "The bottom line is they did it God's way. It may sound corny, but my mom respected my dad and let him lead, like we're supposed to let Christ lead our lives. And my dad loved and sacrificed for my mom, like Christ loves us and laid down His life for us."

"What if my husband doesn't do his part?" Stephanie asked.

"Oh, I saw them struggle at times, but I also saw them show a lot of love to each other. A successful marriage isn't easy, but you have to be committed to doing your part even in the tough times."

In Ephesians 5:22–33 Paul outlines God's pattern for a successful marriage. When a woman submits to her husband as the leader in the relationship, she illustrates how believers respond to Christ as the leader in their lives—with humility and allegiance. And when a husband loves his wife by sacrificing for her, he shows how Christ gave His life for the church. Not only does this pattern illustrate the relationship between Christ and the church; it lays the groundwork for a harmonious marriage. Examine yourself in light of these criteria and see if you are standing on solid ground. Ask God to work in you and your husband to have a God-honoring marriage.

In His Absence

Help me understand Your instruction, and I will obey it and follow it with all my heart. (Ps. 119:34)

Becky washed the last dinner dish, took a deep breath, and fought back the loneliness that sometimes surfaced at this time of day. Becky's husband, Jack, had been deployed overseas for four months, and the evenings were still hard. Her two energetic sons kept her busy during the day, and activities with other military wives provided adult conversation, but the evenings had always been Becky and Jack's time to talk, unwind, and pray together.

During Jack's last deployment Becky had filled the lonely hours by reading romance novels, but she had learned her lesson. The steamy stories tempted her in ways she knew were not pleasing to God. In fact, as the months had gone by, she found herself drawn to men who seemed more accessible: men on favorite TV shows, her Sunday school teacher, and her son's soccer coach. Fortunately Becky realized the cause of her discontent and threw the novels away.

Now as she reflected on those frustrating months, Becky was glad God had shown her some better ways to fill the void. Tonight she would take the boys for a walk and then sit down to study her Bible. When Jack returned, she would be physically and spiritually fit.

If you have a husband who is out of town often for military duty, business, or ministry, you know the frustrations and temptations that come with his absence. You may experience extreme loneliness, resentment, or jealousy. Such emotions, if left unchecked, can lead to temptations that could damage or destroy your relationship. Fortify the walls of your life and marriage by clinging to the truth of God's Word, resisting worldly temptations, and surrounding yourself with godly influences. Even while he is away, you can build your marriage or tear it down.

Pleasant Pastures

The boundary lines have fallen for me in pleasant places. (Ps. 16:6)

When I graduated from college, I struggled with being single. Wedding invitations poured into my mailbox, and many weekends were spent at rehearsal dinners and receptions. My prayer and thought life centered around how and when God was going to introduce me to my future husband. Restless and unsatisfied with single life, I was sure I could only be fulfilled if I was in a meaningful relationship with a man.

One afternoon I heard a radio interview with Elisabeth Elliot, the author of *Passion and Purity*. In response to her interviewer's question about how to accept being single, she quoted Psalm 16:5–6, "LORD, You are my portion and my cup of blessing; You hold my future. The boundary lines have fallen for me in pleasant places; indeed, I have a beautiful inheritance."

Listening to her speak, I realized that my life was indeed pleasant. As a single woman, I lived in green pastures because the Lord was my portion and always provided everything I needed, emotionally and financially. I even had freedoms my married friends didn't. Over the next few months I practiced being thankful for how God provided for me, and I found peace in my singleness. Although I still wanted to marry, I wasn't consumed with finding a spouse.

Sometimes we live much of our lives looking discontentedly over the fence, coveting others' fields. The boundary lines of singleness feel especially unpleasant for many women. We gaze at the lush, fertile pasture of married life, daydreaming about how wonderful it must be in those fields. But in doing so, we miss the beauty and provision of God within our fence. We can say, like David, that our boundary lines have fallen in pleasant places because God drew them, and He has our best in mind.

Breaking Bondages

If you do not do what is right, sin is crouching at the door. Its desire is for you, but you must rule over it. (Gen. 4:7)

Ann left her son's room with the plastic bag in her shaking hand. He ran after her, pleading. As she opened the lid of the toilet, she heard Brian gasp behind her. He reached around and grabbed for the bag. For a second, she was afraid he might become violent, but she couldn't bear having drugs in her house.

"Mom, you don't know what you're doing. That's worth a lot of money!"

Ann opened the bag and turned it upside down. Its contents floated into the water and swirled down the drain. She jumped as she heard Brian slam the wall with his fist before stomping away.

Leaning against the cold tile, she faced reality. She had had suspicions. His attitude and even his personality had changed recently. Even with her suspicions, however, she was still devastated when she found drugs in Brian's room.

Later that evening Ann and her husband prayed together for God's guidance. They knew this was a serious matter that needed to be dealt with immediately and wisely. After praying, they decided to make an appointment for Brian and themselves with a Christian counselor they knew.

If someone close to you is involved in drugs, begin with prayer for that person and for God's wisdom in your role. Encourage the loved one to get help from a counselor, support group, or rehab center. Continue to be supportive and loving as he or she struggles to be free of the bondage of a powerful addiction. Though the road to healing may be long, and you both may feel at times like freedom from addiction is impossible, remind yourself and your loved one that with God everything is possible (Luke 18:27).

United We Stand

*Love . . . bears all things, believes all things, hopes all things,
endures all things. (1 Cor. 13:6–7)*

*My stepdad has cancer. Please pray for us all as I help my mom
care for him.* Angie's brief e-mail touched Sandi's heart as she
remembered past conversations with her friend. Angie had been
young when her mom remarried, and the last thing she had
wanted was a stepdad. As a teenager, her rejection and hostile
attitude made everyone miserable. But her stepdad's persistent
love and faithful walk with God eventually broke through to
Angie, and she finally opened her heart to him.

Now in her adult years, Angie knew he was a blessing to
their family. In fact, they had become so close as adults that they
even exercised together. When her husband died unexpectedly,
her stepdad was one of the people she turned to for assistance
and encouragement. Angie would now walk with her stepdad
and her mom through this trial, just as he had stood with her in
those years of resistance and rebellion.

Sandi e-mailed her friend with her assurance that she
would be praying and checking back with her often. As she prepared a card for Angie's stepdad, she prayed for their family and
thanked God for His goodness in allowing them to be a wonderful example of a family that had overcome through God's love.

Blended families are everywhere, and no one would pretend it is easy to merge those relationships, regardless of how
they were established. But often only the difficult, initial adjust-
ment is the focus. The truth is, many families speak of healed
relationships and loving commitment between family members
who have successfully blended. God's grace and mercy can repair
what is broken, restore division, and bring about bonding.

Mrs. Jones

About a year ago my neighbor Mrs. Jones became a widow. Friends stopped by periodically, and on numerous occasions I thought about stopping by to visit her as well, but I let my busy schedule get in the way and kept putting it off.

But now as I stood in the greeting card aisle at the grocery store looking for valentines for my family and friends, I couldn't help but think of Mrs. Jones. I knew she must be lonely. Although I had missed opportunities to show Jesus' love to her, it still wasn't too late. After I had selected cards for my husband, two children, and a couple of close friends, I found a special card for her.

The next day I knocked on her front door. When she answered, I could see that she was pleasantly surprised to see me. She invited me in, and we talked for almost an hour. As I was leaving, I invited her to join our family for dinner that night, and she accepted.

It's easy to get caught up in our own lives and forget about people who are lonely. But we can show kindness to people in need in many ways. It could be as simple as sending a card. Or maybe you've felt the Holy Spirit calling you to serve in a nursing home or to volunteer in helping homebound senior citizens. James 1:27 says, "Pure and undefiled religion before our God and Father is this: to look after orphans and widows in their distress and to keep oneself unstained by the world."

God wants us to care for those who desperately need His love and ours. Choose to make a difference in someone else's life. Not only will they be blessed by knowing that God truly cares about them, but you will also be blessed by serving others.

Faith at Work

Christ did not send me to baptize, but to evangelize. (1 Cor. 1:17)

Geena worked at a university where she was surrounded by extremely educated people, many of whom didn't care about or know the Lord. Her coworkers knew she was different. She didn't participate in gossip, didn't come in late, and didn't undermine the boss. One day Geena was driving two of her colleagues—Tom and Marianne—to an off-campus meeting. Tom, an atheist, asked her if she was religious.

"I'm a Christian, a follower of Jesus Christ," Geena replied.

Marianne laughed. "You don't believe that stuff about a man being born of a virgin, do you?"

"Yes, I do," said Geena.

"And a man rising from the dead?" Marianne laughed.

"I don't believe in God and all that sin stuff. It's just so negative," said Tom.

Geena began to feel uncomfortable—she didn't know how to answer. Never before had she experienced such ridicule! She silently prayed, and feeling a wave of peace wash over her, Geena replied, "I'd love to talk with you about how Jesus has changed my life. And I can't wait to share how He has healed my broken heart, restored my relationships, and given my life purpose."

In Matthew 28:19, Jesus charged believers with sharing the gospel, which includes sharing it with our coworkers. But in the current climate how can we do this? Doors open when we simply live our lives with faith, show compassion to coworkers who are having difficulties, and do our work "for the Lord and not for men" (Col. 3:23). People begin asking us questions because they see we live our lives differently. And by acknowledging we don't have all the answers—even though we are a Christian—we transparently share our life of faith with the lost.

Healthy Conflict

God's chosen ones, holy and loved, put on heartfelt compassion, kindness, humility, gentleness, and patience. (Col. 3:12)

Jessica's parents had a certain way of handling disagreements. Her mother would clam up, not speaking to anyone in the house for three or four days. Her father retreated to his office at work or into his workshop, depending on the day of the week.

Jessica's husband, Nick, had his own stories to share about the "fighting style" his parents used. His mother screamed, hurled accusations, and threw things; his father left the house for hours, tires screaming as he sped away.

So when Jessica and Nick had their first argument as a married couple, they simply slipped into the only patterns they knew. Jessica didn't say anything; Nick brought up every single thing she had done wrong in the past.

Since Jessica didn't know how to resolve conflict healthily, she sought to avoid any hint of disagreement. But by agreeing with Nick when she really didn't agree, she was being dishonest. So she asked the Lord to help her overcome her fear of conflict and teach her how to address difficult issues in constructive ways.

Because we are sinful, conflict is inevitable. Sometimes the conflict is about personalities; sometimes it's because we want our own way. But being a conflict avoider does not bring truth or peace to a relationship. Talking through issues is really about solving a problem, not attacking the other person. When we work through disagreements, we are working to enhance or even save a relationship. Conflict resolution is about listening and speaking respectfully. "You never" and "You always" statements cause defensive behavior. And we should always remember that we are ambassadors of Jesus Christ, who wants our speech and behavior to "always be gracious" (Col. 4:6).

Fear of God

I had heard rumors about You, but now my eyes have seen You.
Therefore I take back my words and repent in dust and ashes.
(Job 42:5–6)

It was Saturday. Christi had been at church, setting up for her three-year-old Sunday school class, when her husband called to tell her their daughter had suffered a seizure. Suzy had been off her medication for six months, but a recent stomach virus had brought on old symptoms.

Months of fear, anxiety, and depression followed as Christi watched Suzy like a hawk. Christi felt abandoned by God. Her prayers, when she prayed, were full of *Why God?* questions laced with anger at Him. She didn't want to go to church; she didn't want to read her Bible. She was mad.

Finally Christi's sister spoke truth into her life. "Christi, read the book of Job. Everything was taken away from him. He felt confused and betrayed. He questioned God, and God answered him. In the end he developed a healthy fear of Him and His power, and he loved and served God the rest of his life."

What does it mean to fear God? There is a fine line, a holy tension, between taking liberties with our Creator and quaking in our boots in His presence. He wants us to recognize His power and authority; yet we can crawl into His lap and call Him *Abba*. By acknowledging that He is God and we are not, we can give Him His rightful position in our lives. Then we can pour out our hearts without fear, without sin, to the One who is all-powerful, the One who understands.

So when we pray, let's remember who we're talking to. He wants our love, and He wants our respect. Just as a child both loves and respects his parents—that's how we should freely approach our Father.

The Neighbor

God . . . gave His One and Only Son, so that everyone who believes in Him will not perish but have eternal life. (John 3:16)

We've lived in our house fifteen years, but I still don't know the man across the street. When we moved in, we were newly-weds, and my husband was in graduate school. Then I had two babies and was in the throes of motherhood and diapers, pre-school and gymnastics, working and taking care of things.

Over the years I saw the man mow his yard, get his mail, and leave for work, but he never got involved in our neighbor-hood get-togethers. In fact, if I ran into him at the grocery store, I wouldn't even recognize him. He kept to himself and was often gone all weekend.

The other day he stopped his truck at his mailbox. Instead of getting out in the normal way, he sort of slid out and slowly, shakily made his way to the curb. He looked like he had aged twenty years. I felt a God-pang in my heart: *The man is sick.* God nudged me to tell him about Jesus. *But Lord,* I protested, *I don't even know his name! How can I even begin, since I've lived across the street from him so long?*

That was two weeks ago, and I'm still trying to decide what to do. Should we take him dinner? Leave a gift in his mailbox? Offer to pick up groceries? While I've been playing this mental game with myself, his car has disappeared, and I've seen no signs of life at his house.

I hope God gives me another chance to tell him about the One who loves him, about the Savior who died for him, about how he can live forever with the Author of goodness.

Happily Ever After

Love is patient, love is kind. (1 Cor. 13:4)

I had just finished watching *Kate and Leopold,* a romantic comedy. As I thought about handsome Hugh Jackman's character, Leopold, I began mentally comparing him to my husband. Leopold had impeccable manners, thoughtful gestures, and perfect diction—not to mention, he was incredibly romantic and chivalrous. Dave's idea of a romantic evening was eating pizza and watching a game on TV.

Lord, I complained silently, *why can't Dave be more romantic and thoughtful?* But while I focused on the negative, God reminded me of the times Dave changed diapers when I was exhausted, fixed the kids lunch when I was sick, and went off to work every day, never complaining. Yet I felt dissatisfied because of Hollywood's fictional (and unrealistic) portrait of a man.

No, life hadn't turned out like I had planned. But instead of complaining about it, I realized that God wants me to be thankful for what I *do* have—a good husband, healthy kids, a full-time job, and a roof over my head. I repented for my ungratefulness and asked God to give me a more realistic perspective about life, marriage, and frail human beings.

"...and they lived happily ever after." Isn't that the fairy tale our parents read to us at bedtime? Hollywood has convinced us we should expect romance, flowers, and candlelight every night. We grow up with the notion that a man should be perfectly groomed at all times, know our every desire, and be ready, willing, and able to meet our needs. Unfortunately, that's impossible, not to mention unfair, to expect perfection from another imperfect human being (just like us).

We serve a God who knows all our thoughts and desires, and He is working to conform us to the image of His Son. The process may be painful at times, but the results will be so worth it!

Bo

I spoke to you, but you didn't listen. (Deut. 1:43)

When I picked up the phone, Emily began telling me of her plans for a much-needed weekend getaway for herself and her husband. "You're my last hope," she said. Then the guilt kicked in—Emily and Ryan would have to cancel their plans unless I helped by pet-sitting for their dog. "It's the weekend after Christmas, so all the kennels are booked. My in-laws agreed to watch the boys, but they can't take Bo because they have allergies." (Bo is short for Bonaparte—as in Napoleon. The name should have been a clue.)

I agreed. Rick and I love dogs, so how much trouble could one small canine be?

While little Bo was in our care, he chewed through two electrical cords, demolished our son's video game, barked incessantly, and wanted to sleep in our bed. Bo also lifted his leg on the kitchen cabinet, the corner of our bed, and horror of horrors—our Christmas tree.

After Emily picked up the obstreperous little tyrant, I collapsed in a chair, exhausted. I silently asked the Lord, *Why do people always come to me when they need something?* Almost immediately, I felt the Holy Spirit saying, *Did you bother asking Me if you should say yes every time someone asks you for a favor?* I realized that a big part of the problem was me. I had a hard time saying no. I prayed and asked the Lord to help me listen to His voice and to heed His instructions.

In spite of our busy schedules and fatigue, some of us still have a hard time saying no. Sometimes we assume it's our Christian duty to say yes to everything that comes our way. If this is a problem area for you, pray for wisdom and guidance before taking on any new tasks.

Floyd

Be kind and compassionate to one another, forgiving one another, just as God also forgave you in Christ. (Eph. 4:32)

Because of the close relationship my dad and mom shared, I didn't think she would ever remarry when he died. But a couple of years after his death, she hastily tied the knot with a man she had only known a few short months. Needless to say, I was shocked. I guess I had underestimated the depth of Mom's loneliness.

Mom and Floyd had a small wedding at the church where they met. My husband and I thought it was odd that none of Floyd's family showed up, especially since he had two brothers and three of his four grown children living in the area.

We soon found out why. Floyd is one of those irritating, sandpaper people determined to bring everyone else around to his way of thinking. If you express an opinion that differs from his, he'll launch into a lengthy retort on why he's right and you're wrong.

In the twenty-eight years I've known Floyd now, not much has changed. He's still rude, opinionated, and full of bitterness. Mom is still passive and lets him have his own way, but I continually bite my tongue out of respect for her. I've prayed about my attitude and asked the Lord to help me to be patient and forgiving, but it's been difficult. Yet, although I can't control the way Floyd acts, I can control the way I respond to him. Every encounter with him is another opportunity to rely on the Lord and His strength.

No matter how unpleasant it may be, we will always have sandpaper people in our lives. When you encounter such a person, remember Jesus' admonition to forgive "70 times seven" (Matt. 18:22).

Trina

The fear of the LORD is the beginning of knowledge;
fools despise wisdom and discipline. (Prov. 1:7)

One Saturday morning, my neighbor Jane stopped me at her mailbox as I was taking a walk. She was not only my neighbor and friend, but she was also my sixteen-year-old daughter's English teacher.

Jane hesitated as she nervously looked at me. "I don't know if you're aware of this or not, but there's a boy in Trina's class who has been showing a lot of interest in her." Jane wasn't smiling, and I waited for her to continue. "Kyle is very personable, good looking, and popular, but . . ." Jane sighed. "I really shouldn't be telling you this, and if the administration finds out I said anything, I'll deny it."

Lord, I prayed silently, *give Jane the courage to tell me what's going on.* "What is it?" I asked.

"Kyle has been accused by two different girls of date rape. No charges have been brought against him yet, but I wouldn't want anything to happen to Trina. So please don't let her go out with him."

That evening I told my husband about what Jane had said. We were both in agreement that Trina would not be allowed to date Kyle. Trina was angry with us for a while, but later, when the truth came out, she was grateful that we had said no.

Adults aren't the only ones to suffer in abusive relationships. Teens are also vulnerable to violence and may not have the wisdom or experience to realize they are in danger. Know what your children are doing and who their friends are. Pray for wisdom and protection.

Not Forgotten

Can a woman forget her nursing child, or lack compassion for the child of her womb? Even if these forget, yet I will not forget you.
(Isa. 49:15)

Thirty-six and single, that's me. I didn't think I'd be single at this age, and honestly, until I turned thirty-three or thirty-four, it didn't really bother me. But now it bothers me. All of my friends are married, and some even have teenagers. And now that I'm on Facebook, reconnecting with high school friends, I'm confronted with the fact that I'm much further behind the pack as far as marriage and family are concerned.

I envy their children and the struggles and triumphs of parenthood. I envy their partnerships, connections, inside jokes, stolen glances, and gracious gestures they exchange. I even envy their arguments over who picks up the milk or who will file the taxes—at least they have an option. I have no one to share the responsibilities of life—no one to help shoulder the load of the everyday mundane.

I was explaining all of this to the Lord a while back, and as I prayed, I was impressed with the expression: *I am not forgotten* (see Luke 12:6). As soon as I realized the fullness of this sentence, I repeated it out loud, praising Him: "I am not forgotten. God, You see me, You know me, and You have not forgotten me." What a comfort this simple sentence is to me. It represents the complex and intense passion God has for me. It lets me know that my story isn't over, and God is walking through it with me.

For singles, it's often too easy to envy ourselves into depression. Satan can easily play on our fears and turn our focus onto what we don't have. We must be constantly in the Word, diligent in staying close to God, and deliberately thankful for His blessings and care.

What Am I Doing Wrong?

Don't stir up anger in your children, but bring them up in the training and instruction of the Lord. (Eph. 6:4)

"I don't know what I'm doing wrong," Cindy said. She sat beside Anita, grateful that nobody else had arrived for Bible study yet. "Whenever I ask Todd's kids to do something or try to correct them, they react like I'm the evil stepmother from a bad fairy tale. Especially Julia. It seems like all we do is fight."

"Sounds like a rerun of my experience with Mike's daughter."

"But you two act like best friends." Cindy tried to imagine Anita and eighteen-year-old Lisa not getting along.

"What we have took work. Looking back, I was trying too hard, and she was at a difficult age—thirteen. Someone suggested we find ways to get to know each other. I also committed to pray for Lisa daily. The combination helped. I discovered she was a good kid, and she saw that I truly loved her. We still have our moments. But hey, she's a teenager. We're supposed to have moments."

Cindy thought about that. *Maybe I'm trying too hard. God, I want to have a good relationship with Todd's kids. Show me how.*

Movies and fairy tales give stepparents a bad reputation. How difficult it must be to adjust to marriage while also learning to parent children you didn't have the advantage of knowing and raising from infancy. If you are a stepparent, know that God put you where you are for a purpose and wants you to have healthy relationships. Take some time to seek His wisdom and learn from those who have been there and seen success. If you know a woman in this situation, pray today for how you might support and encourage her as she helps raise the children who came with her husband.

End of My Rope

When the Lord saw her, He had compassion on her and said, "Don't cry." (Luke 7:13)

Dawn just wasn't getting well. She hadn't skipped a single dose of her medication, she'd rested and drunk plenty of fluids, and I had done everything I knew to do as a mom to help my ten-year-old daughter feel better. But she still looked exhausted and pale. After seven days of tending to her, I felt like a failure as a mother.

As I contemplated taking Dawn to the emergency room, I felt my composure weaken. I was drained physically and emotionally from caring for her all week while also trying to fulfill my other responsibilities. I needed a hug in the worst way, and I desperately longed for my mom and sister who live a thousand miles away.

Suddenly, I began to cry. I started to express my frustrations out loud, weeping all the more. After several minutes of releasing my emotions to God, I felt a gentle reminder work its way into my soul. *I'm here, Belinda, and I care. I have noticed everything you've been through this week, and I see the pain you're feeling now. Let Me care for you.* I may not have received a hug from my mom or my sister, but Jesus had just compassionately given me the strength I needed in order to continue caring for Dawn.

We humans are frail beings who often feel at the end of our ropes. Thankfully, Psalm 103:14 reminds us we have a Lord who is mindful of our frailties and shows compassion when our humanity gets the best of us. In fact, many of the miracles you recall Jesus performing were prompted by His compassion.

Compassion still moves Jesus to respond to our needs as well. Allow your compassionate Savior to minister to your humanity today.

Bitter Heart

*I walk along slowly all my years because
of the bitterness of my soul. (Isa. 38:15)*

Jana smiled as she sat across from me at the coffee shop. "Tell me about your week."

"Not good," I said. The last several months at church, I had seen my ex-boyfriend with a new girlfriend in tow, and I couldn't stop thinking about them. "I know this isn't very Christlike, but I hope she breaks his heart." Tears threatened as I took another sip of my latte.

"Have I ever told you about my cousin?" Jana asked. "Three years ago Michael was passed over for a promotion. He was shocked and angry. Now, instead of being glad he still has a job when so many people don't, he is bitter and defensive."

"Are you saying I'm bitter and defensive?" I asked.

"I'm saying I'm afraid you're on the path to becoming bitter."

"But Craig and I talked about marriage. I was expecting a ring, but instead he broke up with me." I swiped an escaping tear. "I'm never going to let anyone get close again. It hurts too much to love."

Jana squeezed my arm. "See, this is what concerns me. He broke up with you last June. You need to heal, but you don't seem to want to. It's like you're stuck." She was right, but I didn't want to hear it. She kept going. "If you close off your heart to others, you'll be closing it off to God. He can't use us when we're like that. Give Him this pain. He can heal your heart and help you move on."

I realized then that it was my choice—become bitter or trust God with my heart. If you have any bitterness, give it to God for healing. He can turn bitterness that sours into sweetness that can be savored. It's your choice.

The New Atheism

Repent and believe in the good news! (Mark 1:15)

My pastor was recently invited to speak to his daughter Amy's college class. It was a religion class, and he could talk about anything in Scripture, about God, about truth. What an opportunity!

The professor did not allow students to heckle or be rude, but he did set aside time for questions at the end. My pastor told the class that the Bible is God's Word, and it is truth. He explained that there is ample evidence to support the truth and authority of Scripture. Some of the students became visibly upset as he talked. A few asked questions at the end, but no one was particularly combative while he was there.

All of that changed, however, when he left. Since no one knew Amy was his daughter, they felt free to vent. She said some of the students were outraged, especially the two atheists in the class. "I could never believe in a god who lets bad things happen," one said. "I think Christians are dangerous and irrational," said the other. And both agreed that highly intelligent people do not believe in God, the supernatural, or anything miraculous. Even two weeks later the students were still talking about "that pastor and his Bible," especially the atheists.

A movement called "the New Atheism" is hostile to all religion, particularly Christianity. But the psalmist says: "The fool says in his heart, 'God does not exist'" (Ps. 14:1). Atheism is not new; there have always been people who don't want to believe in God and feel no need for a Savior. If you know an atheist, or if you just want to know how to respond to one, seek out some of the great resources available, and be bold in declaring the truth . . . in love.

Pay Attention

Be gracious to me, LORD, for I am weak; heal me, LORD, for my bones are shaking. (Ps. 6:2)

My friend Jeanne was just diagnosed with ovarian cancer. She's the second friend of mine in five years to contract the disease.

Jeanne had been having some symptoms that wouldn't go away. She visited her doctor several different times, and he told her the symptoms were due to menopause. But over a period of time, her symptoms became worse. When she began having doubled-over abdominal pain, she visited a different doctor who performed several tests. The tests showed a large mass, but even then it still seemed to be benign.

Jeanne was scheduled to have a hysterectomy. While preparing her for pre-op, the surgeon thought the tumor might be cancer, but they wouldn't know for sure until the surgery. The tumor, in fact, was cancerous, and now my sweet friend Jeanne is fighting for her life. A young, vibrant woman who just a few months ago was walking three miles a day is now so weak that some days she can't even get out of bed.

As a believer with a tender love for Jesus, Jeanne is remaining strong in her faith. She knows the Lord has a plan for her life, even in the suffering, and she wants to honor Him above all else. And her friends who love her are banding together to lift her to the One who can heal.

Friend, please know your body. Know its ways. Pay attention. If you are experiencing something that is different for you, don't ignore it. And please don't let your doctor ignore it either. If you notice anything out of the ordinary, don't be afraid to seek help. God our Healer gives us doctors and medical technology to help us. So don't wait! Take care of yourself. You are "remarkably and wonderfully made" (Ps. 139:14).

For His Glory

Don't you know that your body is a sanctuary of the Holy Spirit?
(1 Cor. 6:19)

As a recent newlywed—I've only been married for three weeks, and I'm twenty-three years old—I've been asked to speak to a group of middle-school girls at a friend's church. The topic? God's plan for sex and waiting for His choice guy.

"One of the most important things my parents taught me about sex," I began, "was to love God. You see, God's Word isn't really about the do's and don'ts. You have to see His heart behind what He says. And His heart is the best life for you, free from bondage to sexually transmitted diseases, unwanted pregnancies, emotional baggage, and spiritual emptiness. When you love God first, you are able to understand and trust His love for you. Then you don't have to go searching for love somewhere you shouldn't.

"Another thing my mom taught me," I said, "is that a girl's heart is like a fragile teacup. And when you give a part of yourself away, that teacup becomes cracked and chipped. This is what happens to your heart when you don't wait for God's guy.

"It isn't that God is trying to keep something from you. He just wants us to live a life that is abundant and free. The life the world throws at you is a lie. Don't fall for the traps the enemy will set for you. Besides, waiting for the guy God is preparing just for you is so worth it!"

Teaching our children about premarital sex, drugs, and other risky behaviors must be grounded in God's Word. By loving Him first, they will be better able to handle what the world and the enemy throw at them. If they understand His heart behind what He says, they can better see the love—His love—that will keep them safe.

This Is My Story

I hear of your love and faith toward the Lord Jesus. (Philem. 5)

Lacy was on my school softball team years ago, and we recently reconnected. We've enjoyed catching up and talking, but it's been obvious she is struggling to fill a deep void in her life.

"It seems like you're really happy," Lacy told me wistfully one day.

"I haven't always been content. I used to look for answers and meaning in the things around me, but I always came up empty. Then in college I became a Christian, and God changed everything for me. I realized God isn't distant or far away. He's real and He cares about me. He gives my life meaning and purpose." Lacy looked skeptical but interested. "Why don't you drop by my house after you get off work and join us for dinner?" I asked. "I'm making lasagna."

Lacy smiled. "That sounds great."

The command to share the gospel can seem daunting at times. Yet we can take comfort in the fact that the Holy Spirit is the One who changes hearts—not us—and He will give us the words and wisdom we need. One of the most effective ways to share the gospel is simply to share your story. Each follower of Jesus has a personal story of what God has done in his or her life because God is personal and knows and deeply loves each of us.

When we are real and genuine about our walk with God and our relationship with Him, people see what He means to us and that we believe He is who He says He is. Non-Christians will see that if you, a person who is similar to them in some way, can be a Christian, they can too.

Praying with Perspective

The LORD is righteous in all His ways and gracious in all His acts. The LORD is near all who call out to Him. (Ps. 145:17–18)

After trying to conceive a child for years, Annie and her husband, Brad, tried various infertility treatments. But nothing worked. Annie confided in me that she felt like her prayers for a child were just bouncing off the ceiling. She wasn't asking for something outrageous; raising children who love God would be honoring Him. So why wouldn't He answer with a baby?

Yet His lack of an answer was an answer. Annie and Brad decided that if they didn't conceive after two years of infertility treatments, they would adopt. They began adoption proceedings, and everything fell into place quickly. Annie and Brad traveled to the Ukraine to pick up their precious miracle: little Jamie. Then two months after they returned from the Ukraine, another miracle: Annie was pregnant. She delivered a healthy little sister to Jamie later that year.

Annie said, "If we hadn't struggled as we did, we never would have adopted Jamie. Those trials were God's grace to us even though we didn't know it at the time. We wouldn't change a thing."

Many of us spend years asking God for something, and we don't always receive the happy answer we hope for. Sometimes God tells us no or calls us to wait on Him. When we feel He doesn't hear us, we need to return to the truth of Scripture. He does care about each of His children, and He always works for our good and for His glory. Even when we don't understand God's answers, we are called to keep trusting Him and believing that He has a purpose and a plan. He is always at work, making us more like His Son.

The Check

*Kindness to the poor is a loan to the LORD,
and He will give a reward to the lender. (Prov. 19:17)*

As Dan and I headed toward the sanctuary, our two teenage girls went to sit with their friends from youth group during the morning worship service. We found a couple of empty seats next to Gwen and Richard, a younger couple in our small group who just had their first baby a couple of months earlier.

"Hi," Dan said as we sat down next to them. "How are you doing?" Gwen's eyes started to tear up. "Not so good. Our landlord has given us a week to come up with one month's rent or they'll evict us." I reached out to grab her hand and gave it a squeeze. "I'm so sorry," I said.

Gwen and Richard had been having a hard time with their finances. She was staying at home with the baby, and Richard's employer had cut his hours by a third.

During the sermon Dan leaned over and whispered, "I think the Lord wants us to help them with their rent." I nodded, wondering where the money would come from. Between paying for braces, school clothes, and a new refrigerator, we didn't have much left over at the end of the month. But I figured that the money we had set aside for a new sofa would cover what they needed. We would just have to keep making do with the same threadbare furniture we'd been using since we were first married. Toward the end of the sermon, I grabbed my purse and wrote out the check for their rent.

Throughout the Bible, God shows us His heart for the poor, and He wants us to be generous with what He has given us. Pray for wisdom, and if you can't donate financially, perhaps you can give of your time, certainly your prayers.

For You

*Go, therefore, and make disciples of all nations, baptizing them
in the name of the Father and of the Son and of the Holy Spirit.*
(Matt. 28:19)

"What are you reading in your Bible, Grandma?" my six-year-old grandson Chase asked. I read him the verse I'd just finished: "For God so loved the world that he gave his one and only Son, that whoever believes in him shall not perish but have eternal life" (John 3:16 NIV). Then we began talking about salvation. I said a silent prayer and asked God to give me wisdom.

"Let's pretend you did something wrong at school," I began, "and you were sitting in the principal's office waiting for your punishment." Chase's eyes widened as I continued. "I'm sure you'd be really scared and dreading what would happen to you, right?" Chase nodded.

"While you're waiting, what if a man came in and talked to the principal about your situation? What if the man said to your principal, 'I don't want you to punish Chase. Punish me instead'?" You'd be completely off the hook—no punishment because someone else was punished for you. They paid for your sin." Chase looked somber, but then his face brightened. "Wow! That would be great!"

"That's what Jesus did for you. He took the punishment for all the sins you've committed both in the past and in the future." So after we talked about God's plan of salvation, my sweet grandson asked Jesus to be his personal Savior.

We're commanded to "make disciples of all nations" (Matt. 28:19), and we should begin in our own families. Leading our children and grandchildren to Christ is one of life's greatest blessings. We have an opportunity to tell them about the love of their heavenly Father and His incredible plan of salvation.

Playing Games

I will not set anything worthless before my eyes. (Ps. 101:3)

When I heard sounds of explosions and gunfire coming from the computer, I quickly stepped into the family room to see what my ten-year-old son was up to. Zachary was engrossed in a video game containing a level of violence that is usually reserved for R-rated movies. I picked up the case and saw that it was rated "M" for mature players. Not even "T" for teens. "Zach, where did you get that video game?" I asked.

"Austin let me borrow it. He said it was really cool."

"Does Austin's mom know he has this?"

Zachary shrugged. "His cousin gave it to him." I sighed and silently prayed for wisdom. "I don't want you to play this game anymore. You and Dad and I have talked about our rules for TV and video games, and I don't think this one is good for you." Zachary crossed his arms and stuck out his lip. I knew he wanted to argue the point, but he knew I wasn't going to give in.

I spoke with Austin's mom the next day. She hadn't paid attention to the rating symbols when she saw the game and didn't realize it contained such violence and explicit material. She thanked me for keeping her informed, and I thanked God for giving me discernment to discuss the situation with her in a way that didn't condemn her or her son.

Video games have come a long way since the days of PacMan, Super Mario Brothers, and Donkey Kong. Technology has made them much more realistic, and gamers have a vast selection from which to choose. But decide as a family which games are appropriate for your children, and stay informed. Ask God to guide you as you navigate a world of seemingly infinite choices in entertainment.

The Promotion

Abstain from all appearance of evil. (1 Thess. 5:22 KJV)

When my friend and coworker Ann accepted a promotion at work, she knew it would provide a higher salary and a corner office with windows. But it also meant more responsibility and a few additional challenges as well, such as traveling with male coworkers. Ann and I have seen some coworkers make unwise decisions that led to heartache and ruined relationships. She didn't want to be a casualty.

But Ann didn't count on a gossipy neighbor spotting her with a male coworker on a recent trip to Chicago. Dave carried Ann's bags into her hotel room for her. The door shut behind them, but the neighbor didn't stick around long enough to see Dave walk out the door a few seconds later.

The neighbor not only told everyone she knew at the home-owners' association meeting the next week that Ann had been unfaithful to her husband, but she also spread the rumor around their church. And now Ann's reputation is badly damaged.

Ann realizes that simply avoiding evil isn't always enough. She now lives her life before the Lord abstaining even "from all appearance of evil" to protect not only her reputation but God's reputation as well. These kinds of daily, ongoing decisions are critical to keeping our guard up, our consciences clean, and our testimony pure before an increasingly watching world.

If your job requires you to travel with male coworkers or meet male clients, act wisely. Ask God to protect you from temptation and from making decisions that would cause others to draw the wrong conclusions about your situation. Jesus said, "I'm sending you out like sheep among wolves. Therefore be as shrewd as serpents and as harmless as doves" (Matt. 10:16.)

Too Much Information

Maintain your competence and discretion.
My son, don't lose sight of them. (Prov. 3:21)

Daphne glanced over her seventeen-year-old daughter's shoulder to see why she was looking wide-eyed at the computer monitor. Amy's friend had posted some pictures of herself on her Facebook page.

"I told Lindsey she shouldn't put those pictures on her page, Mom. But she didn't see anything wrong with posting pictures of herself in her new swimsuit," Amy said. "She said there's no difference in wearing a swimsuit to the beach and wearing one on her Facebook page."

"But she's doing more than just wearing a swimsuit in these pictures, Amy. She's modeling it provocatively. And now these pictures are permanently in the public domain for anyone to see, including college admissions offices, prospective employers, and strangers."

"I just wish Lindsey had thought about that," replied Amy.

"That's why we need to pray for wisdom," her mom said. "It's so easy to act before we think, especially on the Internet."

As believers our behavior is constantly under inspection. With the advent of the Internet and the various websites where we can post personal information with the click of a mouse, millions of people have the ability to zoom in on our conduct and character. If your teen or your family has an online presence, you are opening your life up to closer scrutiny by others.

First Peter 3:2 says that when people observe our respectful behavior they can be drawn to the Savior we serve. Conversely, our unchecked behavior can cause others to stumble (Rom. 14:21). Consider the image you present of yourself through your blog or personal page, and help your children wisely assess the information they release to the public. Pray for godly wisdom to help your family enjoy the benefits of the Internet with safety and integrity.

Woeful or Grateful?

We, Your people, the sheep of Your pasture, will thank You forever; we will declare Your praise to generation after generation. (Ps. 79:13)

It was one of those weeks. First my car wouldn't start and needed to be towed to the mechanic. Next, it rained, which wouldn't be so bad, except our roof began to leak. Then I fell down on a slippery sidewalk and hurt my lower back. Throw in a sick child, a broken jar of jam all over the kitchen floor, and I had the makings of a terrible week.

At first I resented my sister's cheerful exhortations when I told her my woes. Her reminder to be grateful in the midst of my problems didn't sit well with me. But when I got off the phone, I decided to put her suggestion into practice.

I escaped to my back-porch swing and began to thank God. Initially I couldn't think of much to be thankful for, but gradually I began to list a number of ways He had blessed me and my family. In fact, as I thanked God for His faithfulness, the generous way He has provided for us, my salvation, my children's able bodies, and my husband's tender companionship, my heart began to swell with genuine gratitude.

When I got up from my swing and went inside to prepare dinner, I still had a leaking roof and a sick child, but I was no longer depressed. My joy had been restored.

King David had a way with words, and many of his psalms express his troubles in such a way that we can certainly identify with them. But David knew better than to count his troubles without also counting his blessings. Repeatedly David chose to express his gratitude to God even though his circumstances were daunting. Check out Psalms 13, 103, and 138 to see how David deliberately chose gratitude over worry, depression, or defeat.

Prayers for Justice

*If you offer yourself to the hungry, and satisfy the afflicted one,
then your light will shine in the darkness. (Isa. 58:10)*

"Violent Ethnic Cleansing in Kenya"

"Torture Used to Enforce China's 'One Child' Policy"

"One Innocent Bystander a Day Killed in Rio de Janeiro's Drug Wars"

The headlines caught Libby's eye as she flipped through the newspaper to find her usual read—the Living section. She tried to avoid the depressing stories, but as she pulled out the section on recipes and gardening, she couldn't help but read the opening lines of a particularly sad story in the next section. When she read those stories, she felt angry and helpless. She didn't want to know about all of the evil in the world. She preferred to stay blissfully unaware.

After trying unsuccessfully to focus on an article about azaleas, Libby turned back to the story in the next section. If she got depressed when she read those stories, she couldn't imagine how the people who were part of them must be feeling. And what about how God felt? His heart must continuously break over the suffering He witnesses. If His heart was to bind up the brokenhearted, feed the hungry, and set the oppressed free, shouldn't she be like-minded? Libby pulled the paper closer and began to read with new purpose, praying for peace, healing, and justice for each person as she went.

Though we may become hardened or try to hide from the suffering we see, Christ does not. He allows injustice for now, but He doesn't accept it or become desensitized to it, and neither should we. In fact, God wants us to fight against injustice, to keep our hearts in tune with His on the issues and events around us. Intervene in prayer as you read the paper or watch the news. God works mightily through the prayers of His people!

Reflecting His Strength

Blessed are those who have regard for the weak;
the LORD delivers them in times of trouble. (Ps. 41:1 NIV)

Noticing her friend's tired face as Sandy walked into their prayer group, Beth felt concern. "Hi Sandy," she said, giving her a quick hug. As they moved toward their seats, Beth asked, "How's your mom doing?"

"She's just holding on," Sandy responded. "My sisters and I are trying to set up a schedule that allows someone to be with her at the nursing home most of the time. But of course, our dad needs us, too, and my mother-in-law is recovering from a stroke. It's such a blessing that my job has flexible hours."

"I don't know how you're coping, let alone continuing to work," Beth sympathized.

Sandy smiled. "I don't know either, but I do know God is sustaining me. His grace is amazing. I see it in so many ways as He helps us with our daily decisions. And I see it in my mother's sweet acceptance of her difficult situation."

Beth was glad to hear her friend's testimony of God's goodness. But she also determined to be a better friend and encourager by praying for Sandy's strength and finding ways to help lighten her load.

As baby boomers reach retirement age and seniors live longer, Sandy's dilemma will be shared by multitudes of families. Three out of four caregivers are women, and 40 percent of them may be caring for both children and elderly parents simultaneously. The Bible offers direction and wisdom in a world that shuns sacrifice and encourages self-focused choices. God gives us strength to face tough circumstances with grace and to model servanthood with joy. If your present season of life leaves you weary and drained, seek prayer support, find ways to nourish yourself, and ask God daily to refresh your spirit.

The Back Burner

I will guard my ways so that I may not sin with my tongue;
I will guard my mouth with a muzzle. (Ps. 39:1)

Furious, I slammed down the phone. *I can't believe he's doing this again! The kids will be so hurt!* "Was that Dad?" asked Shelby, my ten-year-old, as she came into the kitchen. Her older brother, Sam, headed toward the pantry.

"No snacking before dinner!" I said. Stirring the spaghetti sauce vigorously, I took a deep breath and tried to steady my voice. "Yes, that was Dad. He can't come get you this weekend."

"What?" Shelby's freckled face fell as it had so many times before.

"I knew it!" Sam said, stomping his foot. "He's probably going to some golf tournament with the latest girlfriend."

"But why would he ditch us for her?" Shelby asked, her blue eyes filling with tears. So many reasons came to mind. Let's see: (1) He's a terrible father. (2) He cares only for himself. (3) He never grew up. (4) He will always hurt and disappoint you. But I didn't say any of those things. I remembered what my counselor said, "Bashing your ex-husband only hurts your children."

So with both the sauce and my anger bubbling, I put my emotions on the back burner. After dinner I would cry in the privacy of my bedroom. But now I would protect my children's feelings—again. *God, help me*, I prayed silently, clamping my mouth shut. Tight.

Regardless of what your ex-husband does, your children love him. For you to denigrate him in front of them will only worsen the pain and confusion they already feel. No matter how hard it is (and it is very hard), don't criticize him or make snide remarks. If your ex-husband isn't a good father, unfortunately they will discover that on their own. You don't need to tell them.

The Boss

*Children, obey your parents as you would the Lord,
because this is right. (Eph. 6:1)*

"You're the boss!" my mother-in-law said with a smile as she handed my son, Chandler, the markers. He snatched them from her hand without a thank-you and started coloring. I shook my head in disbelief at the phrase. It was said with no ill intentions, but Chandler really did think he was the boss. I turned to him and asked, "Chandler, what do you say?"

"Thank you, Grandma," he said without looking up.

Chandler's first word as a baby was *no*. He'd become so used to being told no that he thought he could say it to me and my husband. We mistakenly thought it was cute when he was two, but after a while his disobedience was not so funny. Some days can be a real challenge.

My husband and I pray together and do our best to support each other in disciplining and raising Chandler. I have to remind myself that God will give us wisdom and grace to raise our son. After all, I have a strong will myself, so I at least know how Chandler thinks. And maybe, just maybe, God is still working on my own strong will.

Being a parent of a strong-willed child can be challenging. Parents need to set up appropriate rules and boundaries, especially while their child is young. If not, the strong-willed child will most certainly make some unwise choices. But God can give you everything you need to do the job well. In Proverbs 22:6, He tells us to "teach a youth about the way he should go; even when he is old he will not depart from it." Raising children is not easy—even for the most patient, loving, and devoted parent—but the rewards are immeasurable.

Undue Pressure

Every wise woman builds her house, but a foolish one tears it down with her own hands. (Prov. 14:1)

When my husband and I were first married, I placed some unspoken expectations on him. But before long I realized that many of my expectations were not going to be met. So instead of asking God how He wanted me to handle the situation, I figured I'd manage things on my own.

First I tried simple requests. "Honey," I'd say, "would you please take the trash down to the dumpster?" Michael would agree, but then he'd forget it and leave it by the front door. Instead of taking care of it myself, I'd leave it just to see if he would notice it when he came home from work. He didn't.

When I realized that subtle hints weren't working, I turned to sarcasm. "Are you waiting for the trash to sprout wings and fly itself out to the dumpster?" I'd ask.

"Stop getting so uptight, Shannon. I'll get it the next time I go out."

I was speechless. I didn't understand how someone could be so relaxed and carefree about things. When I looked around our apartment and saw how much needed to be done, I was frustrated. Didn't Michael understand how much these things bothered me? Then I felt the Lord gently persuading me to pray. I began to realize that the problem was not Michael but my unrealistic expectations and my disrespectful attitude.

It's human nature to want others to behave as we would. Sometimes our expectations are unspoken, which sets our loved ones up for failure. Or we may resort to sarcasm, which is often met with resistance or resentment. Jesus said in John 15:12, "Love one another as I have loved you." That means faults and all. We need to focus on becoming the women God wants us to be—conduits of His love.

Leigh

My friend Leigh discovered that her husband was having an affair with a coworker. Leigh suggested that they go to counseling, move, even find new jobs. But nothing worked—he was unwilling to resolve the problem.

So after months of prayer and heartache, Leigh filed for divorce. She and the children would move closer to family, and she would find a new job. However, in the process of a routine physical checkup, Leigh found out that she had a sexually transmitted disease.

"I've just about had all I can take," she told me. "When I'm tired, the darkness rushes in and threatens to overtake me. I begin to wonder if God even hears me or cares about me anymore."

"Leigh, I don't have any easy answers, and I don't want to give you a canned response. I know you've been told to 'turn it over to God' and that 'things will all work out.' We know, deep down, it will all work out, but in the meantime I will tell you what I do know: God is good, and He will never forsake you or forget you."

God tells us to cast our cares on Him because He cares for us (1 Pet. 5:7). He is willing to assume full responsibility for our burdens, if only we will let Him. God is good and He is faithful, and when we are drowning in sorrow and fear, we need to hold on to His goodness with all of our strength. The enemy will whisper that God has forgotten us or that He doesn't love us, and he'll even try to persuade us that God isn't good. But don't listen to him! Instead focus on the faithful Promise Giver who promises that He will never forsake us (see Heb. 13:5).

My Mother-in-Law

Your every action must be done with love. (1 Cor. 16:14)

I love my mother-in-law. She is, after all, my husband's mother. Widowed early, she was a single mom, and my husband is her only child.

But ever since I've known her, she's been critical of me, both verbally and nonverbally. My house will never pass her white glove test, my meals will never pass her gourmet meal test, my children will never pass her perfect children test. And yet I still love her simply because of who she is. That doesn't make it easy though.

She's coming for a visit, and I'm anxious. I prayed about it because I want things to go well. *Lord, help me to see her as You do. Help me to realize that my worth, my mothering, even my cooking, is based only on what You think.*

As I prepared for her visit, God showed me that my mother-in-law is a love-starved, lonely person. With no one to take care of and no one to share her life with, her being is compressed into my family. *Invite her into your dailyness*, He said.

So I did. When she came, I asked her to help me make dinner. I asked her to help me bathe the kids. I questioned her about the problems with my rose garden. I told her I needed her advice on sewing the new window treatments for the dining room. With a smile as radiant as the sun, she jumped right in. I realized that everyone likes to feel needed.

While we may sometimes see things differently from our in-laws, God says our "every action must be done with love" (1 Cor. 16:14). He wants us to treat even our in-laws with love, kindness, and respect. If your in-laws are lonely, include them in your life. It might make all the difference in your relationship.

Yahweh-yireh

I, Yahweh, will answer them; I, the God of Israel,
will not forsake them. (Isa. 41:17)

"Tessa, I've got bad news. I've been laid off," said Matt. "The economy is so bad, they're closing my entire division."

What followed was two years of complete dependence on and provision from the Lord. Tessa, who had been a stay-at-home mom, went back to work full-time in a job that was heaven sent. She and Matt pinched pennies, examining every single expense to lighten the load. They learned how to garden, repair things themselves, and cook from scratch.

God did many miraculous things for their family during those two years. He didn't provide a job for Matt, He didn't keep the cars or appliances from breaking, and He didn't keep them from having medical bills. He didn't leave envelopes of cash in their mailbox or groceries on their doorstep, but somehow, some way, God always showed up to take care of them. He kept them in the palm of His hand, never forsaking them, always providing just when the days were the darkest.

Matt and Tessa learned that their Provider is the Lord, not a job, not a savings account, not their own ingenuity. They learned how to accept help from others and, in turn, how to help others in need. They learned that this world with its material trappings is not their home. They learned what is truly important.

When your husband loses his job, it is terrifying. You wonder, *How will we survive? How will we pay the bills, save for retirement, put the kids through college?* But your Father is crazy about you and knows your "impossible" situation provides an opportunity to demonstrate His faithfulness, goodness, provision, and unconditional love. So relax in His strong arms: He will come through for you!

Peace and Quiet

*Come to Me, all of you who are weary and burdened,
and I will give you rest. (Matt. 11:28)*

The dog was barking, the baby was crying, and dinner was burning. It was a typical five o'clock hour at the Jamison home. Danielle put Hunter in his high chair long enough to pull the casserole out of the oven, but he screamed in protest at being put down. Tyler appeared at the kitchen door with ink all over his face and hands. "Mommy, I did an art project." *Oh, lovely*, Danielle thought to herself. The phone rang loudly. "Hon, I'm going to be a little late. I've got to get these specs out today." *OK, I'm about to lose it.*

Knowing she needed a change of scenery and a moment to pray, she said, "Tyler, put your shoes on. We're all going to go on a walk."

"Now? What about dinner?" he asked.

"I think it needs to cool off," Danielle replied, referring more to herself than the casserole.

As she pushed the double stroller down the street, Danielle took a deep breath and prayed silently. *Lord, life feels like more than I can handle. I know it's just little stuff, but it's adding up and taking a toll on me. Please give me Your peace so I can live for You no matter what my circumstances are. Help me glorify You in the things I do and say, and please grant me wisdom and strength to live by Your grace.*

We've probably all experienced that feeling of just trying to stay afloat, whether we have dealt with more serious problems or just day-to-day difficulties. However, if we are walking with the Lord, He can equip us to live in a way that brings Him glory. We can't do this out of our own strength but only by His Spirit.

Not Stuck on Stuff

"Well done, good slave!" he told him. "Because you have been faithful in a very small matter, have authority over 10 towns."
(Luke 19:17)

Our mission trip to Kenya was life changing. One of the most striking lessons I learned was how content the people were without all the possessions we are accustomed to. They had no modern conveniences, no expensive cars, no technological gadgets, and not even manufactured goods like toys or store-bought clothes. Their homes were simple mud or dung walls with thatched roofs, and they didn't eat like kings. Yet in home after home, the families brought out their best harvest—a meal of goat meat for us, their special guests.

When I returned home to the United States, I was challenged to find contentment outside all the "stuff" that so easily gets in the way. My husband and I decided to give a portion of our income above our tithe to our church's ministry in Africa. It will be a sacrifice for us to give this money, but I am trusting that God will continue to provide for us. We have so much, and so many have so little. If we can carefully and intentionally be good stewards of what God has given us, He will bless our offerings and use them in ways that have eternal value.

The Kenyan people gave us the best of what they had; they gave sacrificially. Jesus gave His life as a sacrifice for us. We want to give cheerfully out of the abundance God has given us, seeking to find our contentment in Him rather than in what the world has to offer.

Prayerfully examine your budget to see where your money is going. Is your first priority your tithe to your church? Do you use your resources to help others? Does God have lordship over every area of your life, including your finances?

Click

A generous person will prosper; whoever refreshes others will be refreshed. (Prov. 11:25 NIV)

I clicked off a few frames on my new DSLR (digital single lens reflex) camera to demonstrate to my sister how many frames per second it could shoot. "This will be great at the kids' soccer and baseball games," I said.

"Don't you already have a digital camera?" Kate asked.

"Well, yes, but it's just a point-and-shoot. This one has a lot more capabilities."

Kate asked, "Do you know what kind of camera I use? I get those cheap disposable cameras. I'd like a digital, but we just can't afford one right now."

Later that evening I thought back on my conversation with Kate. *Why don't you give Kate your other camera?* the Lord prompted. *But, Lord!* I protested. *I still want the point-and-shoot so I can toss it in my purse when I need to take a small camera. The DSLR is for more serious shooting.* (As if He didn't know.)

Silence. He was waiting for me to obey. Then I thought about how it took me just a few hours working at my job as a nurse to earn the money I had paid for that basic camera. With all the medical bills Kate and Charlie had accumulated, it might be years before they could afford a nice one. I took the point-and-shoot out of the closet and set it by my purse to give to Kate the next day. I felt the Lord smiling.

When the Lord asks us to give away something we're attached to, we may struggle to obey His prompting. But be obedient. Jesus said, "Give, and it will be given to you; a good measure—pressed down, shaken together, and running over—will be poured into your lap. For with the measure you use, it will be measured back to you" (Luke 6:38).

Good Things

Nor should we complain as some of them did. (1 Cor. 10:10)

I set a platter of chicken down on the table, and before I could sit down, my seven-year-old daughter, Emma, crinkled her nose and said, "Ewww. Do I have to eat that?"

"Yes," my husband, Dan, replied. "If you're hungry, that's what's for dinner. Your mother is not fixing everyone separate meals."

Emma and my nine-year-old son, Jack, had been doing a lot of complaining lately, and frankly I was tired of it. They complained about the meals I served, their toys, their clothes, our family rules. So after the kids were in bed, Dan and I talked about how we could teach the kids to stop complaining and be more grateful. We knew the Lord wanted all of us to be grateful for the blessings He has given us.

I began to realize that I did more than my fair share of complaining. I complained about waiting in line at the grocery store, driving a well-used car, my wardrobe, the low speed limit on Clarkson Road. Yet each of these is an example of my heavenly Father's love and provision—abundant choices at the grocery store, a car that runs, plenty of clothes, and rules for my protection, not to mention a healthy family and many other blessings.

Being a parent to a complaining child can give us a little insight into how God feels when we are ungrateful. In Exodus the Israelites witnessed God perform incredible miracles: the plagues, deliverance from slavery in Egypt, the parting of the Red Sea. Yet they complained. When God sent them manna, they demanded meat. We're really not much different on most days. And if "His anger burned" against them (Num. 11:1), as ours does at times against ungrateful children, we should know why our calling is to be thankful in all things (Eph. 5:18–20).

God Provides

The LORD will provide what is good. (Ps. 85:12)

Erica peeked in on her napping two-year-old, then turned and walked into the den. The last few weeks she had been researching day-care providers. As much as Erica wanted to be a stay-at-home mom, she and her husband, Reid, felt it was necessary for her to go back to work and put little Joey in day care.

But with stories on the news cropping up of babysitters who abused and neglected the children they were hired to care for, Erica and Reid wanted to make sure they chose the right person to watch Joey. *Lord,* Erica prayed, *it's scary to try to find day care for Joey. Please give me wisdom to find someone who will give him the kind of loving care he needs.*

Later that week Erica heard about a Christian woman at their church who wanted to provide day care for one child. When Erica went to the young woman's house to meet her, she was delighted to learn that she and Karen had a lot in common. Karen's daughter was just two months younger than Joey, and Erica and Karen had mutual friends. Both women had attended the same Christian university and had similar viewpoints and values. Erica began to realize that in the midst of a difficult situation, God was working on her family's behalf to provide for their needs.

In today's economy many parents must leave their precious children in someone else's care while they work, trying to make ends meet. Finding appropriate day care can be a daunting task. Are the caregivers qualified? Is the environment clean and safe? Will my child receive adequate attention and nurturing?

If you are in need of reliable care for your precious little ones, pray for wisdom. Check references, talk with other parents, and be diligent in making your choice.

Just Trying to Relax

Wine is a mocker, beer is a brawler, and whoever staggers because of them is not wise. (Prov. 20:1)

"How many glasses of wine have you had tonight?" John asked his wife at the end of a nice dinner out. Leslie's mood switched from relaxed to defensive. "No more than usual," she snapped.

Leslie took a sip, letting the warmth soothe her. With three kids, a part-time job, and caring for her mom, her stress level was through the roof. Wine had become a quick fix. "My dad always drank to unwind. That's all I'm doing. Hey, it's cheaper than therapy." Leslie laughed.

"Not much. And your dad died of liver failure."

"I don't go for the hard stuff like he did. John, what's the deal with you?"

"I'm just worried. You seem to need wine to relax, and you jump all over anyone who expresses concern. That tells me there's a problem."

Leslie grabbed her purse. "Let's just go." As she stormed out, she felt the stares of everyone in the restaurant. Later, as she tried to sleep, John's words raced through her mind. Did she need wine to relax? If she did, did that make her an alcoholic?

Tears welled up as she replayed the scene in the restaurant. She'd never been the type to make a scene in a public place. What was happening to her?

At the end of a busy day of work, caring for kids, ministry, and activities, we all need to unwind. Many people in our society condone the use of alcohol, but the dangers of addiction go undisputed. Proverbs offers many warnings about the effects of alcohol. If you or someone you know has a problem, pray and seek professional help. Pray that God will keep you aware of signs of addiction, whether it's alcohol or any other substance.

One Year Later

The LORD is near the brokenhearted;
He saves those crushed in spirit. (Ps. 34:18)

"You'd think it would have gotten easier by now." Shelley bit her trembling lower lip.

"Anniversaries are the worst," Kim said as she reached across the kitchen table and took Shelley's hand.

"Thanks for spending the day with me." Shelley tried to smile. It had been a year since her three-year-old daughter died of a heart defect. Everyone at the support group for moms who had lost children had warned her that today would be difficult.

"I'm glad you called." Kim moved her chair closer and wrapped her arm around Shelley. "When the one-year anniversary of losing my baby rolled around, I didn't have anyone to call. I promised myself I'd never let a friend go through that alone."

Shelley wiped a tear before it dripped down her cheek. "I just don't understand. I mean, I prayed. . . ."

Kim handed Shelley a tissue. "I had a long list of questions too. Finally I realized that I might not ever understand why, but I have a faithful God who sympathizes with my pain, shares my grief, and is strong enough to handle my questions and my anger. He is also kind enough to send friends who understand this kind of heartbreak." Shelley's tears started to gush. *God, thank You for being a Father who understands*, she prayed silently.

In times of crisis or unspeakable loss, those with similar wounds are the ones who fully understand the depth of our pain. And we have a heavenly Father who loves us enough to send the exact friends we need at the moment we need them.

If you have experienced a significant loss, God can use you to help someone else through her grief as well. Pray for an opportunity to provide sympathy and support to one who desperately needs to hear, "I understand."

You're Worth More

Husbands, love your wives, just as Christ loved the church and gave Himself for her. (Eph. 5:25)

Barb patted the couch cushion. Ruthie flopped down beside her. *God, where do I begin? I could give a dozen reasons why C. J. is all wrong for her. But when I was sixteen, would I have listened?*

"Ruthie, about C. J. . . ." Ruthie rolled her eyes. "Not again, Mom. C. J.'s a nice guy. You just don't know him."

"Nice guys don't put you down." During that one evening C. J. called Ruthie a dork, made jokes about her curly hair, and commented that certain body parts were not what he considered perfect. "Is C. J. the type of guy you want to spend the rest of your life with? And if you have a daughter, do you want him criticizing your little girl for the way she looks?"

Barb watched her daughter's expression soften. *God, please let her see my point.* "Think about what kind of qualities you want in your future husband. Why settle for less, even when you're dating?" She squeezed Ruthie's hand. "You are worth so much more than that."

Ruthie twirled the ring on her thumb. "It would be nice to have a guy who compliments me instead of calling me names."

How many of us had the qualities of our future husband in mind when deciding whether to date a guy? Some of us can look back on enough heartbreak to understand the importance of thinking ahead. *What kind of man do I want to spend the rest of my life with?*

If you have a young woman in your life (a daughter, niece, neighbor, or a girl you are mentoring), encourage her to begin thinking about what kind of man she hopes to marry. Commit to pray for and with her.

Desperate Times

God, deliver me. Hurry to help me, LORD! (Ps. 70:1)

Tina clutched her purse and left the middle school principal's office. Though she had told Mr. Chapman about her son Pete's difficulties with some of the boys in his PE class, she didn't feel her meeting had accomplished anything. It seemed to Tina that the principal's remarks about "boys being boys" indicated he didn't grasp how intense the bullying had become.

She started the car but didn't drive away from the school immediately. Instead Tina talked with God about her frustrations over the bullies who taunted Pete almost every day. *Lord, I don't know what to do about this situation,* Tina pled. *Pete is becoming increasingly sullen and fearful, but no one seems to be willing or able to intervene. Please do something!*

Sitting in the car, Tina began to feel God's presence. Hope and strength started to fill her heart again. She switched off the ignition and headed back into the school. She knew that God was working on her behalf, but Tina also was determined to enlist Mr. Chapman's cooperation. Pete was too important to her to "just wait and see what happens," and she felt God prompting her to be her son's advocate.

Bullying has become a widespread problem and must be addressed. Counselors suggest that you begin with a child's teacher and move up to the principal and beyond if the problem continues.

Throughout the Gospels we see examples of hurting, confused, and desperate parents coming to Jesus for help with their child (see John 4:46–54; Luke 8:40–56; and Mark 9:14–27). In each situation Jesus expressed compassion and reassurance. He took the concerns of these weary and frightened parents seriously. He takes your concerns seriously too. Let Him walk you through those crisis moments as a parent. He'll give you wisdom and grace to carry on.

A Healthy Mom

May the Lord be praised! Day after day He bears our burdens; God is our salvation. (Ps. 68:19)

I thought I had unusually mature teenage daughters who enjoyed the tight bond we had developed since their father and I divorced. I thought my relationship with my daughters was mutually satisfying for all of us. I thought wrong.

After Scott left me, the girls and I moved to a different part of the state where I could afford a house, so I didn't have friends around to help me through the divorce. My daughters struggled with attending new schools. Our collective neediness created an unhealthy codependence.

Recently, as I helped them pack for a week with their father and his wife, I heard myself spewing venomous comments about Scott. By the grace of God, I suddenly recognized my sarcasm and disdain for what it was: a sad reflection of my bitter heart. I had developed an unhealthy habit of confiding in, venting to, and needing my daughters in ways that were completely inappropriate for a mother to relate to her children. After my girls left that day, I sat down and repented to God for the way I had dealt with my emotions. Then I called my pastor and asked him for the phone number of a good Christian counselor.

Some single parents unintentionally make the mistake of turning to their child for emotional support, confiding in them instead of turning to other adult friends and family. We forget our children need to be children.

Mothering is hard work. Single mothers carry an even heavier load and often lack the emotional support they desperately need. If you are struggling as a mom, resist the temptation to unload on your child. Seek out a godly friend, Christian mentor, or professional counselor.

Rotten Talk

*A contrary man spreads conflict, and a gossip
separates close friends. (Prov. 16:28)*

Krissy and her husband, Todd, waved good-bye to their friends from church and got into the car. The uneasy feeling she had been ignoring all evening returned. They had enjoyed Adam and Amy, discussing Amy's excitement over her pregnancy and Adam's recent appendectomy. They were so easy to talk to, and everyone had laughed a lot.

At some point, however, Krissy and Todd had shared with them a struggle they were having with another Christian couple, the Smiths, who happened to be mutual friends. More than that, in their frustration over their disagreement, they had told Adam and Amy things that painted the Smiths in a bad light. Adam and Amy had politely listened, but Krissy could sense they felt a little uncomfortable. Since then she had been feeling convicted, and now that she and Todd were alone in the car, she couldn't ignore it any longer.

"I feel really bad about what we shared about the Smiths," she said.

"Me too," he agreed. Later, after praying together about it, they acknowledged to Adam and Amy that they had been gossiping and asked their forgiveness. Then they took steps to improve their relationship with the Smiths.

Ephesians 4:29 says, "No foul language is to come from your mouth, but only what is good for building up someone in need, so that it gives grace to those who hear." When we share personal negative information about others, we plant a seed that will affect how our listeners view and treat that person. Within the body of Christ, these seeds have been responsible for broken relationships as well as divided churches. When we gossip, we tear others down, and somehow that makes us feel important. Where's the grace in that?

Dirty Dishes

God resists the proud but gives grace to the humble. (1 Pet. 5:5)

Natalie was mortified. Gina, a woman she barely knew from church, was doing her dishes.

Since Natalie had been on bed rest for most of her pregnancy, she had been unable to keep up with the housework. As a result, the kitchen was a disaster when Gina showed up to bring her a meal. Because they were new in town and had no family nearby to help, Gina had generously dived into the task. Natalie could do nothing except protest meekly from the couch. She was wishing she could have made a better first impression. It was all an embarrassed Natalie could do to give a tight smile and a short "thanks" before the woman left.

As soon as the door shut, Natalie began to feel convicted. She had been so focused on her humiliation that she knew she had come across as ungrateful. As the Holy Spirit spoke to her, she realized that pride often hindered her prayer life. She knew intellectually that she needed grace and mercy, but sometimes it was hard to accept that she had nothing to offer God but a dirty house she was unable to clean. She tended to avoid God when she felt guilty. Just as she'd had a hard time accepting Gina's help today, it was hard for her gratefully to receive God's provision of help, which came through Gina. Natalie was learning, however, to come to God humbly each time, dirt and all. She decided to write Gina a note of heartfelt thanks.

To have true intimacy with God, we must approach Him just as we are, flawed and in desperate need of Him. As we wholeheartedly submit to God, embracing Jesus as our Savior, He removes the reproach of sin and replaces it with the righteousness of Christ.

Fixated on God

I will meditate on Your precepts and think about Your ways. (Ps. 119:15)

I'll admit it. I recently bought several issues of a popular magazine, which I almost never read, because each issue's cover story was about a certain celebrity couple. For some reason I have an atypical (for me) fascination with the stars' marital problems and their effect, as reported by countless gossip reporters, on their children. Not only have I bought the magazines, but I've also searched the Internet for more intimate details and have watched news stories about them. I have even found myself thinking about what advice I would give them if they were to ask.

During a recent quiet time, it occurred to me that my fixation on this couple looked a lot like how I should be fixated on God. If I spent the same amount of time reading about God in Scripture, digging deeper by going to commentaries and concordances, discussing God's Word and His character with others, and thinking about Him throughout the day, such habits could have a profound impact on my walk. It sounds a lot like what God told Joshua and the Israelites as they were going into the promised land: Think about Him and His commands day and night, talk about them, recite them, write them all over the house as reminders.

We are influenced by whatever fills our minds. The psalmists talked of meditating on God's instruction (Ps. 1:2), His love (48:9), His works (77:12), and His ways (119:15), basically every aspect of Him we can think of. If you're not sure what meditating on God looks like, Scripture memorization and inductive Bible study are ways to start. Any way we think about or ponder God and His Word is meditation. And it's always a better way of spending my time and thoughts than on celebrity gossip.

Weakness and Strength

He gives strength to the weary and
strengthens the powerless. (Isa. 40:29)

Lynn was actually relieved to have a name for the symptoms she had been battling for so many months. The doctor phoned to tell her the diagnosis: fibromyalgia and chronic fatigue syndrome. She spoke with a specialist the next week to receive tips for managing her symptoms and was referred to The Arthritis Foundation to gather more information.

Over the next few weeks, Lynn educated herself about this painful illness that drained her energy and robbed her strength. She learned to pay attention to her nutritional needs, to pace her activity, and to accept her limitations. She also learned to find support in her family and friendships and to run to God, whose power is perfected in weakness (2 Cor. 12:9).

While Lynn's ongoing prayer was for healing or remission, she was also thankful for an understanding family and good medical care.

Fibromyalgia and chronic fatigue syndrome (CFS) often occur together. They are difficult to diagnose and frustrating to both the victim and their support system because the disability does not "show" and treatment success varies. Depression often accompanies this loss of strength and productivity, so it is essential to seek accurate information and learn good self-care.

For believers battling such illness, a prayer support system is vital. Learning to draw near to God and even embracing the limitations as an opportunity to know Him better can bring acceptance and meaning to such a trial. It might be helpful to seek out other patients for support and to learn together about battling CFS or other similar conditions.

If you are dealing with chronic pain or disability, ask God for the courage to remain a blessing to those you meet and live with.

What Can I Give?

Show family affection to one another with brotherly love.
Outdo one another in showing honor. (Rom. 12:10)

When I read *The Five Love Languages* by Gary Chapman, I learned that I am a gift giver. I express my love for others by finding the perfect gift. But after becoming a stay-at-home mom five years ago, I realized I would no longer be able to give people expensive gifts. I had to find new ways to show my love for my family on their birthdays and holidays.

In January, right before my mother-in-law's birthday, we were broke. So I prayed about what I could give Margaret that would be inexpensive but meaningful. It occurred to me that Margaret and Joe's house needed some TLC, and I had some free time. She had a stroke several years ago, and my father-in-law now had to work both outside and inside the home. He just didn't have time to take care of everything.

I tentatively approached Margaret about the possibility of cleaning her house. She seemed genuinely excited about the idea. Not only would I be blessing her in a personal way on her birthday, but I would also be taking some of the burden off Joe. So I collected some cleaning supplies from my house and spent a full day cleaning Margaret and Joe's house.

God has shown me that there are ways to bless my family besides just giving gifts. I can give something even more valuable than money—I can give my time. He reminds us in Colossians 3:23, "Whatever you do, do it enthusiastically, as something done for the Lord and not for men."

Prayerfully seek God's will about what you can do to help someone in need. While you don't need to say yes to every request for help, be open to the possibilities He brings your way.

Constant Companion

A fool gives full vent to his anger, but a wise man holds it in check.
(Prov. 29:11)

My sister Judy married the first man who came along and promised to love her. When her first marriage failed because of Stan's alcohol addiction, she and her three children were left alone. Soon she turned to the next man who swept her off her feet. Unfortunately for Judy, husband number two was even worse than the first.

As in her first marriage, Judy called me day and night with stories about the cruel things her husband said and did to her. I urged her to consider her children's welfare, if not her own.

I felt helpless, and I kept pleading with Judy, telling her to go to a therapist or visit with a pastor, but she refused. I didn't know what to do to help her, other than to listen.

Since her second divorce, anger has been Judy's constant companion and has damaged her ability to trust people. I still pray for her every day, but she seems unwilling to forgive and to release her pain. So far she hasn't turned the situation over to God and asked Him to heal her. Instead she has chosen the path of bitterness.

The dictionary defines *anger* as a strong feeling of displeasure and belligerence aroused by a wrong. If we have been wronged in any way, we need to ask God to help us forgive those who inflicted the hurt. This doesn't excuse the harm or abuse others caused us, but it allows us to find freedom in spite of their actions.

In Ecclesiastes 7:9 we are told, "Don't let your spirit rush to be angry, for anger abides in the heart of fools." God knows the hurts we bear, and He wants to help us. We need to be willing to admit to Him that we cannot do it on our own.

The Budget

Godliness with contentment is a great gain. (1 Tim. 6:6)

My husband's business has been slow lately, and my part-time hours have been reduced, so this year there will be no vacation. For the first time in our marriage, we're forced to prepare a formal written budget, spending our reduced dollars before they ever reach our hands. Oh, we've always had a budget, but it's been in my head and not on paper.

Over the years we've tried to be good stewards of the money God has given us—tithing, saving, preparing for the kids' college, lowering our credit card debt. We've also tried to live below our means, but since things are so tight right now, we're having to make some really tough choices. We totally cut out some expenses (we took our children out of the private Christian school they were attending), and we cut way back on other expenses (no more eating out). We've had to choose between good things and better things in order to prioritize our spending.

This process reminds me to be satisfied and content with what I have, "for He Himself has said, 'I will never leave you or forsake you'" (Heb. 13:5). James tells us to remember those in need: "If a brother or sister is without clothes and lacks daily food and one of you says to them, 'Go in peace, keep warm, and eat well,' but you don't give them what the body needs, what good is it?" (James 2:15–16).

Many families today are making tough sacrifices in order to stay afloat. Some families must even decide between eating and paying the electric bill. So let's not forget our brothers and sisters who are in need, even as we struggle ourselves. Remember that our good God is in control. He is aware of every trial and circumstance and is working toward the restoration of all things.

Long-term Lessons

Whatever a man sows he will also reap, . . . the one who sows to the Spirit will reap eternal life from the Spirit. (Gal. 6:7–8)

Becca was frazzled. Grocery shopping with three boys in a crowded store when it was almost dinnertime was a recipe for trouble. Jamie, her five-year-old, reached for a pack of candy while they waited in the endless checkout line. "Mom, can I please have this?"

"No, buddy, it's almost time for dinner. We don't need any sweets right now."

Jamie got that look in his eyes—a tantrum was brewing. "But I want it!" When he threw the candy on the floor, Becca said, "I know you're hungry, and you're ready to get out of here. I am too. But we're not getting candy right now. Mommy decides what we buy at the store. If you have a tantrum, you will sit in time-out when we get home."

It wasn't pretty, but Becca managed to finish checking out and head home. She knew, however, it would have been far worse on a heart level for Jamie to get his way. After time-out, Becca talked to Jamie about obeying even when you don't get what you want, trusting that Mommy knows what is best for him.

Parenting is full of teachable moments, reminders that our children need instruction about the way they should go (Deut. 6:1–9). When we deal with their struggles, we're not only dealing with their actions and choices; we're dealing with their hearts. Instead of taking the easy way out by not addressing sin in our children's lives or in our own lives, we need to remember that more is at stake than just this moment. As you instruct your children in God's ways and His Word, look for opportunities to point them to Jesus, the only One who can change their hearts.

Are You Listening?

There is one who speaks rashly, like a piercing sword; but the tongue of the wise brings healing. (Prov. 12:18)

"Sometimes I feel like Seth doesn't listen to a word I say," I told my friend Jessica. "We were talking after we got home from work last night. Pretty soon it turned into an argument, and I could tell he'd tuned me out. Do you and Nick bicker about petty things very often?" I asked.

"It depends a lot on me," Jessica replied. "I can get a little testy at certain times of the month. When I started journaling, I realized that my irritability increased at about the same time each month. Don't underestimate your hormones. They might be playing a bigger part in your relationship that you think."

"You're probably right. My period is due any day now, and I guess I've been taking my frustration out on Seth." I was grateful that God had used Jessica to help me see it wasn't all about Seth.

Although hormonal fluctuations can definitely make women more sensitive or irritable, it doesn't mean we can use those times to unleash every negative thought on those around us. Proverbs 14:1 says, "Every wise woman builds her house, but a foolish one tears it down with her own hands." Another way we can interpret that verse is: "Every wise woman builds her house, but a foolish one tears it down with her own words."

Keeping our thoughts to ourselves may be difficult, but we can do that by recognizing when we are feeling hormonal and do our best to keep peace. We are encouraged in Proverbs 14:29 that "a patient person shows great understanding, but a quick-tempered one promotes foolishness." Listen to God, and let your hormones take a backseat.

The Lord Cares

I will never leave you or forsake you. (Heb. 13:5)

I remember the day my dad left. It was a steamy summer afternoon, and I was six years old. He grabbed a couple of suitcases, tossed in his clothes and toiletries, and screeched out of the driveway. I only saw him a few times after that—usually on holidays. He was busy with his new wife and kids.

When I began dating, my insecurities went into overdrive. I was always afraid my boyfriends would leave, and they did. Looking back now, I realize now that dealing with my neediness couldn't have been easy.

My husband and I married when I was barely twenty. I hadn't healed sufficiently from my past and brought a lot of baggage into our marriage. The first time we disagreed, I thought the relationship would end. It didn't. Every time we went through turmoil, I expected him to leave. He didn't.

Four years after we got married, we became Christians. I began meeting with a counselor at church, and she helped me learn to deal with my insecurities. She said that as I began to trust in the Lord, because of who He is and His faithfulness, my fear of abandonment would heal. It's been a long process, but as I grow in my walk with the Lord, I'm trusting in Him to provide for me and to meet all of my needs.

Many people deal with a fear of abandonment. We bring this fear into our relationships, and frequently we may believe we are not worthy of anyone's love—not even God's. But in spite of the fact that people are bound to let us down, God never will. He always loves us, always wants the best for us, and He promises never to leave us.

Good Advice

The one who walks with the wise will become wise, but a companion of fools will suffer harm. (Prov. 13:20)

"You shouldn't put up with that!" Helen insisted. "You ought to get a lawyer and file for divorce." *Maybe that's what I should do*, Dina fumed silently.

But later when Dina had time to cool off, she wasn't so sure her neighbor Helen was giving her sound advice. Even though she and Jeff had been having some strong disagreements lately, was it really reason enough to get a divorce? Should she break up her family over a few heated words and a slammed door? What's more, did she want to put her two children through a painful divorce when she and Jeff could work things out?

Dina prayed about her marriage and began to realize she should look for advice elsewhere—not from someone who was still bitter from her own divorce and didn't have a relationship with the Lord.

The following week Dina sought out Kim, one of the women in her Bible study. They began meeting on a regular basis, and Kim shared with Dina how she coped with ups and downs in her own marriage. As they talked, Dina began to realize that while she and her husband both needed to work on some things, preserving her marriage was worth the effort.

When a man and a woman marry, bringing two completely different people from different backgrounds together to form a new relationship can be a challenge. But when a wife needs advice, she should turn first to God's Word and prayer, asking the Lord to provide a godly Christian woman to help her navigate the sometimes difficult terrain. Look for someone who is like the woman in Proverbs 31:26: "She opens her mouth with wisdom and loving instruction is on her tongue."

Dark Hair, Nice Smile

Surely You desire integrity in the inner self,
and You teach me wisdom deep within. (Ps. 51:6)

"Describe your ideal husband," I remember my high school friend Diane asking during a sleepover at my house years ago. "Oh, about six-foot-two, dark hair, a nice smile." I went on to describe all the glowing characteristics I thought were important at the time.

A few days ago I asked my seventeen-year-old daughter, Sarah, the same question. Happily, she has more sense than I did when I was her age.

My husband (who is not six-foot-two but does have dark hair and a nice smile) and I have been talking to our daughter for some time about what she should look for in a prospective husband. Sarah replies thoughtfully, "I want a guy I can trust—someone who will be faithful, honest, and kind. Someone with a lot of integrity who will be a hard worker. He needs to love kids. And of course, he has to be a strong Christian. That's a must."

Good answers, I thought. She's also been known to add, "It would be nice if he had dark hair and a nice smile. But whatever he looks like, I want him to be someone God chooses for me."

We are often judged according to our physical appearance. Unfortunately, when choosing a marriage partner, many people don't look much further than that. And before looking beneath the surface, they marry based on chemistry rather than character and a mutual commitment to Christ.

There can be a lot of physical attraction between people who are not well suited to each other. The most handsome man in the world could be dishonest, lacking integrity, or much worse. Prayer, patience, and a true understanding of love (1 Cor. 13:4–8) can help believers avoid making marriage mistakes.

Monday Morning

*When you lie down, you will not be afraid; you will lie down,
and your sleep will be pleasant. (Prov. 3:24)*

Rushing into the conference room at the last minute, Meg grabbed her usual seat at the table and sat down for the weekly Monday morning team meeting. She was exhausted from worrying about everything under the sun and hadn't been sleeping well for weeks on end.

Gordon, head of the department, began droning on in his usual fashion. Meg squirmed in her chair trying to stay alert. *Why can't he just get to the point so we can get back to work?* she wondered. *Why does he spend an hour and a half talking when anyone else could say the same thing in ten minutes?*

The next thing she knew, she had nodded off, and Gordon was staring at her intently. The room was unsettlingly still until he leaned toward her and demanded, "Am I boring you, Ms. Johnson?" Startled and embarrassed, Meg snapped to attention.

Later she scheduled an appointment with her doctor. Although he said everything seemed to be fine physically, he recommended seeing a counselor to help her deal with the stress so she could experience better sleep. Meg found a good Christian counselor through her church, who has been working with Meg on letting go of things over which she has no control and trying to work on things she can change. Now when Meg lies down at night, she pictures putting all her worries into God's capable hands, and she finds herself sleeping much more peacefully.

If you are having difficulty falling asleep or if you experience excessive daytime sleepiness, you may want to consult your doctor. If the matter is stress related, counseling may be helpful. Quality of sleep enables us to give our best to God and others.

Numbing the Pain

Don't get drunk with wine, which leads to reckless actions,
but be filled by the Spirit. (Eph. 5:18)

When Jill's mom died after a long illness, Jill's grief spiraled into depression. Her friend Lynn wrapped her arms around Jill after an especially tearful talk. "I hate seeing you hurt this much," she said gently. "Maybe you should consider getting some help."

Instead Jill stuffed her pain down deeper. One sleepless night she sneaked into the kitchen, remembering her father's old remedy for stress. Careful not to wake her husband, she poured a glass of the wine that was set aside for cooking. Just a little wouldn't hurt.

A few months later Lynn found Jill crying in the church bathroom. Heated arguments with her husband over changes in her behavior, the sneakiness and dishonesty, had forced her to accept the awful truth. "Roger says I need to stop self-medicating and get help before I ruin our family. How could I let myself do this, Lynn? I hated it when my dad drank, and I hated all those family reunions where half my relatives left in a huff because of alcohol-induced fights. Now I'm just like them."

"No you're not." Lynn hugged Jill. "You're admitting that things got out of control. Now you can let God help you overcome this."

The Bible is clear on this point: God does not want His children to abuse alcohol. Anyone who has spent time around an alcoholic or an intoxicated friend will most likely understand why the Bible warns against it. Who can deny how it alters judgment and makes everyday activities like driving dangerous? So take a moment to pray for anyone you know who has been affected by alcohol abuse. And when you're the one who's hurting, turn to God alone for comfort.

Bridges, Not Barriers

How good and pleasant it is when brothers live together in harmony! (Ps. 133:1)

"I enjoyed meeting your new neighbor when she visited our Sunday school class last week," Beverly said as I sat down next to her in choir practice. "Is she going to visit again, or will she be finding another church to attend on a regular basis?"

I was just about to respond to Beverly's comments when I realized the implications of her second remark. Did she really assume that because my friend Joy is black, she would automatically go to a predominantly African-American church? Worse yet, was she implying that Joy wouldn't fit in at our church? "Actually," I measured my words carefully, "Joy really felt welcomed here and plans to come back next Sunday."

Beverly smiled. "I'm so glad. She'll be a great addition to our class."

"I think so too," I said, realizing I'd misinterpreted her question. "She's looking forward to getting to know everyone better."

While racism may seem a thing of the past, some people still carry subtle prejudices that affect the way they think of and treat people who are different from themselves. Even in our churches—local outposts of God's kingdom—unseen barriers and unwritten rules can still exist, making some people feel excluded, dividing rather than unifying.

Depending on the geographic location of your local church, your congregation may be made up of people who are of the same color and ethnicity, or it may be quite diverse. But regardless of who regularly attends your services, you can be an agent of love and unity by intentionally making everyone feel welcomed and included. Prayerfully evaluate if you harbor any prejudices that keep you from extending love and kindness to people of other races. Consider what you might do to tear down those barriers and build bridges instead.

Handling Pressure

Don't set foot on the path of the wicked; don't proceed in the way of evil ones. (Prov. 4:14)

Kristie tried to remain calm as she listened to her teenage daughter's account of the party she had attended the previous night. She didn't want to shut the conversation down by over-reacting, but she also didn't want Emily to make the same mistake again.

As Emily explained how her friends had convinced her to go to the party against her better judgment, Kristie remembered back to the previous week when her own friends had invited her to go to a movie that she had already decided not to see based on its rating and reviews. She declined the invitation, but it was difficult. "I know how you felt," Kristie said. "Let's think about what you might do differently the next time you encounter a similar situation."

The mother and daughter talked about the pressures and consequences of following others. When Emily left for soccer practice, they weren't in agreement on every issue, but Kristie felt like God had guided her to say what was needed. She prayed for her daughter and confidently trusted Him to do the rest.

Teens long for the approval and companionship of their friends. And just like in adult friendships, peers can frequently encourage them to take wrong paths and make faulty decisions.

We all struggle with peer pressure, but our children often lack the wisdom and maturity to navigate it successfully. You can help them steer clear of unhealthy pressure by building their confidence in their own decisions, especially when going against the crowd. Ask God to help you set a good example of standing firm on biblical precepts when it isn't culturally cool. Then ask Him to guide you as you help equip your children to fight their battles with peer pressure.

Career Counseling

Seek His kingdom, and these things will be provided for you.
(Luke 12:31)

Katie rubbed her eyes. It was already nine o'clock. She had worked late every night this week and was looking at working Saturday as well. A vision of her young daughter, Madison, popped into her head, tucked in bed, already asleep when she got home. She hadn't said good-night to her all week.

When her husband, Doug, had sounded disappointed on the phone at the news she was working late, Katie had reasoned with him that it would only be until her upcoming presentation. Then if all went well and she got the promotion she'd been longing for, she might be able to cut back on her hours. In reality she knew she would probably have to work long hours more often to keep up and remain competitive. Katie had always thought God honored hard work, but lately she felt convicted over her long hours.

God does want us to work hard, but if we're honest, our careers can become our idols, a source of misplaced ambition and pride or perhaps a symptom of materialism. Single women with few family obligations can be tempted to find their identity in their careers instead of in Christ. Pressure from coworkers and bosses can cause working moms to invest more into their work than in ministering to their families. If you think your career may be consuming your life, taking precedence over God or family, pray for His help in prioritizing your life, opening yourself to His wise counsel. And be certain you're finding your identity only in Him.

"The path of the upright is a highway," the Bible says (Prov. 15:19), not a closed course with no off-ramps. Ask God what choices He wants you to make.

Not What They Seem

Where envy and selfish ambition exist, there is disorder and every kind of evil. (James 3:16)

As Trudy and I stood waiting for the three o'clock bell to dismiss our kids from school, Nina glided toward her luxury SUV. "Look at her," I said to my friend. "She has a perfect life. She's gorgeous. Her kids are smart. Her husband is wildly successful. They even have a second home. I wouldn't mind a life like that."

"Do you know her very well?" Trudy asked quietly.

"Not really. We haven't talked much beyond the usual mom chat."

Trudy paused. "Well, let's just say, sometimes things aren't what they seem." The bell rang, and students came flooding out of the building, just as Trudy added, "You might want to pray for Nina and her family."

"About what? How can I pray if I don't know what to pray for?"

She gave a little wave and started toward her car. "God knows," she called.

Frankly, I didn't think about Nina again until the following week. That's when I heard two moms in the pickup line saying that Nina's husband had moved out. Shocked and saddened for them and ashamed of my envy, I prayed—really prayed—for them this time.

Envy can start with one seed and grow to monstrous proportions, leading to all sorts of other sins, like covetousness ("I wish I had that house or her car"), gossip ("Listen to what she did to get that promotion"), discontent ("Why didn't God give me a husband like hers?"). If nurtured, envy can overtake a believer's heart and choke the life and light right out of it. Follow the advice in 1 Peter 2:1: "Rid yourselves of all malice, all deceit, hypocrisy, envy, and all slander." Ask God for a grateful heart and a generous spirit in its place.

God Is in Control

I sought the Lord, and He answered me and delivered me from all my fears. (Ps. 34:4)

I remember my first major panic attack like it was yesterday. My friend Angela and I were spending the weekend sightseeing in Chattanooga, Tennessee. One day we visited Ruby Falls, a 145-foot underground waterfall located more than 1,100 feet beneath Lookout Mountain.

When Angela and I stepped into the elevator with about twenty other people and began our descent underground, I looked through the screened elevator door, watching the earth and rock as we journeyed into the depths of the cave.

Although I had never before had a problem with enclosed spaces, my breathing became shallow, and my palms began to sweat. I had difficulty focusing my eyes or my mind. I just wanted to escape. As soon as the elevator stopped, I tried to focus my eyes in the darkness. Angela asked what was wrong, and I assured her I'd be fine. But I wasn't.

When I could no longer control my feelings of panic, I broke away from the rest of the group and literally ran back to where I thought the elevator was located. To my horror I couldn't find it. I panicked. Finally a tour guide came to my rescue and escorted me back to the surface, where I ran outside to catch a breath of fresh air.

If you find yourself in a situation where you feel you have no control, keep the words of Psalm 46:1–3 memorized and close at hand: "God is our refuge and strength, a helper who is always found in times of trouble. Therefore we will not be afraid, though the earth trembles and the mountains topple into the depths of the seas, though its waters roar and foam and the mountains quake with its turmoil." Choose to believe those words of truth.

Remembering Rocks

Fasten both stones on the shoulder pieces of the ephod as memorial stones for the Israelites. (Exod. 28:12)

"Mama, what are these rocks for?" my daughter asked. We were working outside, making piles of rocks in different flower beds.

I explained to her that in the Old Testament, God told the Israelites to set up stones of remembrance. In Genesis, Abraham built altars to the Lord in places where he had memorable spiritual experiences. In Joshua, God instructed the people to set up a memorial to Him by the Jordan River because He had dried up its waters so they could cross safely to the other side. God even wanted two memorial stones fastened to the shoulders of Aaron's priestly garment, the ephod. The Lord wanted His people to remember all that He had done for them. And God knew that seeing those piles of rocks would cause others to ask what they were. In this way His people could tell of His faithfulness and goodness.

"Daddy and I decided to set up some memorial stones of our own. This pile is to thank Him for healing you of seizures; that pile is because God helped Daddy find a job; and this pile is just because God has been so good to us. Our rocks are sort of like a journal without words."

"Cool, Mama! Let's call them our remembering rocks!"

When we remember what God has done in the past, we can trust Him more completely with our present. When we reflect on His faithfulness in both good times and hard times, when we look back on how He has delivered us from sickness or financial difficulties, we praise Him with our lives and hearts. Those spiritual stones sharpen our faith as we grow in the confidence of His promises. We are reminded, and He is glorified.

Set up some "remembering rocks" before the Lord.

A Deep Connection

My love is mine and I am his. (Song of Sol. 2:16)

Shawna and Trey had it all: successful careers, beautiful children, a dream home. They were busy at church, busy in their neighborhood, busy with their family. On the surface everything seemed perfect, but God had been working on their hearts. They knew something was missing in their marriage. They had lost their deep connection.

"We never spend time together or talk anymore, Trey," said Shawna.

"I know. I think we need to subtract some things from our schedules," Trey said. "And if we got the kids to bed earlier, even just one night a week, we'd be able to carve out some quality time for ourselves."

Deep connection with your husband can slip away in busy, stressful times. Careers, children, home, church—all of these are good things, but they're not the best thing. If you're married, second only to your relationship with God is your relationship with your husband.

You've read of basic ways to spend time with your husband, like a date night or a weekend away. But think outside the box too. What kinds of things did you enjoy doing together when you dated? Did the two of you play golf? Ride bikes? Sit at the coffee shop and talk? Perhaps some things need to be cut out of your schedules so you can make time for each other. Ask God to show you if something needs to go.

Your time together doesn't need to be expensive or planned. Get up a few minutes earlier, take a walk in your neighborhood together, or sit outside at night and watch the stars. But spending time with the one you love is worth it! Your children also need to see that you love each other, to know what a godly marriage looks like.

Patiently Pure

Pursue righteousness, faith, love, and peace, along with those who call on the Lord from a pure heart. (2 Tim. 2:22)

Charlotte took her seat next to the window for the flight home. She sighed and closed her eyes. Another wedding, another bridesmaid's dress, another friend who found the love of her life. But Charlotte was still single, with no prospects on the horizon. *Maybe I should just give up on finding Mr. Right and look for "Mr. Right Now,"* she thought. It was so hard to be alone.

Some of the singles she knew spent their time at clubs and having one-night stands. But as soon as the familiar temptation and desperation surfaced, Charlotte knew where this line of thinking would take her. The catch in her spirit caused her to pray, *God, I know that obeying You means keeping myself pure, in both mind and body. Please help me trust You to meet all my needs and to be my first love. Help me keep my heart pure to honor You.*

Purity isn't just being chaste and sexually upright; purity is a state of the heart. No matter our situation in life—single, married, widowed, divorced—God wants our hearts and lives to reflect the purity of Jesus. How can we keep our way pure? The psalmist says, "By keeping [God's] word" (Ps. 119:9).

God says that sex outside the covenant of marriage is sin; this is His design for our protection and for His glory. God wants to be Lord of every area of our lives, including our sexuality. If you face struggles in this area, protect yourself with prayer, hide Scripture in your heart, and make a game plan for fleeing from temptations that may arise. Also seek accountability from a trusted Christian friend who will help you uphold God's standard for purity as given in Scripture.

No Longer Enemies

While we were enemies, we were reconciled to God through the death of His Son. (Rom. 5:10)

I was so nervous. My high school reunion was about to begin, and not only would I be seeing old friends; I would also be seeing Gillian for the first time in ten years. Gillian and I had been best friends since kindergarten, but when we entered high school, she told me she was determined to join the popular crowd and didn't have time to hang out with me.

I enjoyed high school very much, but I struggled with the pain of this broken relationship. Then in college God showed me my need for Jesus, and I began a personal relationship with Him. He taught me that while I was still a sinner, Christ died for me. And now He gives me forgiveness I don't deserve because of what Jesus did.

I wanted to be bold enough not only to approach Gillian in true, caring friendship but also to share how Jesus had given me life and peace. So when I saw her, I swallowed the lump in my throat and made a beeline for her. I gave her a hug and a big smile. We talked about family, careers, and how everyone had changed. When I told her that God had changed me a lot since high school, the door was open to share what He means to me.

Forgiveness means we choose to release someone who has wronged us or sinned against us. We don't do it because they deserve it or have earned forgiveness. The Bible says that we ourselves were God's enemies, dead in our sins, yet God sent Jesus to pay our debt on the cross. Jesus has made peace between us and God, paying the ultimate price so that we could be restored to the Father. Who else needs to hear this news from you?

Media Fast

Teach us to number our days carefully so that we may develop wisdom in our hearts. (Ps. 90:12)

My grandmother washed clothes in an old-fashioned washing machine. It didn't have a spin-dry cycle; instead she put the clothes through a wringer that extracted the excess water when she cranked the handle. Grandma never owned a dryer; she hung clothes outside to dry when the weather was nice. During cold Midwestern winters, she hung the laundry on clotheslines Grandpa had hung in the basement. She didn't have the modern conveniences of a dishwasher, color TV, computer, cell phone, or DVD player.

Today most of us have more gadgets than our grandmothers and great-grandmothers could even dream of. But there is a downside to all of our modern conveniences. Recently the Lord showed me that while things like cell phones and computers can be convenient, they can also be time wasters. I began to realize that I spent far more time sending text messages, surfing the Internet, and watching TV than I did praying and reading my Bible.

So I began a weeklong media fast. It was hard not to run to the computer to check my e-mail a dozen times a day or text a friend with the latest news. But the Lord showed me that spending time with Him is as vital as air and water. It requires time and a quiet heart. So now I slow down from the busy pace, turn off all the noise, and listen for His still, small voice.

If you're struggling with your schedule, submit it to the Lord and ask Him to help you use your time wisely. Psalm 31:15 says, "My times are in your hands" (NIV). Get off the treadmill of frantic activity and learn to be still in His presence.

Chat Room

Everyone who looks at a [man] to lust for [him] has already committed adultery with [him] in [her] heart. (Matt. 5:28)

"I met this really nice guy in a chat room," my sister said.

"And what does Ken have to say about that?" I asked, already knowing what the answer would be. There was silence on the other end of the line for a moment. Then Linda said, "He doesn't know." She launched into a defensive mode. "You know Ken and I have been having a lot of problems in our marriage."

"That's no excuse for getting involved with a man online."

"Robert and I are not 'involved,'" Linda replied. "When I talk to him about what's going on in my life, he's so understanding. He's such a wonderful man."

"Linda," I asked cautiously, "are you developing feelings for this guy?" More silence. Then, a quiet "Yes, but I'm not committing adultery!"

"But you also aren't giving your marriage a chance if you're emotionally involved with this guy. Besides, he could turn out to be a nutcase for all you know. You may not be physically having sex with Robert, but if you have feelings for him, you're having an emotional affair."

Internet relationships might seem harmless in the beginning, but when opposite sex friendships are involved, you need to break the connection. Whether you are married or single, know who you're chatting with online. Don't give out personal information. And if you are having problems in your marriage, don't confide in another man—whether it's a friend, neighbor, coworker, or online acquaintance. Reserve those discussions only for trusted female friends and/or a Christian counselor or a pastor.

Personal Mission

Happy is a man who finds wisdom and who acquires understanding. (Prov. 3:13)

My young friend from church was frustrated with her mother-in-law. Since Callie and Tim's wedding four years ago, Sharon has made it her personal mission to instruct her daughter-in-law in all things domestic. Sharon critiques Callie's housekeeping, cooking, and organizational skills. After the birth of their first baby, Sharon even blamed Callie when he got diaper rash.

"I just don't know how to handle it without offending her," Callie lamented to me one morning. "I feel like Sharon thinks no one is good enough for her son—especially me. I get so angry and want to lash out at her, but I know that's not how the Lord wants me to handle it. So I just clam up and keep everything inside."

Since my husband, Brett, mentors Tim, I suggested the young couple join us for dinner one evening so we could share some similar struggles we had when we were first married. In time Tim began taking more responsibility for supporting Callie and establishing boundaries for his mother.

While most parents have the best intentions, sometimes letting go of their adult children can be hard. The Bible makes clear that a husband and wife should put each other before their mothers and fathers. Genesis 2:24 says, "This is why a man leaves his father and mother and bonds with his wife." Setting appropriate boundaries with parents and in-laws is important to the health of the marriage. The bonding spoken of in Genesis 2:24 will be more challenging if husbands or wives let their parents criticize their mates or treat them with disrespect.

If you are experiencing difficulties in your marriage due to boundary issues, pray for wisdom. Discuss the situation with your husband and come to an agreement about how to handle the situation.

Our Marine

The day my husband and I saw our son leave for boot camp was a bittersweet mixture of pride, sadness, and fear. Alex grew up with a strong sense of right and wrong. He always stuck up for the underdog and defended the weak. Now, all grown up, he was willing to put his life on the line to defend the cause of justice and liberty for people he has never met and to ensure our freedom here at home.

Several months later our Marine in his military buzz cut was on his way to Afghanistan. "I'll be OK, Mom," Alex said in a recent phone call. He couldn't possibly know the hours I'd already spent on my knees, pleading for his safety and asking our Father for His divine protection.

Military doctors gave Alex every immunization imaginable and took a sample of his DNA. He was issued a helmet, a Kevlar (bullet-proof) vest, and an M16. So while every earthly precaution is taken to assure Alex's safety and well-being, there are no guarantees. Only God can truly protect him.

While we wait for Alex's return, we pray for the Lord's protection, wisdom, and blessing on our son as well as others serving our country. As Americans, we have the privilege of living in a country where we enjoy unparalleled freedom. And to protect our freedom, brave men and women are serving in all branches of the military across the globe. We owe them and their families a debt of gratitude.

If you know of someone who has a loved one serving our country, ask what you can do to help, especially during an extended absence. Pray for the men and women in our military and their families.

Lies Have Short Legs

There is nothing covered that won't be uncovered, nothing hidden that won't be made known. (Luke 12:2)

Recently I thought about an incident that took place when I was sixteen. As I was driving home from high school, I took a turn too sharply, going too fast, and skidded on the rain-drenched asphalt. I tried to regain control but slammed into a guardrail. No other cars were involved, but my fender was crunched. But because I was afraid, I told my parents that another car hit me and drove away. The police were called, and a report was filed—a report filled with lies.

Obviously the police never found the phantom car that hit me, and I thought I was home free until my friend Tricia asked about the accident at church in front of my parents. Unknown to me, Tricia was nearby and saw me hit the guardrail. So when she asked how much damage my car sustained from the guardrail, my parents were confused. I mumbled through an answer to Tricia and excused my parents and me as quickly as possible.

There is an old saying: Lies have short legs. My lies found me out in a matter of days, and I damaged the trust of my parents. When I lied, I was hoping to avoid repercussions. Instead, by lying, I caused a rift in my family.

The Bible calls Satan the father of lies. The Bible also says that all lies will eventually be exposed. Even if the truth is ugly, uncomfortable, and painful, there is strength in honesty and integrity. Telling the truth allows us to be transparent and open with others. And this transparency draws people in and attracts others to us. When we choose honesty over lying, we are choosing God and reflecting His presence in our lives.

Anchor of Peace

The peace of God, which surpasses every thought, will guard your hearts and your minds in Christ Jesus. (Phil. 4:7)

In January, I decided to look forward and think about what I would like my life to look like over the next twelve months. To be honest, I didn't make it a matter of prayer, but each time I asked myself the question—*What do I want my life to be about in the coming year?*—the same answer kept coming to mind. The answer I envisioned was the word *shalom.*

I researched the word *shalom* to find out exactly what it meant. The most encompassing definition I could find was this: completeness, wholeness, health, peace, welfare, safety, soundness, tranquility, prosperity, perfectness, fullness, rest, harmony, the absence of agitation or discord. This definition resonated with me, and I sought the Lord on how He would like for me to move forward.

Having never had a regular daily prayer time, I decided this would be my first action. Every morning I spend at least thirty minutes praying through Scripture and reading a devotional like this one that helps me apply God's Word to everyday life. In my time alone with God, I've experienced clear leadings, godly insight, inexplicable peace, and an ever-growing trust and devotion to my Lord. Our time together is precious and fulfilling, and because of God's growth in me, my anxious heart has found peace, safety, rest—in other words, *shalom.*

We get to know people by spending time with them and learning about who they are. As the relationship grows, so does a level of understanding, peace, safety, and rest. Spending time with God does the same thing. As we seek Him by intentionally spending time with Him, we have an opportunity to learn about Him, hear His heart, and be transformed.

A Mother's Heartache

*The younger son gathered together all he had and traveled to a
distant country, where he squandered his estate in foolish living.*
(Luke 15:13)

Anna had dreaded this conversation ever since she'd agreed to attend her husband's family reunion. The women were gathered in the kitchen, cutting up vegetables and updating one another on the lives of their grown children. As the conversation worked its way around the circle, Anna tried to hold back her tears and muster the strength to tell the others about her daughter, Lisa. Though she was proud of her daughter's accomplishments, Anna daily grieved the choices Lisa had made in the past few years. She had drifted further and further from the Lord.

"How is Lisa doing?" someone asked. Anna smiled weakly, shrugged her shoulders, and started to answer, but the words got caught in her throat. Then she felt a soothing hand on her shoulder. Her sister-in-law Janice stepped to her side.

"Anna and Jake are experiencing what several of us have endured with our own grown children," began Janice. "But we're going to trust that God has His hand on Lisa and He'll battle for her all the way." Anna was relieved to see genuine, empathetic smiles and nods of encouragement.

Parenting comes with no guarantees. Many parents, though they raise their children to know and love God, must endure the heartache of watching a child walk away from the Lord. Some parents get angry and confused because they believed Proverbs 22:6 to be a sort of parenting warranty: "Teach a youth about the way he should go; even when he is old he will not depart from it." But this Scripture, like all Proverbs, is a biblical maxim or principle, not a promise. You cannot force a grown child to go to church, choose a godly mate, or live a holy life; but you can wait, pray, and hope in the Lord.

Bridging the Gap

Janet had encouraged me to invite her twenty-year-old daughter, Megan, to assist me in Vacation Bible School. I'd rarely seen Megan in church and doubted she would say yes, but I was wrong. Not only did Megan take off a week from work to help, but she proved to be an enthusiastic and creative assistant.

As the week drew to a close, I decided to ask my new young friend why I didn't see her in church very often. "I want to come to church, but I've had a hard time finding my place since I graduated from high school," said Megan. "Everything seems to be geared toward older, married people or children and teens."

I've learned young people are especially drawn to ministry opportunities like Vacation Bible School, mission trips, and children's ministries. They want to make a difference. But I also found that people like Megan will participate in fellowships and small-group Bible studies if they are personally invited and made to feel included. Most important, I learned that plugging into their lives is very rewarding.

Studies suggest than nearly two of every three teenagers who participate in church will disengage after high school and college. While researchers and strategists have yet to agree on the one thing that would keep more of them in church, they concur that something is amiss and the church, which is you and me, needs to do something about it.

Ask God to make you aware of young adults struggling to find their place. Intentionally include them in ministries, fellowships, small-group Bible studies, and worship services. Pray for opportunities to reach out to a searching young adult. Then step out of your comfort zone and into their world to bridge the gap.

How Did I Get Here?

My help comes from the LORD,
the Maker of heaven and earth. (Ps. 121:2)

As Danielle unpacked the box of kitchen gadgets and put them in the cabinets, she wondered how she had gotten here. Just over a year ago she had been unpacking these same items in a different home, a home she shared with her two children and her husband, Dave. But Dave wouldn't be opening these cabinets looking for the juicer or the toaster. He had his own kitchen now.

Dave had left Danielle and the children shortly after moving into their last home, insisting he no longer wanted to be married. Danielle begged Dave to see a Christian counselor with her, but he refused and filed for divorce. Months later she still felt the effects of the emotional whiplash she had incurred with Dave's sudden exit from their lives. Their marriage had been far from perfect, but Danielle never thought her Christian husband would abandon her.

She emptied the box just as the phone rang. "I was hoping I could take you and the kids out for a burger tonight," offered Julie, a friend from church. Danielle silently thanked God for good friends and His provision for her family and gratefully accepted Julie's offer.

Circumstances change, people disappoint, illness replaces good health, and jobs are lost. Such crises can arise so fast, you feel like a rug has been pulled out from under you. Like Mary and Martha in John 11, we may be tempted to feel that Jesus is nowhere to be found in our crisis situation. We may feel betrayed by His seeming absence.

But rest assured He is aware of your dire situations and is working behind the scenes to give you comfort, guidance, assurance, and love. In due time He can even breathe new life into the most desperate situation, bringing God glory and renewing your joy.

Ping-Pong Paige

Cast your burden on the Lord, and He will sustain you;
He will never allow the righteous to be shaken. (Ps. 55:22)

After her dad dropped her off, Paige, my nine-year-old, gave me a halfhearted hug. "Did you have a good time at Dad's?" I asked.

Nodding, she took her backpack and headed toward her room. She called, "Mom, do we have to go to church today? We go every week." I sat down beside her on her bed. "Yes, we do. We've talked about this before."

"Dad says when I'm older, I don't have to go if I don't want to." Pausing, I forced myself to sound calm. "Paige, we go to church because we want to worship and know the Lord better and be with other Christians." She laid her head on her arms.

"What is it, honey?" I asked, stroking her curly hair.

"It's so hard having two families," she said, through tears. "I go back and forth between houses. You and I do stuff together, but Dad and I don't. We go to church, but he and Tiffany don't even believe in God. I feel like a Ping-Pong ball, and nobody understands!"

Wiping her tears away, I said, "I know it's hard living in two homes—I'm sorry. I know it hurts that Daddy doesn't believe in God anymore, but God does exist, and He knows what you're feeling. He's with you always, even when I can't be. I love you so much, and God loves you even more."

Kids of divorce have it tough. Being shuttled between parents is hard, and stepparents and stepsiblings complicate matters. Different parenting standards and expectations can be confusing and difficult. Allow them to voice frustration and pain, and listen. Offer advice when you can, and pray for and with them regularly.

Noah

You will be blessed, because they cannot repay you; for you will be repaid at the resurrection of the righteous. (Luke 14:14)

Last year my son's school started a program where parents and grandparents could come in and help the second-graders who were behind their peers in reading. I felt God urging me to help, so I signed up. It turned out to be one of the most rewarding things I've ever done.

Although I helped three students, I connected with one boy in particular. Noah had light brown hair that was cropped short, and when he smiled, you could see emerging permanent teeth. His laugh was contagious, and he was a sweetheart.

The first time I heard him read aloud my heart broke. We read a book about a trash truck, and Noah had a difficult time pronouncing even some of the most basic words. I could tell he was embarrassed. But I assured him that those words would come more easily in time. Soon his confidence grew, and I saw how positively the individual tutoring helped him. I prayed that Noah and the other children I worked with would realize how precious they are in God's eyes.

Can you imagine what it would do for a struggling child if you could help him or her in some way? Have you thought about using your special gifts to help children? Maybe you have a gift of reading or writing. Or maybe your gift would be helping them learn to play soccer. Whatever talents and gifts God has given you, be open to using them as He directs. You'll never know how much you can truly bless others until you step out in faith to serve.

Matthew 10:42 says, "Whoever gives just a cup of cold water to one of these little ones because he is a disciple—I assure you: He will never lose his reward!"

Unexpected Kindness

The one who does not love does not know God,
because God is love. (1 John 4:8)

When Aaron and I were first married, I went out of my way to do things for him, even when he didn't ask me to. I wanted to be an excellent wife, and I enjoyed meeting his needs. But after a few months we began arguing about money. It was a constant source of friction between us.

Soon I began focusing on Aaron's faults instead of his strengths. Since I knew I was part of the problem, I asked God what I could do to improve our relationship. I needed help getting back on track with my attitude, so I purchased *The Love Dare* by Stephen and Alex Kendrick. I was a bit skeptical when I first got the book. I mean, how much can you really change a relationship in forty days? But the challenges required in this book were exactly what we needed.

On day two of *The Love Dare* my assignment was to show Aaron at least one unexpected act of kindness. That evening while we were watching TV, I quietly reached over and placed Aaron's feet in my lap. He seemed genuinely pleased that I initiated a foot massage. By taking the time to show him I cared, I opened the door a bit more to help our struggling relationship.

Showing kindness and love in our relationships takes consistent prayer and sacrifice. Sometimes we show more kindness toward strangers than we do to our own loved ones. But in Romans 12:10 we are reminded, "Show family affection to one another with brotherly love. Outdo one another in showing honor." God wants us to show our love to one another through unselfish devotion. Once you let go of selfishness, you can be more in tune with the heart of God.

The Love Story

Look at how great a love the Father has given us that we should be called God's children. (1 John 3:1)

We don't have cable at our house, and the government TV box isn't working so well. So in the evenings, we've been watching movies or reading. The theme of love runs through lots of books and movies. I've seen friendship love with Sam and Frodo in the *Lord of the Rings*; I've seen romantic love with Darcy and Elizabeth in *Pride and Prejudice*. These love stories move me to tears while my husband mutters something about chick flicks.

But of all the love stories ever told, the greatest love story happened two thousand years ago on a hill called The Skull. It's the story of the pure, blameless Son of God dying for sinful, undeserving sons and daughters of men. It's about the Hero rescuing His beloved, the Creator redeeming His created, the Spotless murdered for the stained.

God knew before He ever created us that we would sin, causing an impossible gap between Him and the people He created. Jesus knew before time began that He would come to earth to save us. As the great rescue mission played out, did Jesus ever wonder if we were worth it? As God the Father poured out His wrath on His beloved Son for our sins, did He ever think twice about saving us? I don't think so. Why? Because God is love.

God loves us because He chooses to. And that's why Jesus went to the cross—because of love. He knew our desperate need, our utter hopelessness, our certain doom. He willingly went to the cross, and love held Him there. His love story moves us to tears, but His love changes us forever.

Hungry for God

I was one of those women who thought she had it all together. *No need to worry about me, God. I can handle this. Those people over in Africa need You more. I'm OK here on my own.* Of course, I didn't really think that out loud, but my actions proved otherwise. Then during a series of events and circumstances, God showed me that I didn't have it all together.

My youngest daughter was born with a seizure disorder, my husband's business failed resulting in extended unemployment, and I was diagnosed with melanoma. I have now come face-to-face with my failures and disappointments with myself, some of my relationships, and yes, even my walk with the Lord. I've prayed for direction and guidance, but heaven remains silent. My sister suggested that I fast, as the ancients did.

Though I was raised in the church, I didn't know much about fasting. I knew that Jesus told His followers "*whenever* you fast," not "*if* you fast" (see Matt. 6:16), signifying it was a practice we should follow.

After doing some research, I found that the children of Israel and Christians through the ages fasted because of repentance, need, sickness, national deliverance, and many other reasons. Fasting should not be done to get what we want but as a way to step back from the clutter and noise of our everyday lives to draw close to Jesus.

Fasting seems to be an abandoned practice, possibly because we don't understand what fasting is, how to do it, or what it will accomplish. But in using our own forsaken desires to feast on God alone, He teaches us about ourselves, and He reveals His heart to us. Fasting is not something we do for God; it's a way of reconnecting us with our Father.

Be Still

Be still, and know that I am God. (Ps. 46:10 NIV)

I only *thought* I was overloaded before. I was now working part-time, carting the kids back and forth to school, taking care of the house, the yard, the bills. I just knew that if one more thing was added to the mix, I wouldn't be able to handle it. But necessity drove me back to work full-time, and I find myself on the balance beam of too much to do, too many responsibilities, too much stress.

"Be still," the Lord said.

But there's no time to be still. If I'm still, something will fall between the cracks, like the bill I forgot to mail, the project I'm late on, the empty pantry.

"Be still, and know."

Know what? Know that there's no light at the end of my to-do-list tunnel? Know that there's no household help on the horizon coming to my rescue?

"Be still, and know that I am God."

Ah, yes, Lord.

The Lord called to my aching, burdened heart. Against all human logic, I made time for Him in my overfilled, overextended schedule. He showed me what was important, what could wait, and how to ask for and accept help. The best part is that I know He sees me and my struggles and my to-do list.

Yes, many things must be done daily, weekly, monthly. But other things don't have to be done. Too much busyness makes us miss the important, beautiful things of life—like spending time with the Master, watching our kids growing up, meeting our husband's needs, enjoying our friends.

Tight Times

Some trust in chariots and some in horses, but we trust in the name of the LORD our God. (Ps. 20:7 NIV)

Bruce and Aimee called their daughters into the kitchen for a family meeting. "Girls, things have been slow at work lately, and our budget is tight. So we're very sorry to tell you we won't be doing our annual beach trip this year."

The girls looked worried and disappointed. "I understand why we can't go, but are you going to lose your job, Dad?" Lauren asked.

"No, sweetie, I don't think so. It's just important for us to be wise with our resources. This is a prime time to remember that God is in control and He always provides for us."

"My friend Kayla's dad lost his job, and now they have to move," Cassie said fearfully.

"Many people are facing tough times, but our future is in God's hands. He knows our needs, and He cares for us," Aimee explained. "Now, about spring break—how about a camping trip to the mountains? That's easy on the budget, and we'll have a blast. Maybe you could invite Kayla along."

Both girls grinned at each other. "S'mores!" they yelled in unison.

God puts us in families to love one another, support one another, and point one another toward Him while glorifying Him in our decisions and actions. Difficult times are often when we learn to trust Him the most, leaning hard on His promises and drawing near to Him in prayer. Emphasize to your kids that you are not alone; God cares for His children and provides for them. Then when God comes through with an unexpected blessing, share the joy and thank Him together as a family. Be honest about changes that will impact each of you, but demonstrate faith in God's provision and His care. Your children will learn from your example.

The Healer

This is what I command you: love one another. (John 15:17)

Brenda heard the door slam as Erin stormed outside to board the school bus. Erin was Brenda's fifth foster child, and she had been more of a challenge than the other four put together.

At age eleven, Erin was not only dealing with the normal adolescent issues and insecurities, but she was also dealing with an abusive past and a mother who wouldn't stay away from drugs. Erin was angry and scared—she was broken. Anger punctuated many of her interactions with others, and fear kept her from trusting the people who could help her. Brenda prayed for Erin daily and frequently told the girl of God's love for her. Brenda knew that while there were people who wanted to help Erin, only God could heal her wounded spirit.

After numerous counseling sessions and many hours spent on her knees, Brenda finally began seeing a breakthrough. Erin began asking Brenda questions about God and seemed more attentive during church. Brenda knew that Erin would be available for adoption soon. In spite of the difficulties, she was grateful for the time she had to share God's love with a child who was in desperate need.

People experiencing deep emotional pain can be difficult and frustrating to deal with. While hurting people need someone who can help them, only God can truly enable them to overcome their problems and begin a work of restoration.

The Bible is full of examples of God's healing power. The book of Psalms contains many powerful passages that comfort, encourage, and offer hope to those in deep distress. During difficult times when we're tempted to give up, let us instead remember whom we worship and how the Lord of the universe specializes in fixing people who are broken.

So Hard

Theresa sighed in frustration as she learned of her mother's condition. Two months earlier Michelle and Scott, Theresa's daughter and son-in-law, along with their two little boys and their dog, moved in with Theresa, her husband, Jim, and their two dogs. Scott had been laid off and was unable to find a job. With mounting debt and unexpected medical expenses, eventually their house went into foreclosure. Now Theresa's mother was no longer able to care for herself and needed someone to care for her.

"I want to help Mom, but right now we don't even have space for an air mattress on the floor, much less a place Mom would find restful," Theresa said to her sister Janet.

"Bob and I have an extra bedroom, but I think we should talk to Mom's doctors and see what they recommend before we make a decision." Janet paused and then added, "Her doctor may recommend a nursing home."

Theresa was silent for a moment. "Maybe Jim and I should meet with you and Bob so we can all pray about it together. I just want what's best for Mom. This is so hard."

When an elderly parent or loved one becomes less independent, steps must be taken to secure the best care possible. This is a stressful time for everyone. Regardless of the solution, be especially sensitive to the feelings of your loved one who may grieve the loss of independence.

If you have an elderly relative who needs special care, seek God's will and pray for wisdom. Proverbs 2:6 says, "For the LORD gives wisdom; from His mouth come knowledge and understanding." Check with your local church or government to learn about programs that provide assistance for the elderly.

Perfect Fit

I was hungry and you gave Me something to eat; I was thirsty and you gave Me something to drink. (Matt. 25:35)

Once a year my friend Judy takes two weeks of vacation from her job as a pediatric intensive care nurse and goes on trips with a Christian organization that provides desperately needed surgery free of charge to people in various parts of the world. I admit I was a little jealous that Judy got to be a part of God's amazing plan to minister to needy people. So I began to pray and ask Him what I could do.

I don't have any medical training, and I don't have anything special to offer—just my willingness to serve God and to help others.

A couple of months after I prayed that prayer, my husband, Kevin, and I began attending a new church. One Sunday the pastor spoke about their annual mission trip to Haiti where they would be taking medical supplies and children's clothing to a Christian orphanage. Volunteers from the church would help the overworked Haitian caregivers clean and repair the building, as well as feed, bathe, play with, and share Bible stories with the orphans. Our children are grown, and I miss having a little one to hold and care for. Kevin turned to me and smiled. "Sounds like a perfect fit for you."

It's easy to get so wrapped up in our own schedules and agendas that we sometimes lose sight of what God is doing beyond our own community. Opportunities abound to minister to the poor and the needy. If you haven't been involved in missions, ask God to enlarge your vision. Jesus said, "Whatever you did for one of the least of these brothers of Mine, you did for Me" (Matt. 25:40). Ask Him to give you a heart to serve those who are in need.

Numb

Save me, God, for the water has risen to my neck. I have sunk in deep mud, and there is no footing. (Ps. 69:1–2)

After Mike left for work and the kids got on the school bus, Debbie sat in the chair wondering, *What's wrong with me? I don't have any energy, I can't seem to concentrate, and I haven't been sleeping well. I just feel numb.* The phone rang, but Debbie didn't feel like talking to anyone. Finally, just before the answering machine took the call, she picked it up. It was her sister Cheryl.

"Hey, Deb, you seemed pretty down the last time we talked. How are you doing?"

Debbie described the way she'd been feeling. Cheryl said, "Maybe you're depressed. Have you seen a doctor?"

"I don't need to see a doctor. I'll be OK. I just need some more sleep."

"Depression can be serious," Cheryl said. "Besides, it can't hurt to see your doctor. Please promise me you'll go."

When Debbie hung up the phone, she prayed as tears stung her eyes. *Lord, please help me. I want to be at my best so I can be the person You created me to be. Reveal Yourself to me so I can feel hopeful again.*

It's perfectly normal to occasionally feel sad or upset, or to be unhappy with situations in your life. But with depression these feelings linger for weeks, months, or even years. They are much more intense than just "the blues" and can interfere with relationships, work, and daily activities. If you know of someone who may be suffering from depression, prayerfully urge them to seek help. Just as you would go to the doctor to treat diabetes or high blood pressure, depression is a serious medical condition that requires proper diagnosis and treatment. While we are to trust in the Lord (Ps. 37:5), He also expects us to do our part to properly care for ourselves.

We'll Do It

The fear of the LORD is the beginning of wisdom, and knowledge of the Holy One is understanding. (Prov. 9:10)

Scanning through the mail, Vicki noticed her car payment, cell phone bill, and two credit card bills. Her heart sank. *How are we going to come up with the money to pay all of these bills?* With a big mortgage, Ed's gas-guzzling truck, lots of restaurant dinners, and both boys enrolled in hockey, the money seemed to disappear as soon as their paychecks were deposited.

That night Vicki and Ed sat down to talk after the boys were in bed. They agreed that their finances had gotten out of hand when they bought their new house. Then they purchased new furniture on credit. The list went on. Even with Vicki taking on a full-time job, they wondered how they were going to make ends meet. "I can get a second job," Ed suggested. "But we've got to cut way down on our expenses and start living within our means."

Ed reached for Vicki's hand and began to pray, "Lord, we've gotten ourselves into a mess, and we need Your help. Please give us wisdom so we can start living within our means. Forgive us for spending money needlessly, and help us to be satisfied with what You provide. Just show us what to do, and we'll do it."

It's easy to spend more than you make. Sometimes just paying for the bare necessities is a challenge. So how do you survive in a world where the cost of living goes up faster than salaries, and necessities such as groceries and gas take a huge bite out of the household budget?

God has promised to provide all of our needs—notice that He said "needs," not "wants" (see Phil. 4:19). Pray for wisdom and take serious steps to get out of debt and cut down on current expenses.

A Call for Help

Carry one another's burdens; in this way you
will fulfill the law of Christ. (Gal. 6:2)

Melanie had never called anyone besides family members for help, but her mother and sisters were out of town at a women's conference, and her husband was on a business trip.

After a few rings a pleasant voice answered on the other end of the line. Melanie glanced at her daughter dozing peacefully in her wheelchair and almost hung up the phone, but instead she said a quick, silent prayer and spoke quietly into the mouthpiece. After exchanging greetings with Jessica, she told her why she had called.

"I need a couple of hours out of the house this afternoon to take care of some business," explained Melanie. "I can't leave Dawn with just anyone, but, since you told me you've looked after your niece who has special needs similar to Dawn's, I thought maybe you'd help."

"Like I told you," replied Jessica, "I know how hard it is to get the kind of help you need. And I know what a blessing it's been to my sister to have a few people she could trust with my niece. Would you like for me to come right now?"

Melanie breathed a sigh of relief. "That would be great, Jessica. You're an answer to prayer."

All children are gifts from the Lord. Still, parenting a child with special physical, emotional, or mental needs presents unique challenges for a mom. Round-the-clock care, strict adherence to schedules, unpredictable problems, expensive treatments, and isolation can drain and discourage even the most committed mother.

Isaiah 40:11 paints a beautiful picture of God tenderly embracing children and those who take care of them. When you are weary, allow yourself to rest in His strong arms. Also, ask God for suitable, safe, and loving people to help you. Don't be afraid to ask for help.

He Comforts Me

May Your faithful love comfort me as
You promised Your servant. (Ps. 119:76)

Just a few years ago, the use of the word *barren* would send me into a tailspin. My husband and I had not been able to conceive a child, and I felt ashamed, forgotten, and damaged. Then one day God lovingly taught me a firm but sweet lesson. I had focused so much on the desire to become pregnant, I had neglected to nurture the One who already resided within me. I read 1 Corinthians 6:19 that morning and saw something I had never seen. I was not barren or empty. I had been filled with the Holy Spirit!

I dedicated myself that day to nurturing the Life that resides in me. I began to memorize Scripture, enrolled in a Bible study, and began asking God to produce His fruit in my life. Later, when God sent two precious Chinese orphans into our lives, I was more prepared to parent them because I had nurtured the Holy Spirit within me.

Sometimes women experiencing infertility feel that their bodies are defective. For believers it often creates a crisis of faith and a feeling of isolation, especially if most of their friends have children.

While the cultures represented in the Bible sometimes shunned women who could not bear children, the God of the Bible never does. God values and loves every woman. Just as Jesus wept for Lazarus with Mary and Martha, He weeps with those who long for children. If prayers for a child go unanswered, it is not because He does not love the childless. We live in a fallen world, and every life is impacted by it. Even when there is no longed-for infant, God has given us His best—His one and only Son, Jesus. Even when our heart feels as though it is breaking in two, we can entrust it to Him because of the cross.

Looking My Age

*Gray hair is a glorious crown; it is found
in the way of righteousness. (Prov. 16:31)*

At a recent gathering with several other young moms, a friend told us she had asked her doctor about having a tummy tuck. After bearing three children, she felt she needed this procedure. After just one child, I could empathize. We listened as she explained what her doctor had said.

As a new parent, I have endured the late nights and sacrifice of my freedom with love, but accepting my body's changes after pregnancy has been tough. After bearing a child, my body will never naturally be the way it was when I was younger. I have stretch marks on my stomach. My clothes fit differently, and despite my running, gravity already seems to be winning. Some of my friends are having injections, liposuction, even face-lifts. Sometimes I feel the pressure to conform, even though I can't afford it. I don't want to be the only one looking my age.

I admit, I would like my body to look like it did in my twenties. It's tempting to do whatever it takes to maintain my youth. But in the New Testament, Peter says true beauty consists of "what is inside the heart with the imperishable quality of a gentle and quiet spirit" (1 Pet. 3:4). Psalm 139:14 reads, "I will praise You because I have been remarkably and wonderfully made." When we shift our focus from ourselves to Christ, we begin to glow with an inner radiance and confidence.

Plastic surgery is sometimes appropriate and needed, I'm sure, but before undergoing an expensive cosmetic procedure that involves risk, spend time in prayer and reflect on who you are in Christ. Ask Him if this choice is the right one for you.

Having Attitude

Rejoice in the Lord always. I will say it again: Rejoice! (Phil. 4:4)

Laura rubbed the back of her neck. "Your approximate wait time is ten minutes," the automated voice informed her through the phone. She had already been on hold for fifteen minutes, trying to sort out an error on her bank statement. While cradling the phone between her chin and shoulder, she carefully picked up a dish of raw chicken and marinade. With one finger, she pulled open the refrigerator door.

"Squeak!"

Her daughter's toy underfoot, Laura jumped at the unexpected noise. Disaster! The phone slipped into the marinating chicken dish and splattered everywhere—floor, door, her legs, and feet.

Something is always going wrong for me. I wouldn't even be on the phone if the bank hadn't messed up, and now this! Laura grumbled to herself as she wiped up the mess, but before her attitude got any worse, she stopped and took a deep breath. Her memory verse for the week, 2 Corinthians 10:5, stuck haphazardly on the fridge, reminded her to take every thought captive. Laura took a moment to recite it out loud and then asked God for the grace to obey.

Whether you're dealing with minor annoyances or major difficulties, having a godly attitude isn't always easy. However, as you learn to abide in Christ, your responses will reflect the fruit of the Spirit more frequently. Since your attitudes are shaped by the thoughts you entertain, you can foster bad attitudes by indulging in negative thoughts. The only way you can have the attitude God desires is by stopping thoughts that aren't pleasing to Him as soon as you recognize them. Then ask God to replace them with truth from His Word. If you practice taking every thought captive, you will soon see the fruit in your attitude.

Woman to Woman

Older women are to . . . teach what is good,
so that they may encourage the young women to love
their husbands and to love their children. (Titus 2:3–4)

The committee chairman had just asked me, "Would you consider serving as our women's ministry leader?" As I wrestled with that question, I watched my dear friend walking across the church parking lot. How I thanked God for Jane's input into my life! Now widowed and in her seventies, I could still see her welcoming smile and hear her quiet voice asking me, a young Christian mom, her favorite question: "And what has God been showing you lately?"

God had filled my life with older women who showed me how to live for Him. Jane had taught me to pursue God and to share my faith with others. I had watched Marie as she extended hospitality and joyfully served others. Wanda's love for home-making and care for her family had taught me so much. And Leslie's commitment to the special needs children she taught reflected God's love and tenderness.

When I was a young Christian woman with no spiritual background, these women poured into me the wisdom, faith, and nurturing they had developed in their years of walking with Christ. Perhaps now, in my middle years, it was my turn to give back to other young women who needed mentors, role models, and encouragers.

Today our teens, single women, and young wives and mothers need mentors and healthy role models. They have grown up in a culture that does not value truth or godliness. Young women, do you need to seek out the friendship of older, godly women so you can learn from them? If you are mature, are you passing on your wisdom and love for Jesus to another generation of women?

Singles Savvy

Be as shrewd as serpents and as harmless as doves. (Matt. 10:16)

"What did you do this weekend?" Pam asked Shelly before small group started. Shelly sighed. "Nothing. Dan and I had plans, but he had to cancel."

"Again?" Pam asked. "Isn't this the third time in a row? Why do you go out with him?"

Shelly replied, "I go out with him because he's very spiritual."

Pam said, "Spiritual isn't the same thing as Christian. The Dalai Lama is spiritual. Buddha was spiritual. Dan treats you like he doesn't know the Lord at all. He breaks dates and makes hurtful comments about your weight."

Shelly was silent for a moment and then said, "I know he has his faults, but everybody does. He sings praise songs with such emotion. He's even talking about going on a mission trip."

"None of that matters if he doesn't know and love Jesus. Where is the fruit that reflects a growing relationship with the Lord?"

"But I met him at church!" Shelly protested, tears gathering. Pam said softly, "Just because you meet a guy at church doesn't make him a Christian. Some of the people in the singles group are just there to meet people—not to put God first. It shouldn't be that way, but unfortunately it is. We have to be as savvy and discerning in our singles group as anywhere else."

Some people come to singles groups just to find a date or a mate and will do whatever is necessary, even donning a religious mask, to attract other singles. Don't assume a man is a Christian just because you meet him at church. Be sure his life reflects what he says he believes, and be sensitive to the Spirit's leading. If he doesn't walk the talk, run the other way. A life yoked with an unbeliever will always be difficult (see 2 Cor. 6:14).

Mother's Day Mercy

All of you should be like-minded and sympathetic, should love believers, and be compassionate and humble. (1 Pet. 3:8)

My ex-husband pulled up in his convertible. Late as usual! Lili, my five-year-old, skipped up the walk. "Hi, Mommy! Happy Mother's Day!" Rather than make a scene in front of Lili, I held my tongue. "Tell Daddy 'bye," I said, hugging her. "We have a special day ahead." Inside our apartment I changed her clothes, wiped her face, and tamed her curls. Then off we went.

At church the pastor's message was not what I expected. Instead of speaking to mothers, he talked to fathers, urging them to be better husbands. *What about those of us without husbands?* I wondered. *Am I the only single mom here?* Never had I felt so left out at church.

For lunch Lili and I went to our favorite restaurant. I wanted to give us both a special memory. As we stood in the crowded lobby, Lili started talking to a little girl named Alice. "My mommy and daddy aren't married anymore," Lili told her. I felt tears prick my eyes as I gently pulled Lili into a hug. A moment later Alice's grandmother leaned over and whispered, "Alice's parents aren't either." Then she added, "Would you like to join us for lunch?" I smiled through tears at the woman who gave me a gift of mercy on Mother's Day.

Although Mother's Day is meant to be a day of celebration, it can be painful and isolating for some women, such as singles and women struggling with infertility. If you know a single mom, reach out to her by inviting her family to dinner or offering to help in some other way. Also be sensitive to women who want a family but have not been able to have children. If you are in either of these situations, take your heartache to God so He can comfort and encourage you.

Lack of Respect

Wives, too, must be worthy of respect, not slanderers,
self-controlled, faithful in everything. (1 Tim. 3:11)

My alarm blared loudly, and I reached across my night table to shut it off. After a brief stretch I silently got out of bed so I wouldn't wake Darrin, pulled the door shut behind me, and made my way to the first light switch. *Click.* After my eyes adjusted to the light, I saw Darrin's video game machine lying on the family room floor. A few of his games were lying next to it. I sighed. I really didn't understand what it was that drew him to these games.

"Why does he leave this stuff all over the place?" I muttered angrily. I didn't expect to hear an audible reply.

"I didn't do it, Mom," my son, Carter, replied as he stood in the hall. "Dad must have forgotten to put it away last night."

"Hi, honey," I replied. "I know. I'm sorry—I shouldn't gripe like that. God doesn't like it when we grumble against other people."

"It's OK, Mom," Carter replied, as he shuffled off to get ready for school.

I prayed silently, *Lord, please forgive me for complaining about Darrin like that. I know You want me not only to respect him but also to show our son what respect looks like.*

The enemy usually starts his dirty work in our thought lives. A simple thought, such as, *What on earth was he thinking?* or comparing your husband to the neighbor next door or to a coworker can eventually grow into a lack of respect. If you find yourself thinking or speaking poorly about your husband, ask God to help you focus on the positive things he does. If you have an issue, ask God to show you how to approach it in a way that shows respect and a willingness to listen.

Serving at Home

Whatever you do, in word or in deed, do everything in the name of the Lord Jesus. (Col. 3:17)

Celeste opened a birthday gift from her twin sister and was shocked to see a gift certificate to a glamorous day spa. Her twin, Sonya, had just opened *her* gift—a bag Celeste had made herself.

Sonya was a successful executive, and Celeste was a stay-at-home mom. They had always had so much in common, but right now Celeste felt like they inhabited two different planets. "I don't know what to say, Sonya. This is really generous. I feel pretty hokey giving you a handmade purse." Celeste started to tear up.

"I gave you a day at the spa because you work harder than anyone I know. How did you even have time to make me this beautiful purse? I'm not trying to make you feel bad with my gift; I'm honoring you because I think you're amazing."

Celeste gave her sister a huge hug. "In that case, will you keep the kids while I'm at the spa?" she asked with a smile.

Being a stay-at-home mom is both challenging and rewarding. It is kingdom work with eternal implications. Staying home with children requires a multitude of skills—teaching, managing the home, administrating, creating, cooking, and so much more. A newscast once reported that a stay-at-home mom would pull in $138,646 a year using her "mommy" skills in a workplace.

As Christians we know that whatever position we hold, we are working for God's glory and out of love and obedience to Him. Moms, rest assured that God is honored in your labors of love, and He is the only One who can give strength and wisdom to fulfill such an important role. If you know a mom who is discouraged, affirm her today with the knowledge that God loves her and is with her in her daily work.

No Shame

*Their end is destruction; their god is their stomach;
their glory is in their shame. They are focused on earthly things,
but our citizenship is in heaven. (Phil. 3:19–20)*

My husband, Jack, and I wanted to go out to dinner and a
movie, so we looked online to see what was playing. There were
horror films, R-rated action flicks, movies geared to teens, and
an animated film. After considering our choices, we decided to
come home after dinner and watch a movie on TV instead.

Later when Jack started flipping through the channels, the
movies we found on TV contained excessive profanity and violence, sex scenes (between unmarried couples, of course), and
women dressed in skin-tight clothes with plenty of cleavage
showing. Out of the dozens of channels available, we couldn't
find one decent movie. Instead, we watched a program about the
Hubble telescope.

During a commercial break I said, "Doesn't anyone have any
shame anymore? The TV and movies are bad enough, but yesterday when I took the kids to the pool, we saw teenage girls and
even grown women wearing bikinis that barely covered them.
And the language some of the people were using! It makes me
want to keep the kids in a bubble sometimes."

Gone are the days of *Leave It to Beaver* and *Little House
on the Prairie*. Now instead of seeing positive father figures like
Ward Cleaver and Charles Ingalls on TV, we see the likes of
Homer Simpson and others. Modesty and common sense have
been replaced by downright shamelessness. But God's Word still
says the same thing it did thousands of years ago: "I will not set
anything worthless before my eyes" (Ps. 101:3). And Colossians
3:8 tells us, "Put away . . . filthy language from your mouth." The
world's standards may change, but God's Word and His expectations for His people do not.

The Fine, Painful Line

When I am filled with cares, Your comfort brings me joy. (Ps. 94:19)

My sister Barb and her husband, Clint, worked hard to send their children to college. Their youngest daughter Gina's grades were good, and she received a scholarship for tuition from a state university, but they paid for books, room and board, and other expenses. Unfortunately, the university had some extremely liberal professors who pushed their own agenda. And Gina soon discovered that her roommate was gay.

Far from the influence of her Christian parents and the church in which she grew up, Gina became involved in the homosexual lifestyle. During her junior year she arrived home for spring break. She made the crushing announcement to her parents that she was gay.

"How do I handle this?" Barb asked tearfully one evening after Gina went out with friends. "If I remind her what God's Word says, she'll think I'm condemning her. But if I'm too accepting, am I condoning something the Bible clearly says is sin?"

Five years later Barb and Clint's state legalized homosexual "marriage," and Gina and her partner recently "married." Barb and Clint are still walking the fine, painful line between letting their daughter know they love her and accept her as a person without agreeing to her chosen lifestyle.

Over the years our culture has gone from keeping homosexuality in the closet to glorifying it in public. Yet God's Word clearly states that homosexuality is a sin. And sin, any sin, causes pain. Discovering a child is gay can be devastating to parents. If you know someone in this situation, pray for God to intervene. He is stronger than any sin, and His capacity to forgive and restore is infinite.

Opportunity?

I didn't come to call the righteous, but sinners. (Mark 2:17)

"How did you meet Cody and Brendon?" I asked my son Christian when he shut down the computer after playing an online game. I'd heard the two names as he spoke into his microphone.

"School. They're in my AP classes." He filled me in on what they were like and how they acted in class. "They're cool. Don't worry, they don't party or anything. I don't think they're Christians though."

At first it concerned me that my son was spending big chunks of time with guys who didn't attend church or believe as he did. Until this year all of his friendships had grown from our church youth group. What if they swayed him away from his faith or exposed him to things we didn't want him involved in? But he attended public high school. How could I expect him to hang out only with believers?

I fretted and prayed before finally considering that maybe God brought Cody and Brendon into Christian's life for a reason, just as He had sent me some nonbelieving friends during my teen years. Instead of discouraging Christian from hanging out with these kids, I prayed for God to protect him, allow him to be an example, and help him stand firm when he needed to.

As much as we would like to surround ourselves with only Christian friends, we encounter nonbelievers at school, work, activities, and in our neighborhoods. What is more Christlike, to avoid them or to pursue friendship? Jesus spent His days with the "nonbelievers" of His day—tax collectors, fishermen, and women with dark pasts. What if He had associated with only those who knew and believed God's Word? While God wants us to fellowship with other believers and make sure our kids have Christian friends, He also sends non-Christians our way so we can shine for Him and share the difference He has made in our lives.

Plugged In

I am teaching you the way of wisdom;
I am guiding you on straight paths. (Prov. 4:11)

I could see Sean's computer from the kitchen, but that did me little good. He was moving from one website to another so quickly I couldn't tell what he was viewing, much less discern whether these sites were appropriate. If I asked my teenage son to slow down or tell me what he was doing, he might get defensive. So I decided on another tactic.

"Sean, I see you're able to navigate between websites really fast," I said. "I'd like to be able to do that too. Can you show me how?"

My son looked surprised, but I just smiled and waited patiently. "Sure," he finally replied. "See, you can open multiple tabs at the same time." I listened as my techno-savvy son explained something new to me once again, grateful that God was helping this technologically illiterate mom keep pace with her children in more ways than one.

Many parents struggle to keep up with the advances that come so easily to our children. Not only is this learning curve frustrating, but it can also leave an otherwise conscientious mother clueless about much of her child's interaction with the world. The uninformed mom is left to wonder, *Is my child erasing her Internet history? How can I tell? Who is my son texting? Can I find out? And is "sexting" what I think it is?*

First Chronicles 12:23–37 lists and describes army divisions that were equipped to wage war. Interestingly, among those listed are "the Issacharites, who understood the times" (v. 32). Today parents must be similarly aware of trends, technology, and influences. Don't be left ill equipped for the battle. Ask God for wisdom, ask your children appropriate and timely questions, and seek to understand the times we live in.

Med Alert

The turning away of the inexperienced will kill them, and the complacency of fools will destroy them. (Prov. 1:32)

I wonder why I didn't find seventeen-year-old Kara's intense desire to babysit for my son to be strange. I remember being surprised that my disclosure of Josh's attention deficit/hyperactivity disorder didn't send Kara running but actually seemed to pique her interest in staying with my children. Now I understand what was behind it all.

The morning after Kara babysat for Josh, I noticed my son's prescription bottle had been drained of all but a few pills. I knew this because I keep meticulous watch over his medication. I'm aware there is a growing trend of children and teenagers abusing Ritalin and other prescription drugs.

My first reaction to the missing pills was, admittedly, anger. But during my quiet time with the Lord that morning, I realized I should lovingly confront Kara about the missing medication and her potential use of it. After all, the bigger problem was not that Josh was now short on pills but that Kara could have a life-threatening addiction.

Prescription drug abuse is on the rise among teens and young adolescents. One reliable source reports that one in five teens admits to having abused pain medications, prescription stimulants, and/or tranquilizers. Because many young people are not familiar with the dangerous side effects of these legitimately prescribed drugs, they assume their flirtations are harmless. But when taken incorrectly, prescription drugs can have dangerous results, such as seizures, respiratory depression, decreased heart rate, cardiovascular system failure, and feelings of paranoia.

Ask God to help you be an alert parent who's aware of signs of drug misuse, and ask Him to show you other avenues through which you can help put a stop to this dangerous situation.

New Dreams

You have put more joy in my heart than they have when their grain and new wine abound. (Ps. 4:7)

Ruth is a warm, gentle woman with a maternal instinct toward the young women in her Sunday school class. I just assumed she was a wonderful mom. But on Mother's Day I happened to glance her way as the pastor asked all mothers in the congregation to stand. Ruth remained seated beside her husband.

Because my husband and I had struggled with infertility issues for several years, I decided to broach the topic with Ruth. Maybe she could help me overcome some of the resentment and frustration I was battling. When I spoke with her, she offered me wise counsel, but it wasn't what I expected.

"I wasn't able to have children because I've been on potent medications since I was a girl," Ruth admitted. "Even though I had dreamed of being a mommy and felt motherhood was the noblest calling of all, I had to trust that God had another plan for me. The hardest part was letting go of my plan for my life. But God taught me to dream new dreams, and He has given me a life more wonderful than I ever imagined."

While motherhood is certainly a noble calling and blessing from God, it's not the only means through which women can serve Him and find fulfillment. When we elevate motherhood to the level of being our greatest source of joy, we actually erect an idol. Thus we make assumptions such as, "If I can't have children, God must be displeased with me about something."

If you are unable to bear children, God is mindful of your situation and still has great plans for you. If you know of someone who is struggling with infertility, pray that God will comfort her and that she will find her greatest joy in drawing close to the Lord.

Be Prepared

Precious treasure and oil are in the dwelling of a wise person, but a foolish man consumes them. (Prov. 21:20)

During my first visit to the Grand Canyon, I was intrigued by the number of large warning signs exhorting hikers to take plenty of water and food with them even on short hikes. I wondered why there were so many of these reminders since I had not encountered anything like those signs on trails back east.

My friend, a much more experienced hiker, explained that because it was so dry and hot in the canyon, you could lose up to two quarts of fluids without realizing it. Without the physical reminder of sweat-dampened skin, it is easier to become severely dehydrated. Every year park rangers rescue more than three hundred people due to injuries and illness such as dehydration. Here it was a matter of life and death to be properly prepared.

Armed with several large bottles of water and a bag of trail mix, we had a challenging but great hike that morning. As we headed back up the trail after our descent into the canyon, I saw a few other hikers who had not heeded the sign and were sitting exhausted and even crying on the side of the trail. As we neared the end of our hike and caught sight of the trailhead, I remembered that God's Word teaches, "Careful planning puts you ahead in the long run" (Prov. 21:5 MSG). Having planned for the rigors of the hike by filling our water bottles and bringing energy food, we ensured our hiking experience was different from those who did not.

Though Jesus taught that we aren't to worry about tomorrow, many Bible verses emphasize the importance of planning for the future. In fact, taking some steps to prepare for the unforeseen, while also trusting God's sovereignty, can help eliminate needless anxiety.

Image Investment

Those He foreknew He also predestined to be conformed to the image of His Son. (Rom. 8:29)

Wendy looked at the price tag on the couch that had caught her eye. She groaned. It was so expensive! She imagined it in her living room. The colors and fabric would be a perfect match to the rug she had just paid off. She sat down on one of the plush cushions to calculate in her head how many extra hours she would need to work to pay for it. It would mean taking some early morning and late evening hours.

"Wendy! I was just thinking about you." Wendy looked up and saw her friend Gwynn from church walking toward her. "I was putting together an e-mail list for our next Bible study and wondered if you had decided whether to participate. From what I hear, a lot of women have grown closer to the Lord through this one."

Wendy had forgotten all about the women's summer Bible study. She wouldn't be able to do it if she worked more hours. In fact, she was already struggling to have her daily quiet time with her current schedule. She rubbed her hand longingly over the couch's fabric. In her heart she knew the answer. Jesus didn't care if her house looked like a picture out of *Better Homes and Gardens*. He did care about what she looked like inside. "I'd love to participate, Gwynn."

In an image-obsessed world, we women are especially susceptible to believing we and our homes need to look like the perfect pictures in all the latest magazines. God, who does not look at our outward appearance but at our hearts, wants us to look more like His Son. "For where your treasure is, there your heart will be also" (Matt. 6:21). Are you investing in a worldly image or in looking more like Christ?

The Choice to Forgive

Just as the Lord has forgiven you,
so you must also forgive. (Col. 3:13)

Allan's thoughtless words stung like a blow. The day that had started as a promising getaway now had a shadow threatening overhead. I mentally rehearsed his painful remark and settled in to freeze him out.

Almost immediately I felt the Holy Spirit say, *You need to forgive him.* But if I did that, how could he understand his mistake? He had hurt me and needed to know better than to treat me like that.

I wish I could say I immediately responded in obedience, forgave my husband, and enjoyed a wonderful day. But I did slowly determine to let go of the attitude I was nursing. Sometime in the course of our time together, I finally surrendered my "right" to be offended and my thirst for justice. Later that evening, free from attitude, I cuddled up next to him. Then I found the freedom to voice my hurt in a way that allowed him to understand and gain awareness of the impact his words had on me.

Even in the best marriages spouses will sometimes rub each other like sandpaper. For a believer, the question will always be: *How can I respond to my spouse in a way that pleases Christ and reflects my commitment to Him?* Forgiveness is often the answer to that internal question.

Choosing forgiveness will no doubt be desperately difficult in some situations. And forgiveness does not mean freeing a spouse from the responsibility and consequences of their actions. It means releasing our condemnation, our demand for "justice," and letting God do His work. In most marriages forgiveness is staying caught up on releasing the daily irritations and our tendency to keep score for future reference.

Why Can't That Be Me?

*Rid yourselves of all malice, all deceit, hypocrisy, envy,
and all slander. (1 Pet. 2:1)*

"Kasey, you've got to come and visit me! It's been so long since we've seen each other," my sister Valerie said.

"I'll try sometime next year," I promised, although I had my doubts if I could afford it then. My financial situation seemed hopeless.

"I'll pay for your plane ticket," Valerie said. "All I have to do is work one extra day, and it's paid for." She had such a giving heart, but her generous offer made me feel frustrated that I couldn't afford it myself. I replied with a quiet, "Um-hmm." I was having a hard time not envying Valerie's financial success. She had a wonderful job as a nurse, and her husband made a great salary, but she didn't understand that I couldn't just book a flight to come and see her. And I didn't feel right accepting her money. I wanted to see my sister, but I didn't want her to have to foot the bill.

"Call me soon," she said and hung up before I could answer. I prayed silently, *God, please help me be content with my life. I don't like feeling jealous of Valerie's financial success. Help me be happy for her instead of envious that it's not me.*

It can be tempting to envy another person's financial success. But God doesn't want us wasting our time feeling dissatisfied. He wants us to be grateful for the blessings He has given us. Proverbs 14:30 reminds us that "a tranquil heart is life to the body, but jealousy is rottenness to the bones."

Maybe you're struggling with envy of some kind. If you are honest with yourself and with God and confess your jealousy, He will help you overcome your dissatisfaction and gain a new appreciation for all of the blessings you do have.

Relationship Strains

Wives, submit yourselves to your own husbands so that, even if some disobey the Christian message, they may be won over without a message by the way their wives live. (1 Pet. 3:1)

"Sharon, I need some advice," I confessed to my mentor one day. "I've been overly critical of Joe lately, and as a result he's been acting distant. I've apologized, but our relationship still seems strained. I've felt the Holy Spirit telling me that I need to accept Joe the way he is and show him more respect. But it's not easy to keep my mouth shut when he's constantly glued to the TV watching sports."

"Have you tried sitting down with Joe while he's watching a game? Just spending time with him would let him know you're willing to show an interest in something he really enjoys."

"No," I admitted.

Sharon said, "Well, I'll tell you from firsthand experience, showing an interest in what your husband likes should help you and Joe grow closer. It really helped Ed and me open the lines of communication again."

Every relationship has its rough spots. If you find that you're at a point where you're struggling, earnestly seek God's guidance about how you and your husband can reconnect. He promises in Psalm 32:8, "I will instruct you and show you the way to go; with My eye on you, I will give counsel."

If you're tempted to focus on your husband's shortcomings, think about his strengths instead and thank God for them. If you do your best to accept him the way he is, you'll be showing him that you value and respect him. When something bothers you about him, resist the temptation to criticize, nag, and condemn. Instead, communicate your concerns with honesty and kindness. Showing your husband love and admiration will help set your relationship on the right track.

Thank You

"I've been there before, Marcia," Denise said. "I know you and Bryan are going through a rough time since he lost his job. When I was going through a particularly dry time, I remember one Sunday school lesson about how Jesus healed ten lepers but only one came back to thank Him. I felt convicted about how little I thank Him for all He has done for me, and I've never forgotten that story."

Marcia listened as Denise continued, "I'll tell you what has helped me. I made a commitment to write in a journal every day for thirty days. Each day I wrote down five things I was grateful for and thanked Him for each one. The next day I wrote down five more things, and so on for thirty days. After the first few days, I got past the usual things we're thankful for like food, a house, and clothes. And at the end of that month, I was down to the nitty-gritty of thankfulness for all that God has done for me."

"A gratitude journal?" Marcia asked.

"Yes," Denise said, "and when you do this, your whole perspective will change. Just think about how you feel when you give something to your kids and they're ungrateful, or when you cook a good meal and everyone's grumbling about having to do the dishes. That's how God feels when we don't thank Him for all He's done for us."

We please the Lord when we thank Him for His goodness, His provision, His loving care. Find a pretty notebook and take a few moments each day to write down what God has done for you, and then thank Him for those things. When we develop a heart of gratitude, the Father is honored and glorified, and we find joy and contentment.

Memorial Day

He Himself bore our sins in His body on the tree, so that,
having died to sins, we might live for righteousness;
you have been healed by His wounds. (1 Pet. 2:24)

One morning I heard a popular radio announcer talking about Memorial Day. He said that many Americans don't know what Memorial Day is all about, that Americans think it's just a three-day weekend marking the beginning of summer or a day to be off from work and have a barbecue.

The announcer went on to explain that Memorial Day is all about remembering and honoring those who have bled and died so we can enjoy our freedoms in this country. He asked for a moment of silence in gratitude to these men and women who gave their all. Yes, those who died in service to our country deserve our remembrance and respect. Without their love and sacrifice, who knows where this nation would be? I will remember.

But what about a Memorial Day for the One who bled and died for my spiritual freedom? The One who willingly, humbly, lovingly suffered unimaginable cruelty and death so I could enjoy freedom for eternity? I whispered my thanks to Him for His sacrifice that enables me to live, free from captivity and slavery and bondage to sin and eternal death. I will remember!

For as long as America has been in existence, we have had enemies, many intent on our destruction. We have also had people who have sacrificed to protect us from terrorists, foreign dictators, religious zealots, or entire nations. We do well to remember their sacrifices.

But we also have a powerful spiritual enemy, intent on our destruction. And we have a Protector who has loved us with an "everlasting love" (Jer. 31:3), who loved us "while we were still sinners" (Rom. 5:8). Let's honor and remember Him every day for His ultimate act of sacrifice.

Flight Test

He watches over His nest like an eagle and hovers over His young.
(Deut. 32:11)

Our next-door neighbors have a huge hedge separating our properties, and birds nest there. Our cat sits and stares at the birds as they go about their business.

Today I watched a drama unfold from my front porch. A baby bird decided he was big enough to leave the nest. Flying as far as our driveway, he got tired, and his baby wings weren't strong enough to go any further. He desperately flapped, but he couldn't get off the ground. All of the birds in the hedge were strangely silent—no calling, no chattering, no fluttering. It was as if they were holding their collective breath, wondering at the outcome. The bird's mama was hovering and chirping and fussing around her baby as he feebly tried to take off.

He hopped, he rested, he flew, and so it went for what seemed like hours. He finally got close to the hedge—his mother accompanying him all the way—and flew into the relative safety of the lower limbs. My family cheered. The other birds resumed their chattering. Thankfully, our cat was otherwise occupied. All was well.

This little scene reminded me that soon my own baby birds will leave our nest. Will they be able to see hidden dangers, or in their innocence will they be certain prey for the enemy? Will I hover and chirp and fuss, unwilling to let them go? Will I allow them to make their own mistakes, knowing when to step in for a rescue or just walk alongside?

But this is God's plan. All baby birds, including my sweet children, have to leave the nest sometime. I have to trust the precious jewels of my nest to His care and His plans. He, amazingly, loves them even more than I do.

Fun without Funds

Don't worry about your life, what you will eat or what you will drink; or about your body, what you will wear. Isn't life more than food and the body more than clothing? (Matt. 6:25)

"Hey, Mom!" Jarrett called as he ran in the house after getting off the bus one afternoon.

"Hey, buddy. You sound excited! What's up?"

"It's Friday! That means Family Fun Night!" I had to smile. Since we started sticking to a pretty strict budget a few months ago, we instituted a night of inexpensive fun for the whole family every Friday night. Although I had my initial misgivings when we gave up going to the movie theater and eating out on weekends, I came to realize that our penny-pinching actually had unexpected benefits. We were spending more time together, learning to be creative with our time and resources, and really enjoying ourselves in the process. Each week we let one person decide what we would cook for dinner and what activities would follow—board games, a walk to the park, hide-and-seek, or maybe renting a movie. I realized that family fun didn't have to be expensive because just being together was the fun part.

Lean times can actually teach us to value the things that are most important in life, things that don't have a price tag—like love, togetherness, fun, encouragement, making memories, and having a place to belong. If you are struggling financially, take an honest assessment of your situation and decide on a reasonable budget. Then choose to make the best of your situation, looking for ways you can get more for your money, be creative with what you do have, and be a good steward of what God has given you. Trust that God will sustain you, and use this tough time as a refining tool in your life, teaching you more about lovingly following and believing Him.

The High Cost of Sin

The wages of sin is death, but the gift of God is eternal life in Christ Jesus our Lord. (Rom. 6:23)

"Is she two?" the teenage girl at the ticket booth asked about my daughter. I quickly realized that if I said my just-turned-three-year-old was still two, she could get into the amusement park for free. "Um, yeah," I said. I reasoned that Jillian had been three for less than a month, so it wasn't a big deal. I handed over cash for the remaining tickets, feeling slightly guilty, but knowing I would get over it.

"Mom," my older son, Nicholas, pulled at my arm. "You forgot that Jillian isn't two. She had a birthday. She's three now." The ticket seller didn't hear Nicholas's comment, but I felt horrible.

"Excuse me. You do need to charge us for her ticket. She is actually three." The teenager looked at me like I was crazy. "OK, no problem," she said. "I'll just ring it up again."

After I paid what I owed, I considered what I had done and asked God to forgive me for trying to cut corners dishonestly. Even though it's a little thing that people probably do all the time, it's lying and stealing, and that makes it a sin.

Sin is serious—all sin. We tend to categorize sins into more and less tolerable categories. But the truth is that all sin leads to death; all sin is abominable in God's sight. And for all our sin, even the littlest lie or the tiniest cover-up, Jesus died.

Because of the great price God paid to put our sin to death, we should live in gratitude for the debt He has paid on our behalf, even in the small things. We obey Him not out of fear or compulsion, but as a response to the astounding love, grace, and mercy He has freely given to us.

One Who's Been There

He comforts us in all our affliction, so that we may be able to comfort those who are in any kind of affliction. (2 Cor. 1:4)

"I don't know what to do with him," I told my friend Kathy. "It's like one night my sweet little boy went to bed and woke up a different kid." We sat in our favorite coffeehouse trying to figure out how to deal with my oldest son's latest phase.

Kathy had already raised her kids and dealt with all the frustrating stages of growing up. For the next hour we talked and prayed. By the time she drove me home, my feelings of failure and frustration were replaced with relief that other moms struggled in the same way and lived through it. Better yet, with persistence and patience their kids turned out just fine.

Kathy is one of several older women God has brought into my life. I consider each one a gift for her wisdom, guidance, and willingness to share what God has taught her about raising children, building a godly marriage, balancing work and household responsibilities, and growing a deeper relationship with God. Some are like big sisters I can vent and laugh with; others are surrogate moms I can run to for comfort and advice. All stand as living examples that we not only survive the daily frustrations of life, but we are also better, stronger women because of them.

When Mary learned that she was to give birth to the Savior, she ran to her older cousin Elizabeth, who was also pregnant with a miracle child. Clearly our Father values relationships that span generations. Who has God brought into your life as a mentor, big sister in Christ, or fill-in mom? What has she taught you about perseverance, being a good wife, or loving Jesus? How can you pass on to others what you have gained?

Powerful Prayers

There is salvation in no one else, for there is no other name under heaven given to people, and we must be saved by it. (Acts 4:12)

Leslie's friend had written to her in an e-mail: *This past Sunday I felt God urging me to call Ava. I responded to that urge; and after we talked a while, I was able to lead her to Christ. She prayed by phone and became a Christian.* Years of prayers for Ava had at last yielded the fruit of salvation.

Leslie's heart was blessed and encouraged as she thought of her own list of lost friends, family members, and even acquaintances she continued bringing before the Lord. She thought especially of her friend Wendy. Their paths had crossed long ago at a conference. In the early days of their friendship, Leslie discovered that Wendy was not a believer.

In the years since, Leslie had stayed in touch. They meet occasionally for a meal or an outing. But most of all, Leslie prays for Wendy. How she looks forward to the day when she can rejoice at her friend's birth into the family of God!

All of us probably have a list (in our head or on paper) of those we know who need Christ. We should be faithfully praying for the salvation of those on our list. We can also be teaming up with other Christian friends, partnering together in asking God to lead these individuals to Himself. We can seek to put authentic believers and godly influences in their path. We can ask God to bring events into their lives that would cause them to seek Him.

Praying for the lost is a true discipline of perseverance. Sometimes the answer comes quickly; other times we wait for years or never see the fruit of that prayer. But our responsibility is to pray faithfully.

Consequences

Trust in the LORD with all your heart, and do not rely on your own understanding. (Prov. 3:5)

The flu bug hit Denise hard, and she arrived home from work two hours early. As she passed by her daughter's room, she heard voices inside. "Nicole?" she said as she opened the door. Denise wasn't prepared to see her sixteen-year-old daughter scrambling to cover herself with a sheet and Nicole's boyfriend, Alex, hurriedly pulling on his jeans. Furiously Denise grabbed Alex's shirt and shoes and threw them at him. He scrambled past her and rushed out the door.

That night Denise and her husband, Jack, had the first of many long conversations with Nicole. A few weeks later Nicole told Denise about a suspicious sore she had developed, and a visit to the doctor confirmed that she had a sexually transmitted disease.

In the car on the way home, Nicole whispered quietly as tears slid down her cheeks, "I thought Alex loved me. He told me that I was the only one. He hasn't even called me in two weeks, and he's been avoiding me at school." Turning to her mom, she asked, "Do you think God hates me now?"

"Honey, God doesn't hate you—He loves you, and He didn't want this to happen. But all of our actions have consequences. We don't always see them ahead of time. That's why He tells us not to do some things. He wants to spare us from the pain that will come when we disobey Him."

The Centers for Disease Control estimates that approximately nineteen million new infections of various sexually transmitted diseases occur each year in the United States, almost half of them among young people ages fifteen to twenty-four. Just as the laws in our communities are designed for our protection, God's law is there to protect us. He is a loving Father who gives us the guidelines for living an abundant and satisfying life.

Guaranteed

Listen, LORD, to my cry for help. Lord GOD, my strong Savior,
You shield my head on the day of battle. (Ps. 140:6–7)

A few summers ago some of the coastal states in the Southeast braced for a major hurricane. While many people decided to evacuate, they first took time to board up their homes and businesses. They knew the storms were coming and wanted to protect the places where they lived and worked. Two days later thousands were homeless, having lost everything to wind and water.

As I prayed for the people who were suffering because of the hurricane, I thought about the storms that come to us all. Just as we know hurricanes will hit America's coastlines from time to time, we don't always know when they will come or what they will harm. We only know that storms are guaranteed.

I asked the Lord to help me prepare for those difficult times when I will go through trials and storms. I prayed for wisdom to know how to prepare and for the strength to endure whatever storms He allows to come into my life. I also asked Him to shape my character and to help me grow during difficult times.

While some people believe trouble will somehow bypass us as Christians, that's not what the Bible teaches. Jesus said, "You will have suffering in this world" (John 16:33). Since we know these storms will come, how can we prepare for them? First, stay connected to the Lord. Take time each day not only to lay your requests before Him but also to listen to Him. Second, stay in the Word. God speaks to His people through His Word (Ps. 119:105). And although pain sometimes makes people feel like isolating themselves, this is an unwise move. Stay connected to other Christians and accept help when it's needed.

Not Alone

Share with the saints in their needs; pursue hospitality. (Rom. 12:13)

Jodi had planned to have the house clean for Linda's visit, but today it looked like something had exploded. On the couch lay a load of unfolded towels. An endless to-do list hung on the refrigerator. Gone were the days when her husband took care of the yard and she took care of the house. Now that he was gone, it was all up to her.

"Sorry about the mess. Now that I'm working, carting the kids everywhere . . ."

Linda hugged Jodi. "Don't worry about it. You have a lot on your plate right now."

Jodi felt the tears well up. The weight of the responsibility only compounded the pain of her husband leaving. "How am I going to do this?"

Linda squeezed her hand. She reached for a napkin and handed it to Jodi. "You know, it's OK to ask for some help. Your kids are old enough to do simple things like folding those towels. And I'm willing to do anything I can. How about if I do the run to soccer practice tonight? I'm going anyway." Relief flooded Jodi as she reached out and hugged her friend. *Thank You, God. I'm not as alone as I feel.*

Many Christian women experience the loss of a spouse through death or divorce. In addition to the loss of relationship, they are hit with the reality of added responsibility. Suddenly the daily routine of carpools, housework, repairs, and caring for children falls on one set of shoulders instead of two. For those in this situation, learning to ask for help can be beneficial. For the rest of us, how can we become more sensitive and helpful? Ask God what you can do to help. None of us were created to tough life out on our own.

He Will Make a Way

The man who trusts in the LORD, whose confidence indeed
is the LORD, is blessed. (Jer. 17:7)

Patricia opened her eyes slowly to the annoying beeps of the alarm clock beside her bed. As usual she began to think through the day ahead but stopped suddenly when she remembered that, as of yesterday, she no longer had a job. She had been "released from her duties" when budget cuts caused the organization to do some extreme and quick reshuffling of personnel. Patricia closed her eyes and moaned slightly as the weight of unemployment fell fresh upon her.

Hearing her cat scratching at the bedroom door, Patricia decided to get up and face the day. But yesterday's shock had left her numb. She had worked at the same place for more than fifteen years and couldn't think of another place in her small town where she would want to seek employment.

After Patricia fed the cat and made coffee, she took her coffee mug into the living room and sat down with her Bible. Opening to a familiar psalm, she allowed the words to wash over her, giving her hope and assurance in her sovereign God. She bowed her head to pray and began to anticipate the new path on which God would take her.

Whenever change is thrust upon us, we may be tempted to struggle against the new and cling to the old. But we can be confident that God still has good plans for us, even when we can't yet see them. God assured His prophet in Isaiah 43 that He would make a way for His people where there seemed to be no way. Likewise, when we encounter difficult changes, we can know that God loves us, is still on His throne, and will make a clear path for us in His time.

Time to Talk

*Two are better than one because they have a good reward
for their efforts. (Eccl. 4:9)*

Recently I flew to visit a handful of my closest college friends whom I haven't seen in six years. However, I left disappointed by how little we seemed to have in common and how much of our previous camaraderie was lost.

It should have been no surprise to me. I simply haven't made the effort to keep in touch with them. To be honest, I find myself struggling to make time at all for my friends. As a task-oriented person in a performance-driven culture, I let career, television, the Internet, and even my reading list get in the way of maintaining my friendships. I have ducked into the house to avoid neighbors or screened phone calls because I felt I had too much to do to take the time to talk.

But I'm beginning to realize my to-do list is a bottomless pit, and oddly, the more I cross off, the longer it grows. As I get older, I'm learning to invest in my friendships because I'm beginning to realize how much I need them. With God's grace I will continue to get better at placing people above projects.

God is relational and created us to be in relationship with Him and others. Friendships are vital to our spiritual, mental, and emotional well-being. Yet both work and play can interfere with maintaining those friendships, so we might just have to put work on hold to call that friend we haven't talked to in a while. On the other hand, a good chunk of our time may be absorbed in meaningless leisure, such as too much television or the Internet. In that case we can choose activities that allow conversation and relationship building. We need our friendships; making time to invest in them is wise.

Perfection

I do not set aside the grace of God, for if righteousness comes through the law, then Christ died for nothing. (Gal. 2:21)

I have a confession to make. I'm a perfectionist. As I write this devotional, I'll revise it until my fingers are sore and finally send it to my editor, unsatisfied. Checking items off my to-do list gives me no satisfaction either. With the completion of each task, I see two more to be done. I often feel that what I have accomplished isn't good enough, and I resist trying new things at which I may fail or that I think could possibly make me look foolish. It's even hard for me to admit I'm wrong because it's so hard for me to deal with failure. The images of beauty, success, and gorgeous homes on the magazines at the grocery check-out lines are reminders of what our culture thinks I should be.

I suppose knowing is half the battle because the more I recognize how my striving for perfection steals my joy, the more I want to change. In the Gospels, Jesus makes clear what He thinks of pharisaical perfectionists. I don't want to make the mistake they did—knowing and doing all the right things while missing God's grace. Though my perfectionism is ingrained, I'm thankful that "I am able to do all things through Him who strengthens me" (Phil. 4:13). I can even change.

As Christian women we should desire to live a life worthy of our calling, but if we make being perfect our focus, we miss the grace and mercy of Christ on the cross—as if He died for nothing! Though trying to be perfect may seem good, perfectionism is actually a works-oriented symptom of ugly pride. We didn't, nor could we ever, earn His love. We can choose to live in His love and grace, not under the tyranny of perfection.

The Perfect Dress

*Your beauty should not consist of outward things
like elaborate hairstyles and the wearing
of gold ornaments or fine clothes. (1 Pet. 3:3)*

Wendy and I stepped into our favorite department store and headed to the sale section, hoping to find something for our double date the next evening. After much sifting through several racks, I noticed a beautiful cobalt blue dress tucked behind some of the other dresses. I pulled it out and admired its beautiful color and modest bateau neckline. I was elated! It was as if God had saved it there just for me.

Wendy held up a silver dress with a plunging neckline. "What do you think?" she asked hesitantly. I could tell she liked the dress, but she also wanted an honest answer.

"You don't like it, do you?" Wendy asked, sounding disappointed.

"It's really pretty, but I think it might be a little too revealing. I think you'd really be uncomfortable in it."

"I suppose you're right," Wendy agreed sheepishly. "I don't want to give Ryan the wrong impression." We both began looking for a more modest dress for her.

Today we see celebrities on the red carpet in designer gowns that may seem beautiful and glamorous but often are downright revealing. Today's fashion icons can also be seen on the covers of magazines wearing tight or skimpy clothing that many women want to emulate. The trend to reveal more and more skin has carried over to our local department stores, and sometimes finding stylish yet modest clothing can be a challenge. In spite of our culture's fascination with celebrities and what they're wearing, God calls His children to a higher standard. Romans 12:2 says, "Do not be conformed to this age, but be transformed by the renewing of your mind." Trust the Lord to help you find stylish clothing that is fit for a daughter of the King.

You're a Great Dad

Encourage one another and build each other up as you already are doing. (1 Thess. 5:11)

When my husband, Mark, and I found out we were expecting a baby, he was excited and worried at the same time. As an only child, he hadn't spent much time around babies or young children. One day he asked me if I thought he would make a good father. "You're a wonderful man, and you'll make an excellent father," I reassured him.

A few days later, as I was dusting our bedroom, I took a closer look at the books on Mark's nightstand. They were all about parenting. One book in particular caught my eye. Curiosity got the better of me, and I picked it up. As I leafed through the pages, I saw that Mark had been taking notes throughout the book. He really did want to be a great dad. He was seeking the Lord for wisdom in His Word and through the sound advice of other godly Christians.

Several weeks after our son was born, I had taken a much-needed nap. When I woke, I saw Mark relaxing in the rocking chair feeding and cuddling with the baby. I quietly made my way over to them and gently hugged my husband.

"See," I whispered, "I told you that you'd make a great dad!"

Mark smiled. "Thanks for reassuring me," he said. "I needed to hear that."

No matter how confident we may be, we all need encouragement. We are designed to respond to sincere, positive comments.

Try to find a way to encourage others on a regular basis, especially your loved ones. Focus on their good qualities and actions. In Hebrews 3:13 we are reminded that God wants us to "encourage each other daily." Obey this command and watch to see what happens.

Waiting for the Rain

Keep knocking, and the door will be opened to you. (Luke 11:9)

My husband and I have prayed for two years about a job for him. But there have been no answers, no interviews, no calls, no nibbles. We've fasted and pleaded about this issue, but heaven has been silent. Hopeless and in despair, I stopped asking God to provide a job for Blake. *What's the use?* I thought.

Last Sunday my pastor preached about Elijah. For many years the land of Samaria had experienced famine. Wadis were dry, cattle were dying, crops were destroyed. In 1 Kings 18, after God had defeated the prophets of Baal, Elijah began to pray for rain. On top of Mount Carmel, Elijah got on his face to petition God. Six times he sent his young servant to go look for a cloud; six times the servant replied, "There's nothing" (18:43). Elijah kept praying expectantly; on the seventh trip, the servant reported there was a cloud "as small as a man's hand coming from the sea" (18:44). And then it rained. In fact, the Bible says "there was a downpour" (18:45).

Deeply convicted, I realized that I had been expecting the downpour, but hadn't gone looking for the wisp of cloud. Giving up on prayer, being discouraged when answers don't come, isn't the way God wants me to live. Giving up is based on sight, not faith. Giving up doesn't give God time to work, both in the circumstances and in my heart. And giving up doesn't teach me to hold my Savior's hand when times are dark.

Giving up, complaining, being angry—these are simply not options for us. They give our enemy a toehold to speak lies into our hearts. Let's keep knocking on heaven's door, patiently waiting for our Father's perfect plan and timing to unfold. He is always working, always for our best.

Wake-up Call

All my days were written in Your book and planned before a single one of them began. (Ps. 139:16)

Have you ever had a wake-up call? Not the hotel kind—I mean a rock-you-to-the-core, humbling wake-up call. I had one last summer.

I'm supposed to go to the dermatologist every six months because of a skin condition, but I got lax and didn't go. Last summer we were on vacation, and a mole on my back began to hurt. I decided I might as well have it checked out.

After her examination the doctor removed the mole I came in for. But the one right next to it, she said, looked like melanoma. I was totally in shock. I hadn't even noticed that the mole had changed. After waiting two weeks I got the results. It *was* melanoma. Thankfully, she'd caught it early.

When I realized that God actually, literally saved my life, I fell on my face, humbled. He could have chosen simply to get rid of the cancer without my ever knowing about it, but He didn't. Instead of just taking care of it, the Ruler of the universe reached down and got my attention so I could learn something about Him.

God saved my life. Yes, my days here are numbered; they are like a little puff of wind, but my Creator says, "Not yet." I am here today because I still have something to do for Him. And He's not going to allow anything to come between me and His mission for me, not even a mole.

One part of the definition of humility is that we see ourselves as we really are. Wake-up calls remind us who we are. So when you get a wake-up call from God, realize who you are, who loves you, and then give Him the glory for it.

Shallow Living

Why this turmoil within me? Put your hope in God. (Ps. 42:5)

Sarah sat down and ordered coffee while waiting for her friend Liz. She checked her e-mail, made a call about her daughter's birthday party, wrote a note for work, and planned dinner. Liz walked in the coffee shop, and after a hug Liz remarked on how tired Sarah looked.

"I am tired. I've got Jill's birthday party to plan. I've got to take Brett to soccer practice. I'm behind on a project at work, and don't get me started about the summer camps and the home projects," Sarah went on. "I just can't seem to get it all done, no matter how hard I try."

"Have you spent any time with the Lord lately?" Liz asked with her typical directness. "Because when we're so stressed and at the end of ourselves, it's probably because we haven't plugged into our Power Source," she said.

"No, I don't seem to have time to do that either," Sarah said. "Something's always more pressing, something that needs to be done right now."

"Setting priority time with Him is important. He says He will direct our paths, and He can help you order your days," Liz said. "Busyness, even if it's for God, can make life shallow and just one long to-do list, so that at the end of the day, all you've done is checked things off. Ask Him, and He will show you what He wants you to do."

Sometimes the expectations of others can place real demands on our time, crowding out the things we should do like spending time with the Lord. So today, think of things you don't need to do, things you can delegate, and things that can wait. Spend time with the Father first. He promises it will be time well spent.

Great Expectations

Love never ends. (1 Cor. 13:8)

This year my husband and I will celebrate our twentieth wedding anniversary. We have come a long way over the years. Despite our struggles he's the guy for me. God had a plan to knit our hearts and lives together before we even met.

That being said, I've finally realized that my husband is not Superman. He has his own quirks, foibles, and oddities, just like me. He does things differently from me—he perfectly aligns his money in his billfold; I just stuff mine in my purse. His interests are not the same as mine—he likes sports; I like books.

My expectations for him were high in the beginning. I just knew he was the answer to my every dream: a big house, fancy cars, great vacations. I expected a handyman who would leap at the chance to fix a faucet, change a lightbulb, and maintain my car. I expected a romancer who wanted to talk to me for hours, who brought me flowers just because, who delighted in going to the mall with me.

But guess what? He's not meant to fulfill all my needs. In fact, he can't; that's God's job. Instead, my husband is my helper, my complement, my best friend. So I can let him just be my husband, the love of my life, the guy I get to do life with.

Sometimes it's hard to see past our spouse's annoying habits and imperfections. When life gets hard, it's easy to think that our expectations are not being met, that he's not doing all he can to make life better for us. But our God-shaped vacuum cannot be filled by anyone else; it can only be filled by God. Give your husband the freedom to love you, to be himself, and to be only who God intended him to be.

Teach Them Well

*Repeat them to your children. Talk about them
when you sit in your house. (Deut. 6:7)*

Our eight-year-old daughter, Leah, asked Jesus to be her
Savior when she was six years old. After talking with her about
it for several months, we knew she was ready. She understood
that she was a sinner who needed a Savior. She understood that
Jesus died for her.

But we didn't count on the fierceness of the enemy's attack
on her baby Christian heart. She began questioning her salvation
and things like how do we know that Jesus lived and that He
rose from the dead. She wanted to know how she could be sure
she belonged to Jesus.

We took her back to Scripture. We showed her where
Paul teaches us to put on the full armor of God (Eph. 6:11).
We showed her where Jesus appeared to more than five hundred people after His resurrection (1 Cor. 15:6). We showed her
where John tells us that we can know we are His (1 John 5:13).
We talked to her about renewing her mind with Jesus' truth
rather than listening to the whispered lies of the enemy (Rom.
12:2). We told her other books were written around that time
that talked about Jesus.

Showing her the truth in God's Word has satisfied her
questions. And showing her how to find the answers for herself
has helped. But we are still working on how to deflect the enemy's fiery arrows with God's truth. I pray every day that my baby
girl will become adept at handling "the shield of faith" (Eph.
6:16) and draw so close to the Lord that she will never doubt
her salvation.

Our children's spiritual growth doesn't stop when they
become saved. In fact, it's just beginning. Discipling your children is an honor, a sacred trust, guiding them as they grow in
the Lord.

Coming Home

Speak up for those who have no voice, for the justice of all who are dispossessed. (Prov. 31:8)

"That's a pretty picture, Kayla," I told the sweet six-year-old. "When you get home, you can hang it on your refrigerator." Our church outreach ministry was helping tutor children at a local after-school program. Kayla and I had spent the whole afternoon together.

"I don't have a 'fridgerator," she said. "My mom and me sleep in the car."

I tried not to act surprised. "Oh. I'll bet your mom will love your picture."

Later, I asked the program director about her situation. "They've been homeless for a couple of weeks," he said. Marty is a single mom who lost her job and had no one to help her out. She's been doing the best she can.

I told the director I would bring by some clothes and school supplies for Kayla, and I asked him how to find Marty, seeing what I could do to help her get back on her feet. That night I prayed, *Lord, help me be part of the solution to this difficult situation, and help me to glorify You in the way I love on this little girl and her mother.*

When we picture homelessness, it's most often in the context of a big city or a third-world country. Yet homelessness exists in every community. God's Word tells us to be compassionate to those in need, to give generously, and to be the vehicle of His love and grace to others. Jesus said that of those to whom much was given, much would be required (Luke 12:48). This is true in terms of material wealth as well as the spiritual riches He has poured out on us. He treated others with compassion, and we are to model Him in the way we respond to those in need.

A Better Plan

Sexual immorality and any impurity or greed should not even be heard of among you, as is proper for saints. (Eph. 5:3)

While Jeff and I were planning a cruise for our twentieth anniversary, our next-door neighbors Ken and Rita were getting a divorce. One night after Ken abruptly left his wife for another woman, Rita sobbed, "Why would God allow this to happen?"

Over the next couple of years, Rita grew bitter about her situation. She had gone from being a stay-at-home mom with a comfortable life to a working, single mom of two teenage daughters. One day Rita announced that she had met a man. She and Paul had been dating for a few months, and he was going to move in with her and the girls. "Rita . . ." I began.

"Please, don't lecture me. I deserve some happiness after all I've been through. Besides, we're not living in the fifties anymore. People just take it for granted that couples are going to live together. It's not a big deal."

I continue to pray for Rita and the girls. I'm asking God to change her heart and let her know He has a better plan for her. Although she's right in saying it's become more common over the last few decades for unmarried couples to live together, this hasn't changed God's opinion on the subject. Even secular research has cited the harmful effects of cohabitation.

According to a study by Rutgers University, living together before marriage increases the risk of breaking up after marriage. It increases the risk of domestic violence for women and the risk of physical and sexual abuse for children. Unmarried couples have lower levels of happiness and well-being than married couples. Pray for people you know who have chosen to live together.

Right Next Door

I rejoiced in the Lord greatly that once again you renewed your care for me. (Phil. 4:10)

My next-door neighbor was in a bind. Monica had recently become a single mom when her husband lost a two-year battle with cancer. Now she and her eight-year-old daughter were on their own.

Monica called me in a panic one evening after she came home from work. "I lost my babysitter," she said, "and I was wondering if you could watch Emma for a few days after school until I can find another one."

"Of course," I replied. Emma and my daughter Chelsea are good friends, and they spend a lot of time together outside of school anyway.

The next morning during my prayer time, I felt the Lord telling me that I should offer to watch Emma *every* day after school. I knew Monica's finances were tight, and I had been asking the Lord to use me to minister to others. I just didn't know I would find an opportunity right next door. When I talked to Monica about it, she said, "I can only pay you twice a month because that's when I get paid."

"I want to do it just as a favor, not for money," I insisted. "I'm always here when the girls get off the bus anyway. They'll enjoy spending time together." Monica protested, but I told her my husband had already agreed, and I wanted to be obedient to the Lord.

Single moms have a tough assignment. Most are working mothers who not only have to put food on the table and pay the rent, but also many must arrange for babysitters, keep up with the housework, help with homework, and hopefully find a moment to themselves once in a while. If you know of single moms in your church or area, ask God for wisdom about what you can do to help them and their children.

A Different Path

Women are to dress themselves in modest clothing,
with decency and good sense. (1 Tim. 2:9)

I met Lori at a class we were taking at a local university while working on our master's degrees. We seemed to have a lot in common—we were both Christians, my two daughters were about the same age as her two girls, and we lived within a few miles of each other.

Lori and her husband, Greg, invited all of us over one summer afternoon for a barbecue. "We have an in-ground pool, so bring your swimsuits," Lori said. John, Amy, Rachel, and I arrived, and I began helping Lori in the kitchen. When Heather, her oldest daughter, walked into the room, I couldn't help but notice that she sported a one-piece swimsuit with a jaw-dropping neckline that barely covered her developing figure. She was all of thirteen years old, yet she was dressed like the typical cleavage-baring celebrities you see on the red carpet. I was shocked, and I didn't know how to respond.

I prayed silently, *What will I tell my girls when they say, "Well, her parents let her do it, and they're Christians"?* Fortunately, all four girls didn't seem to share the same interests and didn't get together again. I was grateful that Amy and Rachel chose a different path.

In our culture seeing women and even young girls dressed in skimpy outfits has become commonplace. Women may feel pressured to keep up with contemporary styles—whether it's plunging necklines or hemlines that show way too much leg. But just because the Bible was written centuries ago doesn't mean its message is out-of-date. Psalm 119:89 says, "LORD, Your word is forever; it is firmly fixed in heaven." No matter what the world may tell us about fashion or any other topic, obeying God's Word is always appropriate.

Seek Him

You will find Him when you seek Him with all your heart and all your soul. (Deut. 4:29)

A few months ago one of the vice presidents at my company wanted to know how employees in his department were spending their time. For several weeks my coworkers and I kept meticulous track of how much time we spent on our various duties. It was a tedious exercise for us, and we were all glad when we no longer had to account for every minute of our workday.

While I was relieved to be finished with the task, it made me wonder how I spent my time at home. I had become increasingly frustrated with the lack of time I felt I had for prayer time, Bible study, exercise, and sleep. So I began my own analysis in which I tracked duties like cleaning, cooking, laundry, entertainment, and so on.

After a couple of weeks, I was surprised to see how much time I spent on activities like watching TV and surfing the Internet. Could I really say I was seeking God with all my heart and soul? Apparently not. I was spending more time with the remote control and my computer mouse than I was with my Savior. I asked Him to help me seek Him first and always make Him my number-one priority.

God loves us and wants to spend time with us, but sometimes we fill the time we should be spending with Him with other activities. While there's nothing inherently wrong with most of these things, we can't allow them to take such a big chunk of our time that we don't spend sufficient time seeking Him. If your schedule has become a problem, ask the Lord to help you put things back into balance and to give Him first place in your life and in your heart.

It's Only Lunch

*Each person is tempted when he is drawn away
and enticed by his own evil desires. (James 1:14)*

Meg put her purse in her desk and turned on her computer. She was tired after another week of being alone with the kids, working, and trying to hold everything together while Brian was gone on another business trip. Their relationship was strained, and she felt neglected.

Daniel, her coworker, stopped by her office. "Hey, how would you like to grab some lunch today?" he asked.

Meg hesitated, then said, "Sure." As soon as the words were out of her mouth, she felt the Holy Spirit warning her, but she ignored it. *It's only lunch*, she thought. But throughout the morning, Meg found herself thinking about Daniel—he was tall, handsome, and fun to be around. *Maybe it will do me some good to get out for a change*, she thought.

During lunch the conversation was lively, but it turned more serious. "I've been noticing that you've seemed kind of down lately," Daniel said as he touched Meg's hand. She pulled away and said, "Look, I shouldn't have accepted your invitation. I'm married."

"I know," he replied. "But I could be a good friend if you need one." Back at the office Meg realized she had used poor judgment. While it felt good to have a man's attention, she knew that flirting with sin could get her in serious trouble.

Our society's standards of what is and isn't appropriate have changed over the years, sometimes blurring the line between right and wrong. As Christians we need to be clear about where we stand and to remember we represent the King of kings. Some things that are innocent in the world's eyes may be areas in which the Lord calls us to a higher standard.

Too Soon?

*God is our refuge and strength, a helper
who is always found in times of trouble. (Ps. 46:1)*

Many were shocked to see our associate pastor at church the day after his wife's memorial service. Not only had he lost the love of his life, but God had taken her suddenly as well. One Sunday she was greeting visitors, and the next she was with the Lord. Was he ready to be around so many people, answering the same questions and rehashing painful events of the last couple of weeks? Was he coming back too soon?

He needs to be around his church family, I sensed God reminding me. While one friend had waited several weeks to return to church after losing her husband, our pastor needed to be around those who loved him, had adored his wife, and would support him through every excruciating step of his grief. His quick return taught me that our responses to a tragedy are as different as our individual personalities. It wasn't my job to keep track of how long a person should stay in isolation or what they could handle when. God called me to love, pray for, and remain attentive to my grieving friends' needs.

When a friend or loved one loses a spouse, it's tempting to play counselor and assess how grief should look. But after watching only a few go through it, we see the vast differences in the way people handle their pain. Some need to grieve alone for a long period of time before returning to work, church, and activities. Others find solace in being around people. While one widow can't smile for months, another finds healing in laughter. Helping a brother or sister through loss provides an opportunity to seek wisdom and practice sensitivity, knowing that God created us uniquely and comforts us in the exact way we need.

Providing for Today

I have been young and now I am old, yet I have not seen the righteous abandoned or his children begging for bread. (Ps. 37:25)

My husband, Norm, handed me a stack of mail. I tossed a familiar envelope aside for another that I knew contained a check. "Thank You, God. Now we can pay Nathan's dentist bill and buy some groceries." On that note I decided against opening the first one until I was ready to face bad news. Checking my IRA statement had become too depressing.

As a freelancer, I don't have the benefit of a 401(k). I must save for retirement on my own. For two years financial stress has kept me from contributing to that account. For part of that time a poor economy ate away at my small reserve, cutting it by almost a third. When I first saw the numbers going in the wrong direction, I knew I wasn't alone. A friend's husband had lost half of his account when the stock market plummeted. I am part of a growing club of men and women learning to trust God to provide for the future. Even today I must focus on this month's bills instead of tomorrow's nest egg.

As soon as we hit the adult work world, we're taught the importance of planning ahead for a house, our kids' college educations, and retirement. But who expects an economic crash, job loss, medical crisis, or some other financial blow to reverse all our planning and saving? Perhaps we all need a season when we are forced to examine whether we trust God completely or our trust in Him stops with our savings. How many of us will reach old age with our needs truly unmet? While we may not know where future funds will come from, God promises to take care of His children.

Doing Some Good

Act wisely toward outsiders, making the most of the time. Your speech should always be gracious, seasoned with salt. (Col. 4:5–6)

Being new to the community, I thought a knitting class would be a great way to make friends. I had envisioned a group where we would not only knit but would also share our concerns and pray for one another. That's what my previous knitting group did. But this group was different from the start. They shared their concerns but usually with heavy doses of criticism and gossip. Still I grew to love the women and our time together. I started praying for them and fully intended to share God's love with them.

Unfortunately, after knitting with my new friends for a couple of months, I realized I'd neglected to share my faith with them; and, I'm ashamed to admit, I was becoming like them. I had developed a critical spirit, and it almost seemed as though my tongue was actually looser in my mouth.

Convicted of my actions, I discussed my alternatives with the Lord. Either I could drop out of the group and safeguard myself from these ladies' influence, or I could remain in the group with a new awareness and fresh resolve to let my light shine. In the end a green light from God and a renewed burden for my friends' salvation compelled me to stick with the group. But I'm humbly on my knees before each class.

As you mix with nonbelievers at work, in the community, and even in your family, ask God to help you resist the lure of the world's ways. Periodically examine your thoughts, words, and behavior to make sure you're living a holy life that reflects well on your God. Then you'll be able to do some real good.

Hearing God

My sheep hear My voice, I know them,
and they follow Me. (John 10:27)

My friend Paige seemed quiet during our morning walk. "Is something bothering you?" I asked.

She nodded. "I'm afraid I'm not really a Christian." *Uh-oh*, I thought. "Why?"

"Beverly in my small group is always talking about how God speaks to her, and I hear people at church saying they hear God's voice. But I never hear God's voice. Ever. I'm beginning to think He doesn't talk to me because I'm not one of His."

"But God doesn't always speak audibly, Paige," I said. "In fact, I've never heard an audible voice. I would guess that most Christians haven't."

"Then how does He speak to you?"

"Different ways. He speaks through His Word for one. That's our chief source of knowing Him. And the Holy Spirit speaks in our hearts. Remember when you said you knew in your heart not to take that new job? You prayed about it, and He gave you your answer—in your heart."

Paige brightened. "Yes! Does that count?"

"Absolutely! And He can speak through godly people. When I wondered whether to keep tutoring those at-risk kids, two friends confirmed it for me. God nudged them to do it."

She paused. "I'm beginning to understand. I think I'm hearing His voice through you right now."

In the Bible, God sometimes speaks audibly. He spoke out loud to young Samuel when he was little (1 Sam. 3) and to Saul on his way to persecute more Christians (Acts 9). But that's not the only way He speaks to us. The key is to be listening for Him, and we do that by spending time with Him in prayer and in His Word, by being still before Him, knowing He wants to communicate with us.

Never My Fault

Make your own attitude that of Christ Jesus. (Phil. 2:5)

"Katherine," my boss said in a flat tone, "you're late to work again, and it's got to stop. This is your last warning." He looked at me and shook his head.

I held back the tears as I walked back to my office. I was getting tired of everyone reminding me that I was frequently late. They made it seem like they were never late a day in their entire lives. I opened my desk and grabbed a tissue. I needed a few minutes to gather my thoughts before I'd be able to work productively.

I glowered at the counseling statement I'd been made to sign, and I began to read my boss's comments. Each time I was late I'd had to write my reason. First tardy, late 37 minutes. Reason given: *Kids missed the bus, and I had to drive them to school.* Second tardy, late 40 minutes. Reason given: *Dog got out of the house, and we had to find him.* Third tardy, late 55 minutes. Reason given: *Got stuck in traffic.* Fourth tardy, late 48 minutes. *Power went out, and alarm clock didn't go off.*

The list went on, but I was done reading it for now. In one sense these were all valid reasons. And yet the thread of excuses revealed obvious, underlying causes. *Lord,* I prayed silently, *please help me to get my act together. I know I've have been blaming my tardiness on everyone but myself. Please forgive me. Help me be more organized.*

If you find that you are blaming other people for your faults or mistakes, pray about your circumstances and ask God to change your heart if necessary. Don't blame anyone else for your mistakes but instead take responsibility for your actions (see Prov. 3:30).

Leap of Faith

*Hear my prayer, Lord, and listen to my cry for help;
do not be silent at my tears.* (Ps. 39:12)

"You should watch this DVD of you and your dad," my mom said. She knew that I was going through a rough time, and she had just found something she thought I should see. The screen came to life, and I heard my dad's familiar voice calling to me. In the footage I was about three years old and was wearing a red-and-white, one-piece bathing suit.

"Come on Sophia, you can do it! Jump!" Dad coaxed me. He smiled reassuringly, but I shook my head no, my brown hair whipping back and forth across my face. "There's nothing to be afraid of," he said. "I'll catch you."

I stubbornly refused, afraid to jump. My dad waited patiently with his arms outstretched. Finally I saw myself bend at the knees and leap toward him. I took flight for a moment as fear enveloped me, but I had faith that everything would be all right. A moment later the cool water splashed me as Dad caught me in his strong, loving arms.

"I knew you could do it!" he exclaimed. I saw myself giggling and trying to break free from his gentle embrace. "I want to do it again, Daddy!"

I smiled to myself. I had faced my fears as a young child, and I knew I could face my fears now. But this time I knew I would have my heavenly Father cheering me on.

Are you standing at the edge? Do you need a little push or some coaxing to keep moving forward? Isaiah 35:4 says, "Say to the cowardly: 'Be strong; do not fear!'" God does not want us to run away from our fears and problems. He promises that He will walk with us through difficult times.

Persecution

*All those who want to live a godly life in Christ Jesus
will be persecuted. (2 Tim. 3:12)*

"Mommy, my teacher said I can't say *Jesus* or talk about the Bible," said Jenna as she got in the car after school. *And so it begins, Lord*, I thought. *She's so young!*

My six-year-old first-grader, who is also a brand-new baby Christian, just got a small taste of persecution. The children in her class were supposed to draw a picture of what they would be doing over the summer break. Jenna's picture was of Jesus and all the things she would do at our church.

"Jenna, when someone becomes a Jesus follower," I said, "many people won't like it. They may say mean things to you, or they won't be your friend anymore. Some of your teachers may tell you that you can't talk about Jesus or say *Christmas* or *Easter*," I said.

"But why, Mommy?" she asked.

"Not all people love Jesus. They may not understand they need Him. They may not even want to know about Him. But you have to remember that when people say or do mean things to you, they've also done that to Jesus.

"The best thing to do," I went on, "is to ask God to help you love them and to help them want to know Him. Remember to always treat people with kindness and your teachers with respect. And never forget that you belong to Jesus."

Teaching our children to expect persecution is hard to do. But the Bible tells us in 2 Timothy 3:12 that "all those who want to live a godly life in Christ Jesus will be persecuted." Even the youngest of us. Remind your kids that Jesus will be with them, that God has a bigger plan, and that He will not forsake them.

Precious Time

*She watches over the activities of her household
and is never idle. (Prov. 31:27)*

I was a stay-at-home mom for ten years. Some days seemed like a year all by themselves. On normal days, though, I spent as much time with my girls as possible. I played games with them; I read to them; I rode bikes with them. My house was never perfect even though I did stress about it. The meals I cooked were never gourmet, and I never did anything as well as I would have liked.

But as I look back on that time, those years seem like a day. Today our girls are thirteen and nine, and I am working full-time. My schedule is too full; my body is too tired; my life is too compressed. But they tell me they miss me; I miss them too.

Even though the days are hectic, I still read to them at night. Yes, even the thirteen-year-old enjoys it. But I want more time with them because soon, I know, they'll be leaving our nest. So now instead of Play-Doh and block towers and swing sets, we're learning how to do some other things together. Like card making and cooking and knitting.

I realize my time with my children is short. Even now I see it as precious time that I will never get back. So I'll just have to figure out how to fit in all the other things that need to be done but are not as important. My house may still be a little messy sometimes, but will they remember? Or will they remember our precious times of reading, games, crafts?

God gives us our children as a sacred trust, a stewardship. And while we have a great responsibility to raise them to know Him, He also wants us to enjoy them and revel in the gifts they are. You won't regret it.

Preserving Marriage

Without good direction, people lose their way; the more wise counsel you follow, the better your chances. (Prov. 11:14 MSG)

"So how have you been?" I innocently asked Sheree as we left the meeting. Her eyes teared up. "Mitch and I aren't doing very well," she admitted. We stepped into an empty Sunday school room. She continued, "We weren't Christians when we got married, and we did so many things wrong. I think God has changed my heart, but I'm not sure about Mitch. I know he's cheated on me at least once, and he says he doesn't love me anymore."

I was completely overwhelmed. I am much younger than Sheree, but she has been married twice as long. What should I say? "Sheree, have you guys talked to anyone? I mean, like a counselor?"

"I'd like to, but Mitch refuses. He's given up on us."

"You can't give up hope, Sheree. Do you remember that verse that says, 'Nothing will be impossible with God'? (Luke 1:37). Listen, I'll go down to Pastor Ron's office with you right now, and we'll talk to him about finding a good counselor for you two to visit. And I'll pray with you that God will begin restoring what is broken."

The Bible teaches that we are all sinners (Rom. 3:23), and our marriages are affected by sin as well. Yet we must remember that no marriage is beyond the saving grace of God. If He can save us from our sins and spiritual death and give us eternal life through His Son, He can bring restoration, healing, and peace to our lives and relationships here on earth.

If you are facing trials in your marriage or you know someone who is, encourage them to visit a godly counselor who will honestly and lovingly point out the truth of God's Word and try to preserve their marriage in keeping with His will.

Receiving God's Provision

The LORD is waiting to show you mercy, and is rising up to show you compassion. (Isa. 30:18)

Katy shared with her friend Sandy about her recent Saturday morning surprise. "When my doorbell rang early, I couldn't imagine who was coming by that time of day. It was the men's ministry from my church—they were there to put a new roof on my house!"

Tears came to Katy's eyes as she said, "I know we needed it, and it was a huge help. But it's really tough to let people help me since Larry walked out. My dad has been doing repair work, and the older kids have been helping out with groceries. Even my friends gave me gift cards for my birthday. It is so painful to know that I can't give back right now."

Sandy reached over to hug her friend. "What you need to understand is that you are not indebted to these people. They are being God's hands and feet as He honors His Word and provides for you. You would be robbing them of a great blessing if you refused their kindness. Be sure, someday God will use you to extend that same blessing to someone else."

Our culture promotes independence as a great virtue. Whereas our society once valued and encouraged interdependence, today "neediness" is considered weakness. But the body of Christ and the Word of God present an opposing view. We are told to "carry one another's burdens" (Gal. 6:2). The New Testament church had a major ministry to widows and orphans.

When a legitimate need is provided, our response is to receive God's provision with thanksgiving and rejoice in His faithfulness. It is a witness to a "me-first" world. If false pride makes it difficult to be a gracious receiver, we need to search our hearts.

Innocent?

You are my shelter and my shield;
I put my hope in Your word. (Ps. 119:114)

It seemed so innocent at first. April thought it was kind of endearing that Ron, her husband of three months, seemed to be possessive of her time and attention. She just thought it meant he loved her. But soon he not only objected to her being with her friends; he also became jealous when she wanted to talk to her parents and her sister on the phone.

April began to feel like she was suffocating. And if she expressed opinions about anything that differed from Ron's, he reprimanded her. Soon the verbal outbursts escalated, and one evening when she arrived home from work twenty minutes late, he pinned her against a wall and squeezed her arms so hard she had bruises the next day. He accused her of seeing another man. He scrounged through her purse and took away her cell phone.

The next day she called her sister from work. April tearfully told Amy about what had happened the night before. "April," Amy answered her, "this can't go on. We've been praying, but we just didn't know. As a police officer, Dave sees this type of thing all the time, and we were starting to suspect."

"Well, it'll probably get better. Ron said he was sorry last night. He was almost crying because he felt so bad."

"No, April, listen to me. It sounds like Ron has some serious problems. We can help him get counseling if he's willing to do it. But while your safety is at stake, we should get you to a safe shelter."

Victims of domestic abuse experience varying degrees of danger and manipulation. If you find yourself on either side of this experience—the abused wife, the caring friend—make sure to seek immediate help.

The Real Issue

*Refrain from anger and give up your rage; do not be agitated—
it can only—bring harm. (Ps. 37:8)*

Jenna always heard there would be ups and downs in marriage, but lately it seemed like she and her husband, Patrick, had experienced a lot more downs. In fact, if she had to rate her marriage—and her husband—on a scale of one to ten, she'd give them no better than a three. Sometimes less.

Increasingly, Jenna's anger was boiling over at what she was going through. She was even starting to fly off the handle over things she would once have considered insignificant—a toilet seat left up, dirty socks on the floor.

One morning she picked up the phone and began rattling off her complaints to her older sister, Monica. After listening for a few minutes, trying to be supportive, Monica finally said, "It seems to me that the problem isn't really whether Patrick leaves the toilet seat up. Perhaps one of the issues here is that you need to deal with your anger. I hurt for what you're feeling, but I just don't hear anything huge in what you're telling me about him."

Jenna protested a bit but finally sighed. "Maybe you're right. You're not the first one to tell me that I've got a bit of a temper. I never intended to be this way."

Unfortunately we sometimes treat strangers with more courtesy and kindness than we do our own husbands. We get past the honeymoon stage and feel comfortable, so we let our hair down and stop trying as hard as we did in the beginning of the relationship.

Instead of letting the worst come out, make an effort to show your loved ones the best in you. Pray for God to give you an extra dose of patience, love, and kindness so you can demonstrate His love to those to whom you are closest.

Greta

We are asking that you may be filled with the knowledge of His will in all wisdom and spiritual understanding. (Col. 1:9)

As I drove to work, I dreaded the day ahead. My new coworker Greta had been assigned to my team to work on a special project. In the month she had been there, I had yet to see her smile. She didn't seem to want to socialize with anyone. I prayed quietly, "Lord, please give me a new understanding and appreciation for this woman. Help me look on her with compassion instead of irritation and criticism."

Later as I passed by Greta's office, I noticed that her eyes were puffy and red, and she looked exhausted. Cautiously approaching, I asked, "Are you OK?" As if a dam had burst, Greta opened up and tearfully told me about her eighteen-year-old daughter, Ali, who had a mental illness and had stopped taking her medication. The previous day Ali had become agitated with a neighbor's child and began screaming and cursing at him. Since this wasn't the first incident, the seven-year-old's parents called the police.

Suddenly I was ashamed. I had been critical of Greta. While I thought she was just a grouch who didn't like other people, she had been doing her best to deal with a situation I couldn't even imagine.

The world is full of all kinds of people, and some of them we just plain don't like—sometimes for good reason. Others just rub us the wrong way for *no* particular reason. But God calls us to treat others with kindness and respect, whether we like them or not.

Jesus said, "Do not judge, and you will not be judged. Do not condemn, and you will not be condemned. Forgive, and you will be forgiven" (Luke 6:37). The next time you're around someone you find difficult, ask the Lord to help you see that person through His eyes.

Two Different Worlds

I do all this because of the gospel,
so I may become a partner in its benefits. (1 Cor. 9:23)

This is one of the happiest times of my life. My husband, Sam, who refused to go to church with me for most of our thirty-two years of marriage, recently committed his life to Jesus. I'm still in shock, but already I've noticed a change in Sam. Simply put, he is joyful!

Looking back over the years, Sam and I seemingly lived in two different worlds. I took the children to church on Sundays, and he did yard work. I would try to tell him about things I was learning in Bible study, and he would change the subject. I grew discouraged many times, but I continued to do the only thing I knew to do—pray for the strength and grace to obey God's Word and pray every day for his salvation.

It's not easy being married to an unbeliever, but as I look back, I recognize God was working in my marriage all along. He's given me grace to handle every disappointment, and now I can see the fruit of obeying His plan to be patient and to pray.

The Bible indicates in 2 Corinthians 6:15 that a union between a believer and an unbeliever will be unharmonious at times. But Christian women married to unbelievers should prayerfully seek to honor both God and their husbands. First Peter 3:1–6 says respectful treatment and a gentle spirit do more to influence an unbelieving husband than persuasive words and arguments.

If you are married to an unbeliever, pray for his salvation and commit to living a godly life before him. Find ways to grow spiritually and plug into your church as much as possible without neglecting your spouse. Above all, don't give up on your husband, but love him in word and in deed.

From Dates to Mates

Who can find a capable wife?
She is far more precious than jewels. (Prov. 31:10)

Debbie's teenage son, Matt, was bringing a girl home after school to play board games and listen to music. But mainly he was bringing her home to meet Debbie and her husband, Steve.

As parents they had begun to lay a godly foundation for relationships when their children were preteens. Watching selected TV shows together provided opportunities for discussions comparing God-honoring relationships with worldly ones. They welcomed their children's friends to their home (as long as a parent was there) so they could get to know them.

When dating loomed on the horizon, Debbie and Steve, remaining open to input from their teens, established clear expectations, firm rules, and appropriate consequences. So far both Matt and his sister were making good choices.

After making sure there were cold sodas in the fridge, Debbie sat down for a moment. "Father, help my kids choose their friends and their dates wisely," she prayed aloud. "After all, any date is a potential mate."

As your children approach the traditional dating years, establish some family guidelines for how you will handle boy-girl relationships. For instance, "group" dating is a good way for teens to mix (as long as the group meets your approval). You will want to establish other guidelines for different situations, such as no car dates until you've met the boy or girl at least twice. Let them know you will come and get them without judgment if they feel uncomfortable in a situation.

Consider how you can encourage your children to choose their friends wisely. Teach them to look for godliness, responsibility, respect, and goodness as they choose people to date. Every girlfriend or boyfriend is a potential marriage partner.

Radical Obedience

One who does good works—this person will be blessed in what he does. (James 1:25)

While flipping through the channels one evening, I came across a documentary about sexual violence against women in the Congo. As I watched the show, I was moved by the brave female filmmaker who traveled through war zones to give a voice to the victims. A survivor of gang rape herself, the filmmaker created environments that gave whole villages of women a forum to tell their stories and a chance to begin to heal. If just being in such a volatile country wasn't dangerous enough, this woman even went to remote areas to meet with the Congolese soldiers responsible for such violence. She had a passion to let the world know what was happening so that more might intervene for these women.

I was challenged deeply by her fervor. This woman was willing to risk her life in a way that I, a recipient of true redemption and healing in Christ, couldn't imagine. Convicted, I began to pray that I would have even half of her zeal in living differently, in showing radical compassion for others, and in service to God. Knowing that fear and apathy hindered me, I asked God to help me conquer those two things. As He began to work in my heart, I realized He wasn't sending me to Africa, but every day in many ways, I could choose to live radically for Him by being faithfully obedient.

Ultimately, being radical for God is the result of surrender and obedience to Him. Instead of ignoring the Spirit's promptings, the Bible says, "Don't stifle the Spirit" (1 Thess. 5:19). Each time you say yes to the Lord, and see how God blesses you for it, you will be encouraged to be bolder. How is the Spirit prompting you today? Will you obey?

Eating Disorder

He has satisfied the thirsty and filled
the hungry with good things. (Ps. 107:9)

I never had a weight issue until my junior year of high school. My mother and stepfather were fighting, and I wasn't happy at home. Through emotional eating and lack of exercise, I gained twenty pounds that year. After reading an article that advised only eating when I was physically hungry, I began to lose weight. It wasn't long before I was addicted to feeling hungry, and I began relishing the sense of control it gave me.

Concerned, my mother lectured me and tried to make me eat more. Teachers told me I looked sickly. But one day my obsession was officially fueled and reinforced when some strangers in the airport asked if I was a model. It was exhilarating to think that my ultra-thinness somehow made me more beautiful in the world's eyes.

I loved eating too much to abstain for long. But as I struggled with vacillation between emotional eating and not eating enough, I began bingeing and purging. Laxatives were my purge of choice, but I occasionally threw up when I was afraid my mom would notice how many tablets were missing.

When I became a Christian in college, I learned my eating issues were not only a result of a skewed view of beauty, but they were also my way of coping with stress in life. As I grew in the Lord, I learned to manage my eating in a healthy way and to trust Him to be in control.

An eating disorder—whether it's anorexia, bulimia, or binge eating—is a way of dealing with difficult circumstances, relationships, and emotions without God. Cultural ideas of physical beauty also make women especially susceptible to this coping mechanism. If you suspect you have an eating disorder, seek competent help. Ask God to teach you how to let Him help you.

Dot.com Dating

*The LORD is my strength and my shield;
my heart trusts in Him, and I am helped. (Ps. 28:7)*

Jackie was finally ready to start over after grieving her husband's death. She had met a few men over the last several months, but none of them seemed to be "the one." Not having any luck finding a man in her church's singles class or in her social circles, a friend had suggested that she try an online dating service.

Jackie was excited that the Christian service said they would scientifically match her with someone based on her personality, and she was assured by the background checks they performed on participants. She had felt it was the perfect solution to finding a husband quickly.

Now, several months later, her enthusiasm was waning. The first man, though his "credentials" had been a match, had just gotten a divorce and talked the whole time about his ex-wife. She had doubts about whether the second man she had met was a believer. The third lived four states away. It seemed the scientific process wasn't so perfect after all.

The dating service was a great way to meet men, but she realized in her eagerness to find someone, she hadn't even sought God's guidance. Repenting, she asked Him to take control, to give her wisdom, and to reveal His perfect will for her, whether it was best for her to marry again or to remain single.

Some unmarried women have a deep desire to be married. Others are content to remain single. If you are single and would like to be married, talk to God about it and be sensitive to His leading. Online or off, it's important to get to know someone you are considering as a marriage partner. There is no substitute for fully surrendering your desire to God and listening to His gentle guidance in the process.

Across the Miles

*This is My command: Love one another
as I have loved you. (John 15:12)*

When my husband, our children, and I moved four years ago, I wanted to make staying in touch with my family a priority. When we first moved away from my hometown, I thought we would be able to travel back and forth between my parents' home and our new location, a three-hour drive. But with rising gas prices and an uncertain economy, I soon found that those weekend visits weren't going to happen as often as I had hoped. So I decided to find ways to keep in touch inexpensively.

I now make it a point to e-mail and phone my parents and siblings regularly. I also send them text messages and pictures. It helps them feel like they are a part of our everyday lives. Having my kids stay in touch with their grandparents is pretty simple too. I just have the kids call them frequently. Not only do those calls brighten my parents' day, but it also helps my children feel connected to their grandparents.

No matter where you live, you can make a conscious decision to stay close to those you love. In Hebrews 13:1 we are told to "let brotherly love continue." Staying in contact even when you live far away can help those family bonds stay strong.

Although nothing beats seeing your family face-to-face, you can still find ways to connect with one another. Receiving a phone call, picture, letter, or e-mail can be a real blessing to family members. Don't underestimate the significance of taking time out of your busy schedule to stay in touch with loved ones. Sometimes a little creativity and planning can make a difference in someone else's day.

Pursuit of Perfection

Charm is deceptive and beauty is fleeting, but a woman who fears the LORD will be praised. (Prov. 31:30)

"Mom, when can I start wearing more than just lipstick and powder?" my fourteen-year-old daughter, Kylie, asked. "Most of the other girls in my youth group get to wear more makeup."

"Why do you want to wear more makeup?" I asked.

Kylie reflected a moment and said, "Well, I've noticed that the girls who wear more makeup seem . . . sophisticated, I guess, and the boys seem to pay more attention to them." She blushed.

"Kylie, women today feel all kinds of pressure—especially the pressure to feel beautiful. We think we have to look a certain way and be a certain weight to be accepted and valued. God wants you to accept yourself just the way He made you. Makeup is just something to add a little pizzazz. But don't fall into the trap of thinking you have to look perfect all the time. Focus on developing your inner beauty, not just dressing up what's already beautiful on the outside."

"I know," she said, smiling. I was glad she and I had a relationship where we could talk about things that were important to her.

First Samuel 16:7 says it best: "Man does not see what the LORD sees, for man sees what is visible, but the LORD sees the heart." While we should make an effort to look our best, God doesn't want us to be consumed with our outward appearance.

The enemy is constantly trying to get us to doubt our true worth. But God wants us to be consumed with only one thing, and that is Him. Don't let insecurities and the pursuit of perfection cloud your perspective. You are priceless, especially in your Father's eyes.

Benefit of the Doubt

Do not judge, so that you won't be judged. (Matt. 7:1)

"Have you seen Jennifer recently?" Amber asked. "She's lost a lot of weight since she and her husband separated. Do you think she's seeing someone else?" Amber raised her eyebrows waiting for my reply.

I paused before answering. I didn't want to get embroiled in starting rumors about a coworker. "I'd rather not speculate about what may or may not be going on."

Amber shrugged. "I'm just curious."

"I understand, but I think if Jennifer wanted to share her situation with us she already would have. Besides, a few months ago, the Lord convicted me about the way I was gossiping, and I asked Him to help me not to do it anymore."

"You're right, Claire," Amber said. "I guess I just love the drama."

When we gossip about others, we aren't giving them grace, and we're setting ourselves up as their judge. Romans 2:1 says, "Therefore, any one of you who judges is without excuse. For when you judge another, you condemn yourself, since you, the judge, do the same things." And Proverbs 20:19 gives us clear advice: "The one who reveals secrets is a constant gossip; avoid someone with a big mouth."

God asks us to follow His example and extend grace to other people who have offended us. In doing so we are following His command to love others as we love ourselves (see Matt. 22:39).

If you find yourself in a situation where someone is being talked about, or if you are the one who started gossiping, stop. Ask God to help you steer clear of all gossip and avoid being judgmental. Give the same measure of grace to others that God has given to you.

He Promised

The flour jar did not become empty,
and the oil jug did not run dry. (1 Kings 17:16)

When I answered the phone, my friend Mindy was crying on the other end. "Jake just lost his job," she told me. "How will we survive? What will we do?"

I sighed. My husband, Alex, and I were in the same situation. In fact, we had been for two years. "Mindy, I know you're really scared right now. You're wondering how you'll pay the mortgage, how you'll support your family, even how you'll retire. But remember, God will take care of you because He loves you and you are His daughter. He promised."

"But I don't understand. We've tried to be good stewards of what He's given us, we tithe, we even sponsor a missionary," she said.

"I don't understand it either, but God knows about your situation. This pink slip didn't catch Him by surprise. He knows how much money you have in savings. He knows you need to put the kids through college. He even knows your bills. He'll give you exactly what you need. I think one of the hardest things we as Christians have to learn is dependence on the Lord and that He has our best interests at heart. He will provide for you because that's His nature. His provision probably won't look like you think it should, but He will take care of you."

When you are staring unemployment in the face, it's hard to wrap your heart around this truth. But ask God to make you aware of all the little things He does every day to provide for you. Write them down; read them when you are afraid. These are faith builders. The stronger your faith grows, you'll find you don't need to "see" the answers because you trust the One who is holding on to you. He will guide and provide. He promised.

I'll Do It Tomorrow

I went by the field of a slacker. . . .
I saw, and took it to heart. (Prov. 24:30, 32)

"I admit it. I'm a procrastinator. I never do today what I can do next week," Julie said. She was the speaker at a women's ministry event at our church. The subject was overcoming bad habits.

"My motto has always been 'Procrastinators unite . . . tomorrow!' But today I'm a rehabilitated procrastinator. With God's help, instead of putting things off, I'm putting good habits in place that bring peace and calm to my marriage, my family, and my job."

I smiled. Julie and I are friends, and I knew she had worked hard to overcome procrastination. She discovered that procrastination is a learned behavior, and in her case it stemmed from feelings of being overwhelmed with life. With so much to do, she was frozen to inaction. She just continued to put things off.

"There were times that I mailed thank-you notes six months late, I had overdue library books accompanied by huge fines, and some days we had no food or clean laundry in the house. I knew my put-it-off habit was hurting my family and even my walk with the Lord. With His help, I'm prioritizing my activities every day, delegating some things, letting some things go, and designating idle time during the evening to get important things done."

Our God is an orderly God. He's never late, and He doesn't forget because He's overwhelmed. And since our goal is to become more Christlike, with His help we can begin replacing our bad habits with good ones.

If you have a habit that increases your stress, is dangerous to your health, or hurts your relationships, talk to the Lord about it. He has provided the Holy Spirit to give you power to overcome bad habits and make better choices.

Dry Bones

He said to me, "Son of man, can these bones live?" (Ezek. 37:3)

Lately my spiritual life seems like Ezekiel's valley of dry bones. I pray, go to church, and try to do all the right things, but I feel as parched as a desert. My service is routine, my quiet times are dull, and my worship seems like something to check off my list. My spiritual emptiness also seems to be spilling over into other areas of my life.

We all get into spiritual ruts, and there are many reasons. Have I overcommitted, trying to do good things but leaving out the best thing? Am I harboring some secret sin like bitterness or anger that keeps me holding God at arm's length? Has He allowed me to run headlong into the wall of my dreams and desires so I will turn to Him to discover His dreams for me? And even worse, are my prayers and quiet times all about me, rarely about Him?

God says in Jeremiah 29:13 that when we seek Him we will find Him. So I sought Him, I got alone with Him. No distractions, no agenda, no phone. What He revealed was painful.

My husband and I have had some tough times lately. Financial and health problems. Various family issues. And while He has brought us through those things, He lovingly showed me that my heart has gotten crusty and hard. I secretly didn't like His timetable and was harboring anger toward Him. I was hiding these feelings—sins—under an oh-so-spiritual façade. The reason for my dry season was sin and pretending.

When your spiritual life seems dry, sometimes He wants to see if you'll pursue Him. Sometimes you may have sin in your life. Or perhaps He wants you to learn to sit quietly at His feet. In the meantime do what you know to do. Pray. Love. Serve. Tithe. Worship.

Imperfect Masterpieces

*He will be with you; He will not leave you or forsake you.
Do not be afraid or discouraged. (Deut. 31:8)*

Deanna wrapped her sweater around her shoulders more tightly and sighed. She was cold, and she knew the tingling numbness in her legs would make it difficult to get up when the nurse called her name. Everything was such an effort now. She fingered the pearl handle on her cane and thought back over the last two years since the onset of her illness and that dreaded diagnosis. How her life had changed. The pleasures of playing tennis, long walks on Saturday morning, and shopping at the mall would never again be part of her life.

In the middle of her sorrow, however, she had found a new and unexpected joy. Her friend Ruth took her to a neighborhood Bible study, and with extra time on her hands, Deanna delved more deeply into God's Word. She began to cultivate new interests also. She was on the prayer team at church, and she started painting again, a talent long neglected.

In each season of life, the Lord provides opportunity as well as challenges. He guides us into new adventures when we allow Him to show the way. When illness strikes, God has not abandoned us. In this new season God will unlatch new doors when we open our hearts and minds to Him. The same physical encumbrances that slow us down can also make us more sensitive to the quiet whispers of God, the nuances of His Word, and the needs of others.

When Michelangelo carved his famous statue of David, he began with a flawed piece of marble. But by allowing the limitations of the defect to inspire his creativity, his resulting masterpiece was all the more beautiful. As God creates a masterpiece in you, He can use the imperfections in your health to sculpt you into a more perfect child of His.

Life-Changing Mission

Let's not just talk about love; let's practice real love. (1 John 3:18 MSG)

Sonya was a little nervous about the week ahead. The singles pastor at church had asked her to join a mission trip to the mountains of West Virginia. They would be repairing homes of elderly people each morning and holding Bible school at a local church each afternoon.

On the first afternoon in a corner of the fellowship hall, a little girl named Natalie sat by herself while the others played games. Natalie didn't say much, so Sonya did the talking. She talked about her life, her favorite Bible stories, and how much Jesus meant to her. Then it was time to leave.

The next afternoon Natalie made a beeline for Sonya and pulled her over to the same corner. She had brought a doll, which she put in Sonya's lap. Each afternoon was the same: Sonya would sit and talk to the quiet girl, playing with the doll, and trying to make Natalie smile. At the end of the week, the church's pastor told Sonya that Natalie had a troubled home life, and he had never seen her bond with anyone before Sonya. Sonya fought back tears when she told Natalie good-bye, and gave her a little Bible to take home.

Mission trips are incredible opportunities for spiritual stretching. Not only do you experience new places, cultures, and people, but you are put in situations you have never faced before. These moments drive us to depend on God's provision and faithfulness, and we see Him come through for us in amazing new ways.

Consider taking a short-term mission trip. Check at your church or denominational website to see what mission opportunities are coming up. If you are unable to go on a trip yourself, you could support someone who is going with prayer and financial help.

Practicing Kindness

What does the LORD require of you but to do justly, to love mercy, and to walk humbly with your God? (Mic. 6:8 NKJV)

"Use kind words, Jack," I reminded my four-year-old.

"But Mom, Matthew knocked down my tower and he's being mean!"

After ironing out the sibling spat, I thought about how often I withhold kindness myself because I think someone doesn't deserve it. For example, there's that neighbor down the street who scowls at my kids every time they ride their bikes near her yard. I've never wanted to show her any kindness because she's never shown me any.

But it suddenly dawned on me that it's easy to be kind to those who are kind to us. The harder thing, the thing Jesus did, was to show kindness to people who were hard and cold and didn't deserve it—like us. He lived a life of love and then provided the ultimate display of compassion at the cross where He died for our sins.

I called the boys into the kitchen and told them we would make some banana bread to take to our neighbor. Maybe we could warm her heart with the love of Jesus. Maybe not. But either way I knew I could reach out in love and kindness to her because the same has been done for me at the cross.

Being kind does not come naturally to us—that's why random acts of kindness often make the nightly news in our society. Kindness simply means you have sympathy for others and you want to do them good. It stems from an attitude of humility, putting others before yourself, and going out of your way to meet their needs. Ask God to show you times when you are tempted not to live or respond in kindness. Hide verses in your heart so you will remember what God's Word says about living out godly characteristics.

Good News

He will wipe away every tear from their eyes. Death will no longer exist; grief, crying, and pain will exist no longer, because the previous things have passed away. (Rev. 21:4)

One evening my husband and I sat down after dinner to watch TV. We heard one discouraging news report after another: "Stock Market Takes a Dive," "US Troops Killed in Afghanistan," "Russia Building Arms Plants in Venezuela," "Corruption in Washington," "National Debt Exceeds $16 Trillion." Todd turned to the local news, and we heard reports of a robbery, a murder, and a missing child. I thought about what I had heard from some of the women in my Bible study recently. They were dealing with heavy issues like children on drugs, a husband hooked on pornography, a pregnant teenager.

We looked at each other, and I asked, "What kind of a world are we handing over to our children and grandchildren?"

Todd sighed and shook his head. "I know it can seem depressing, but no matter how bad things seem, God is in control."

"I know that's true, but with so many bad things happening, sometimes it's hard to focus on the good things," I answered.

If we focus too much on world events without remembering who is in control, it can be downright depressing. Jesus said, "You will have suffering in this world. Be courageous! I have conquered the world" (John 16:33).

If you find yourself disturbed over local and world events, remember who is in charge and be encouraged. Allow yourself to dwell on the good things in your life that often go disguised as forgotten blessings. Turn them into reminders of God's faithfulness, consistency, and love.

Happy Birthday

You must willingly open your hand to your afflicted
and poor brother in your land. (Deut. 15:11)

When my fifteen-year-old daughter's youth group leader challenged students to find ways to help the poor, Jenny took it seriously.

One evening Jenny said, "Pastor Mike showed us a video about poor people in India. So many families live in slums, and the little kids play right by open sewers in the streets." She shook her head. "It's horrible." I could tell that my daughter's heart had been touched, and I prayed that the Lord would continue to give her compassion for the poor.

Jenny began helping organize bake sales at her Christian school and car washes with her friends on weekends. She also convinced several friends to donate a portion of the money they earned from babysitting, mowing lawns, and part-time jobs to the growing fund for the poor.

But I was most proud of Jenny when she invited her friends over for her sixteenth birthday party. She asked them to donate the money they would have spent on presents to a Christian organization that helps people in India and some of the surrounding countries in south Asia. The highlight of the party was when they went through a catalog the organization provided and chose gifts for the needy, such as blankets, garden tools, and water filters. They even purchased livestock—goats, chickens, and rabbits so impoverished families could have a source of income and food, as well as learning about the love of Jesus.

Throughout God's Word, we read of His compassion on others, especially the poor. Psalm 103:13 says, "As a father has compassion on his children, so the LORD has compassion on those who fear Him." Psalm 82:4 instructs us to "rescue the poor and needy."

So Soon

Put to death what belongs to your worldly nature: sexual immorality, impurity, lust, evil desire, and greed, which is idolatry. (Col. 3:5)

Alice was devastated when she heard the news. Although she wasn't planning to be a grandmother so soon, she would have welcomed her seventeen-year-old son's firstborn. But now, instead of holding her first grandchild in her arms, she's grieving for the baby she will never see.

Alice and Craig's son, Dylan, told them recently that his girlfriend, Tara, was pregnant and was going to have an abortion. "I tried to talk her out of it," he told his parents one evening as tears spilled down his cheeks. "I told her I'd help support the baby if she would keep it." Even though Dylan pleaded with Tara repeatedly, she had made up her mind. She was college bound in the fall, and she and her parents didn't want the "inconvenience" of a teenage pregnancy. Eventually, Dylan and Tara's relationship couldn't survive the stress, and they stopped seeing each other.

In the 1950s and '60s, the number of teen pregnancies was far lower than it is today. Most girls who became pregnant out of wedlock either settled for a hurried wedding or were sent to a home for unwed mothers, and the baby was put up for adoption. But along with the sexual revolution came a growing acceptance of pregnant single women. Today it's common to see photos and film clips of unwed celebrities sporting a "baby bump." Famous couples live together and have children together, but they have absolutely no intention to marry.

Teens who become pregnant face the tough road of how to handle school, work, finances, and relationships. But abortion does not solve the problem or whisk it out of our lives. For these young women adoption is a redemptive alternative. Let's pray for how we'll handle these life-altering decisions.

Not Greener

*Marriage must be respected by all, and the marriage bed
kept undefiled, because God will judge immoral
people and adulterers. (Heb. 13:4)*

Eva finished the dishes and sat down on the sofa—alone. Nick was working late again. Opening her laptop, she saw another e-mail notice about her upcoming class reunion. Clicking on the attachment containing the contact information of former classmates, she wondered if her high school boyfriend's name would be on the list. It was. She read that Brent had become a veterinarian. Eva remembered the way he had always loved animals. Reading further she saw that he was currently single.

Eva sensed that she and Nick were drifting apart. She longed for the closeness they had experienced early in their marriage, but she knew it wasn't an excuse to fantasize about a man she had dated more than twenty years ago. She asked the Lord to help her keep her thought life pure.

The ringing phone interrupted Eva's thoughts. "Alone again?" her sister Beth asked.

Eva said, "Yes. In fact, maybe your call is a divine interruption."

"What do you mean?" Beth asked.

Eva told her sister about her struggle. "I know the grass is *not* greener on the other side of the fence, but Nick and I could really use your prayers."

Proverbs 6:32 says, "The one who commits adultery lacks sense; whoever does so destroys himself." Those are strong words, but adultery is serious, and the damage it can do is incalculable. It can not only destroy a marriage, but it can harm the children, other family members, and friends as well. If you know someone who is contemplating straying from their marriage, pray for them and ask the Lord to give you discernment about confronting them in love.

Who Comes First?

I will instruct you and show you the way to go;
with My eye on you, I will give counsel. (Ps. 32:8)

Rhonda tried to keep her voice down as she said to her husband, Bruce, "I used my last personal day yesterday. Sami still has a fever. Can you please stay home with her?"

"I have a huge project due on Friday. Just take the day unpaid."

Rhonda ran her fingers through her damp hair. "But I've missed a week already with both kids getting the flu. My boss is getting irritated. I can't afford to push it, especially now that she's talking about cutting hours. Mine could be the first on the chopping block if I make her mad."

"If I don't finish this project on time, *my* job could be at risk."

God, Rhonda prayed silently, *we can't send Sami to school sick. Should I risk getting in trouble or ask Bruce to put his job on the line?* Bruce let out a long breath and reached for his cell phone. "Tell you what, I'll call and see if they mind if I work from home today."

"Thank you!" Rhonda hugged her husband, but inside, her nerves stirred. *Was it a mistake to go back to work?* she wondered. *Bruce won't always be able to make this kind of sacrifice. Will this be a constant struggle?*

These days it is common for both parents to work outside the home. While the extra income and benefits cut money-related stresses, other frustrations come with the territory. Who should stay home when a child gets sick? Which parent takes time off for teacher conferences, school holidays, or unexpected calls from the principal? Which career should take precedence?

Like so many areas of family life, couples must seek God's wisdom and direction while also respecting each other. Know that He sees and values our efforts, and He promises to send what we need when the unexpected happens.

Still Waiting

While the son was still a long way off, his father saw him and was filled with compassion. (Luke 15:20)

"Have you heard from David lately?" Sharon asked. She prayed that Dana would know she cared and wasn't just being nosy. She couldn't imagine having to ask one of her kids to leave because of his behavior.

Dana nodded. "His roommates are finally paying their share of the rent, but the apartment is in a horrible part of town. He seems happy though." Dana's eyes misted over. "I'd almost rather he not be happy. I expected him to beg to come home by now, ready to give up partying, turn back to Christ, and go to college as he planned. He's been gone over a year, and he's still out there."

"I'm so sorry. Maybe Pastor Bill's daughter can give you some hope. It took five years, and she returned with two children whose father wanted nothing to do with them, but she's home. And look at her now, mentoring teen moms."

Dana wiped away a tear. "I keep reminding myself that the Bible doesn't say how long the prodigal son stayed in that distant country." Sharon hugged Dana. "And my prayer is that you'll be waiting to run to David, just as that father ran to his son."

Parents have a responsibility to invest their time and energy into helping their children grow physically, spiritually, emotionally, and socially, helping them develop healthy patterns that will carry over into adulthood. But there is no ironclad guarantee a child, teenager, or adult will not rebel. Many prodigals will come to their senses and return to the roots of their upbringing. A few will not, using their God-given freedom to continue making poor choices. Parents of prodigals need to maintain hope, give unconditional love, and be ready with open arms to welcome their prodigal home.

A Visual Reminder

Pray for us; for we are convinced that we have a clear conscience, wanting to conduct ourselves honorably in everything. (Heb. 13:18)

On Veteran's Day our church presented a slide show of members who had served or were serving in the military. Next our pastor called veterans and military personnel in the congregation to come forward for prayer. Finally he asked anyone who had family members serving oversees to stand. That final group reminded me that every soldier leaves behind a family—a concerned mother and father, a lonely spouse, children, siblings.

Many of my friends were standing: Susan, whose husband has been serving for several years; Diane and Bruce with two sons in the military; Lindy whose brother was about to leave; Teri, who had one son serving and another who had just joined the army. My own son had just turned nineteen. If circumstances were different, I could be standing too. How could I so easily forget to pray for these families? How often had I glossed over the "Pray for Our Military" list in the church newsletter? Why didn't I ask about their status more often?

Instead of sitting there feeling guilty, I allowed God to use this as a prompt for change. I asked Him to bring these precious families to mind more often, offer wisdom in how to pray for them, and provide ideas for how to offer support and encouragement during this unsettling time. After all, if my son were serving, isn't that what I would need?

How often do we consider that each man or woman in uniform represents a family? They must trust God in a way that many of us can't relate to—placing their loved ones in His hands, praying that He will keep them safe, strong, and firm in faith. Consider today how you can remain consistent in prayer and support for these strong but constantly concerned families.

The Hand of Mercy

Jesus was . . . preaching the good news of the kingdom, and healing every disease and sickness among the people. (Matt. 4:23)

"Thanks for taking care of the kids today," Amy said to Melanie as she hurried her daughters into her friend's kitchen. "Without your help I wouldn't be able to attend this training conference."

Melanie offered a faint smile but shook her head slowly. "What made you decide to work with people with AIDS and HIV?"

Amy remembered her own misgivings about helping AIDS and HIV patients before God began tugging on her heart. She understood why Melanie was questioning her newfound calling for helping those with AIDS. Glancing at her watch, she decided to forego the doughnuts and coffee at the conference. "If you have time, I'll tell you why I'm doing this," Amy said. Melanie nodded, and Amy shared some of what she had learned.

According to Kay Warren, wife of pastor and author Rick Warren, HIV/AIDS is still the greatest humanitarian crisis of all time, killing millions every year and leaving millions of orphaned and vulnerable children behind. Kay became so burdened about it that she began an international ministry to those suffering from the ravages of AIDS. Although treatments are increasingly more effective, there is still no cure for AIDS, which is outranked only by cancer and heart disease as the leading cause of death for women.

Kay has said that Jesus spent one-third of His ministry healing the sick. And we as His followers in this current age, with our current issues, inherit His calling to go to the sick and hurting, to help and minister to them in Jesus' name. How might God be leading you to serve those who suffer today?

Working Nine to Nine

What does a man get with all his work and all his efforts that he labors at under the sun? (Eccl. 2:22)

Although I'm able to offer accounting services from my home, I was still working long hours and weekends. Work was stacking up, and I hadn't cooked a decent meal for my family in weeks. The breaking point came last winter when I noticed my friend Jan was online, and I sent her an instant message. I typed simply, "I need a vacation!"

Jan's response hit me like a splash of cold water. "You just got back from vacation, silly!" Stunned at Jan's playful reminder, I stared at my monitor and recalled that indeed my husband and I had just been to the mountains the previous month.

Sobered by the realization that I was working too much and too long, I shut off my computer and put my head on my desk. I cried out to God and asked Him to help me get my life back in balance. My business was thriving, but my family, health, and relationship with the Lord were suffering as a result. Initially I whined to God that my heavy workload was the culprit. But gently He showed me it was not necessity fueling my work but my own pride.

Jesus said in John 6:27, "Don't work for the food that perishes but for the food that lasts for eternal life." Yet many of us continue to labor to the point of exhaustion for that which does not satisfy. Are you so focused on your work that you are neglecting relationships? Have accomplishments, money, or position become an idol to you? Are you sacrificing health and spiritual growth for success? Are you seeking God and His kingdom first, or do promotions, pay raises, and accolades top your list? Ask God to help you honestly evaluate your work ethic today.

Financially Faithful

Give, and it will be given to you; a good measure—
pressed down, shaken together, and running over—
will be poured into your lap. (Luke 6:38)

Debbie sat down and sighed. *This is not going to be fun*, she thought, looking with disdain at the financial ledger, a stack of envelopes, and the bank statements her husband, Jeff, had gathered. He had decided it was time to get serious about a family budget, and Debbie was dreading the process of reviewing their spending habits and planning their expenditures from this point on.

"Honey, I know you don't like talking about money, and I know a budget seems stifling to you, but I feel like it's the responsible thing to do," said Jeff, taking Debbie's hand in his. "Tell you what; let's pray before we get started."

Debbie nodded, touched by Jeff's suggestion. He began to pray for wisdom and direction. When he finished praying, Debbie squeezed his hand and continued the prayer. "Lord, thank You for giving me a husband who wants to honor You with our finances. Forgive us for all the times we disregarded You and spent our money frivolously. You have been generous to us. Please help us budget in such a way that we can be more generous toward others."

The Bible tells us that our relationship toward all that the Lord has given us is one of stewardship. We are not owners or even rightful earners. In Psalm 24:1 David says, "The earth and everything in it . . . belong to the LORD." We are stewards of that which God has entrusted to us, and we are to give abundantly, sacrificially, and joyfully. Consider how you manage the resources God has provided for you. What changes do you need to make so He will find you to be a good and faithful steward?

Teammates

Submit to one another out of reverence for Christ. (Eph. 5:21 NIV)

One Friday night my husband, Jim, and I, both of us tired, argued about our Saturday afternoon plans. We had all the kids for the weekend—Jim's and mine. He wanted us all to go to a movie, which his kids would love; but I wanted to go to the river, which my daughter would love. He eventually conceded, but we were both mad.

Getting ready for bed, I thought: *I should apologize, but I don't want to!* "Don't let the sun go down on your anger" (Eph. 4:26). *I know, I know.*

When I walked out of the bathroom, Jim was reading in bed. "I'm sorry for the way I acted," I gulped. "I know sometimes my loyalty to Ashley gets in the way. I believe you have the best intentions regarding the kids, but I don't always act like it."

He looked at me. "I'm guilty of the same thing. I'm sorry too. A riverside picnic sounds like a great way to spend the afternoon."

I sat beside him. "This blended family thing is so complicated."

"I know. I had no idea it would be this hard."

I searched his eyes. "But it's worth it. We just have to remember we are on the same team."

Take one couple, add children from previous marriages, mix in ex-spouses, and you can get a spicy stew with unpredictable flavor. Then tension builds in the marriage when there's no time to discuss problems, share feelings, or build intimacy. But if you are in a blended family, be encouraged. The Lord can shape your family into one with a strong bond, where everyone feels safe and loved and God is glorified.

The (Not So) Express Lane

A man who does not control his temper is like a city
whose wall is broken down. (Prov. 25:28)

Even though I'd chosen the express lane, the cashier seemed superslow. There were three people ahead of me, and it took her almost ten minutes to get their purchases rung up and bagged. I fussed and fumed inwardly, as if that would make her go faster. If she didn't hurry up, I was going to be late picking up my son from summer camp.

By the time she got to me, I didn't even try to smile. I had my debit card already in hand as I shoved the groceries across the counter. Still the cashier smiled at me and started scanning the items. She thanked me with a warm smile and handed me my receipt.

I felt a little guilty for so openly displaying my anger. So I just nodded and grabbed my groceries. Although I felt God telling me not to get so upset over something so insignificant, I still wanted to let someone else know how aggravated I was. So I headed to customer service.

When I spoke with the head cashier, she told me that the new cashier, Sheri, had suffered a stroke several months earlier. I felt completely embarrassed and humbled. I hadn't sensed that she was disabled in any way, and I had treated her horribly—not at all like God wanted me to treat her. I thanked the head cashier and went back to apologize to Sheri. I'd already made a bad first impression, and I didn't want Sheri to feel bad about my behavior toward her.

Being able to control your temper is a good thing. So try to remember in the heat of the moment that we shouldn't allow ourselves to lash out at others in destructive anger. If you lose your temper frequently, commit the matter to serious prayer. God can change you.

We Must Tell Them

We . . . must tell a future generation
the praises of the Lord. (Ps. 78:4)

When we brought our first daughter home from the hospital, we felt inadequate, unprepared, and, yes, exhausted. Not only were we responsible for taking care of her, but we also felt the weight of responsibility for her spiritual growth.

Our godly parents reminded us that the Ultimate Parent, God, has given us the "road map" to parenting in His Word. "God teaches us, through Moses, how to teach spiritual truth to our children," said my mom. "He tells us to teach them during everyday life and ordinary circumstances, as we go about loving them and raising them," she said.

So as an infant Carly heard Christian music in the car on the way to the grocery store. I read Bible stories to her from a baby storybook. We told her that God made her and loves her. We took her to church. As she grew, we said "good-night" prayers and a blessing before meals, and when we played at the park, I told her that God made the trees and the birds.

When Carly started preschool, I prayed for her in the car on the way to school (with open eyes, of course!). We asked God to help her find good friends, to learn about Him, to have fun on the playground. I always pointed out to Carly when God answered those prayers so that she would begin to look for His answers herself.

Now Carly and her sister Katie are both at college. And even though we did not parent perfectly, we had the Perfect Parent watching over us, giving us guidance, and forgiving us when we blew it.

It's never too early to teach your children spiritual truth. Use teachable moments to help them apply biblical truth to their lives. And when they have questions, show them truth in Scripture.

A King's Heart

A king's heart is like streams of water in the LORD's hand: He directs it wherever He chooses. (Prov. 21:1)

Last November, city election signs littered the streets and neighborhoods of the small suburban community where I live. The signs implored me to vote for the mayoral incumbent or the city council member who was running against him. Newspaper ads touted one candidate over another candidate I had never heard of. Campaign materials expounded on the fiscal irresponsibility of their opponents.

I did get out to vote during that election. Some of the people I voted for won their election, but some of the people I voted for did not win.

So now, a few months later, I am frustrated by the people in office. The incumbent mayor—who won back his position—is an avid bicyclist. He has received enough votes from the city council to begin a major project which involves widening a road and installing sidewalks so he can institute a citywide bicycle race. The project cost millions of tax dollars, dollars I feel could be better spent.

I complained and fussed to my husband and my neighbors about what I considered to be a waste of money. But God, the very next Sunday, brought to my attention the responsibility I have to my elected officials: to pray for them.

God puts our elected officials in place. No matter if we voted for them or not, agree with their politics or not, or even like them or not, He commands us to pray for them. It's another way to demonstrate our belief that God is sovereign over everything that happens here. Election results, whether they gladden us or make us despair, do not catch God by surprise. And we must always remember that our God can change the hardest of hearts and make them His own, for the good of all of His people.

Magic Number

Watch out and be on guard against all greed because one's life is not in the abundance of his possessions. (Luke 12:15)

Ellen recalled looking at her 401(k) balance on the computer screen and feeling a tremendous sense of satisfaction. Her account was getting closer to the magic number she had in mind. Grabbing a calculator, she had punched some numbers and put them down on paper.

If I earn 10 percent a year over the next four years, maybe I can think of retiring early, Ellen thought. She and her husband, Richard, had worked hard, tithed, paid their bills on time, contributed to their retirement plans, and had always lived below their means. She was already daydreaming about long, lazy days on the beach and traveling to see their children and grandchildren more often.

A couple of weeks later, the stock market plunged dramatically. Within a few weeks Ellen's 401(k) was down by more than 30 percent. She felt sick to her stomach as she checked her balance on the computer again. *Lord*, Ellen prayed, *this financial meltdown has ruined our plans. What are we going to do? Will we ever be able to retire?* She sat in silence for a few minutes.

As Ellen remembered God's promises, she realized that He would always be there and would meet their needs. She breathed deeply and prayed, *Please help me to turn over this burden to You, Lord. You knew this would happen, and You know what the future holds. Help me trust in You and make wise choices.*

In days of uncertainty, many people worry not only about the status of their retirement accounts but also about whether they will be able to put food on the table. But in spite of the shaky economy, international instability, and unemployment, God is still in control.

Listen

Listen and hear my voice.
Pay attention and hear what I say. (Isa. 28:23)

Becky set her purse and keys down on the table. It had been a long week with several disruptive students in her seventh-grade history classes. Grabbing a diet soda from the refrigerator, she looked at the chore list she had posted on the door for her fifteen-year-old daughter, Corrie. Nothing for that day had been checked off.

"Corrie?" Becky called crossly as she went upstairs. "Why haven't you done your chores?"

Corrie was talking on the phone and didn't hear Becky as she approached her room. "My mom and I don't communicate at all," Corrie said into the phone. "She's busy all the time since she went back to work—she's either at school, or when she's home, she's working on lesson plans or grading papers. About the only time we talk is when she's telling me what to do."

Becky stepped back and quietly walked back down the hall to her bedroom. She had always wanted to have a good relationship with her daughter, but between her work schedule and Corrie's teenage mood swings, it had been difficult. She sank down in the chair and thought about the conversation she had overheard.

Lord, Becky prayed, *Corrie's right. I've been so intent on giving her to-do lists and telling her what to do and what not to do that I haven't focused enough on listening to her. Please show me how to turn things around.*

Teenagers are especially concerned with fairness, and if they feel their parents aren't listening, they're not likely to open up. If you're having similar issues, pray for wisdom. Ask God to help you not only communicate your concerns but also listen well. Proverbs 1:5 says, "A wise man will listen and increase his learning."

Confide Carefully

Seek first the kingdom of God and His righteousness, and all these things will be provided for you. (Matt. 6:33)

Kim and Scott had been married seventeen years and had three children, but over the last couple of years, she felt they were drifting apart. Scott focused so intently on his career that Kim felt neglected. But she was tired of nagging him and trying to get his attention. Eventually Kim found herself in a chat room on the Internet and began making a few friends online.

One evening as she talked with her sister Erin on the phone, Kim mentioned one of her new online friends—Brad. "You and I have always confided in each other," Kim said, "but it's really helpful to have a man's perspective of what's going on between Scott and me."

"You've got to be kidding me!" Erin exclaimed. "You don't know who this guy is—he could be a real creep. Kim, this will hurt your marriage—not help it. My best advice as a Christian and as your sister is to keep Scott your first priority and stay away from other men—whether it's a neighbor, a coworker, or someone you met on the Internet. If you need a guy's point of view, why don't you and Scott go in together and talk to your pastor?"

Kim was annoyed, but deep inside she knew Erin was right.

Marriage was designed by God to be a fulfilling relationship between a man and a woman who are both submitted to Him. But because of our fallen nature, our relationships become damaged. When we feel the need to confide in someone about our problems, things can get sticky.

If you are experiencing difficulty in a relationship, pray for wisdom and ask God to direct you to a wise and godly woman who will help and not harm the situation.

I Needed That

Encourage each other daily, while it is still called today. (Heb. 3:13)

Overwhelmed by looming deadlines and drowsy from lack of sleep, I wondered how I was going to accomplish everything that was on my agenda for the day. I pushed myself away from my desk and decided to make a quick trip to the ladies' room. On my way back to my office, I glanced over at Gail as she studied her computer screen.

Gail was a wonderful Christian woman who was likable and friendly and had an infectious laugh. Although she had multiple health problems—lupus and arthritis, as well as suffering from chronic back pain—she always took the time to greet me with a smile.

Before I was a couple of steps past her office, I felt the Holy Spirit prompting me to turn back to give Gail a hug. I hesitated for a moment, thinking of my cluttered desk and crazy schedule, but then I turned back, walked into her office, reached out, hugged Gail, and said, "The Lord told me to stop in and give you a hug."

She hugged me back and said, "Thank you, sweetie. I needed that."

As I left Gail's office, I noticed that I felt better, and the day ahead didn't look quite so overwhelming as it had earlier.

No matter who we are, what we do, or how we feel, we all need encouragement. God didn't create us to live in a vacuum; we were created for relationships—with Him and with others.

The next time the Lord prompts you to encourage someone, be obedient. Speak God's blessings into his or her life and thank Him for the opportunity to be the hands and feet of Jesus to a person who needs kind and encouraging words.

One Less Thing

Who can eat and who can enjoy life apart from Him? (Eccl. 2:25)

I hesitated before sending the e-mail to my writers' group. How could I tell them I needed to take a break? They would be so disappointed. I'd been leading the group for years and considered each member my friend. But my husband had injured his back and would eventually need surgery. He clearly needed me home more.

Long before that, however, I'd sensed God telling me that something needed to go. I was involved in choir and worship team at church, attended a home Bible study and the ladies' study group, in addition to being a mom and working as a freelance writer and editor. "You're doing too much," several friends had pointed out.

Norm's health issues doubled as a last straw and a convenient excuse to slow down. I quickly sent the e-mail before I could change my mind. As it turned out, many in the group welcomed the break. I wasn't the only one who needed one less thing on her weekly calendar.

How do you know when you've crossed the line from an active lifestyle to an overcommitted one? Does it take one "last straw" event or request? A crisis? An out-of-the-blue season of unexplainable dissatisfaction when activities suddenly feel like chores, when what used to be fun is just one more thing to rush to? Admit it: sometimes it's freeing to be forced to cut back.

Interestingly, one of the wisest, most successful men in history, King Solomon, became disillusioned with his work. One day all of it felt like "a pursuit of the wind" (Eccl. 2:26). What drove him to that point? As we read on, it's clear he eventually saw work as a gift from God to be enjoyed. How can we get back to that point? Perhaps only when we are willing to stop juggling more than we can handle.

The Sting of Sacrifice

*If anyone . . . sees his brother in need but closes his eyes to his
need—how can God's love reside in him? (1 John 3:17)*

Mary looked forward to her monthly scrapbooking party
with the women in her neighborhood. These nights always
promised good food and lots of laughter. But now she wondered
whether she should attend that evening.

Mary's sixteen-year-old daughter, Amy, had come home
from cheerleading practice in tears that afternoon. She had been
struggling to fit in with the other girls on the squad and had
discovered that day that she'd been intentionally excluded from
a sleepover at the captain's house.

After comforting Amy for a while, Mary sent her to take a
shower. She knelt beside Amy's bed and asked God to grant her
wisdom for ministering to her daughter's need. As she prayed for
Amy and considered her hurts, Mary knew what she needed to
do. Instead of spending the evening with her friends, she would
take Amy out for dinner and a manicure. It would be a sacrifice
on her part, but this was more important.

When Amy came out of the shower and her mother shared
her plans, Amy's excitement confirmed that Mary had made the
right decision.

Sacrifice is simply part of the job description for wives and
mothers. We give up time, outings with friends, solitude, privacy,
and personal goals almost daily. Out of love and concern for our
families, we often put aside our own plans, preferences, and priorities. But while sacrifice is a sign of our love and devotion, we
need to be careful lest resentment and bitterness take root. Ask
Him to "fill your cup" so your spirit is refreshed. Then, as God
leads, you can continue to serve others with grace and joy.

Keeping Pace

Encourage the young men to be self-controlled. (Titus 2:6)

The colors were eye-popping, and stars floated across the screen. A catchy tune played in the background, and an invitation to take a "Best Friends Quiz" blinked perpetually. How in the world had Katy created something so sophisticated on the Internet, and how could Jodi navigate her way through it?

Jodi had decided to let her fifteen-year-old daughter develop a page on a popular social networking website. Katy begged to join for months, but only recently had Jodi received the "go ahead" in her spirit. When Katy first asked, Jodi had adamantly said, "Never!" She had heard stories of teens posting lurid photos, kids sending one another hateful messages, and predators using the website to find personal information about unsuspecting victims.

But recently Jodi had heard about other kids in their church who had pages. Jodi prayed about whether it would be in Katy's best interest to participate in the website. Ultimately Jodi had decided to let Katy set up her page with a few conditions. Now the fun and the work were about to begin.

Let's face it, many of our kids have outpaced us as far as technology goes, and keeping up requires a fast and furious pace. But if you're going to responsibly raise your kids to live godly lives in the culture they've inherited, you'll have to do your homework.

Daniel's parents in the Old Testament must have done a good job preparing their son to navigate his way through a flashy and advanced culture. Throughout the book of Daniel, we see he was able to plug in to the culture of Babylon without getting pulled into its traps. What do you need to do to help your children safely navigate their tech-savvy and highly charged culture?

The Talk

My daughter and her friend were carrying on a lively discussion in the back of our car when something they said piqued my interest. Tuning in more carefully, I realized they were talking about a visit from a sex educator in their health class that day. The woman is a local educator who goes to schools throughout the area and teaches a pro-abstinence sex-education curriculum. She had been to my daughter's Christian school the year before to address her eighth-grade class and had taught an appropriate program. But the things I was hearing from the back of the car seemed questionable.

"Did she actually say that?" I asked my daughter.

"Yes," she responded. "She wasn't at all like last year. She still told us we shouldn't have sex until marriage, but she used some pretty crazy illustrations and words to make her point. We must have gotten the Christian version last year but not this year!"

As much as we try to prevent harmful information or interaction from coming into our children's lives, parents often find out about destructive influences after the fact. If you discover too late that your child has been exposed to inappropriate teachings about sex, gender orientation, evolution, religion, or any other topic, don't count it all lost. Ask God for the wisdom to know how to address the topic with your child. Seek Him to know if you need to address those in authority over your child about avoiding similar situations in the future.

Most important, be proactive in teaching your child the facts of life yourself. The Bible makes clear in Deuteronomy 6:6–9 that parents should teach their children to know God and live according to His statutes so they will not fall victim to the worldly teachings around them.

Shrewd as Serpents

How can a young man keep his way pure?
By keeping Your word. (Ps. 119:9)

Tracy couldn't believe what she was seeing. While passing her ten-year-old son's room, she had caught him looking at suggestive material on his computer. "Brian, what was that?"

"I was looking up information for my project, and this is one of the websites that came up." After talking to him further, Tracy realized that Brian had stumbled across the site while entering a few innocent search words for his report. He admitted that it wasn't hard to accidentally pull up such pages, but he was quick to assure her that it had not been deliberate.

Later Tracy discussed the incident with her husband, John. Both were appalled at how easily their son had been able to access such explicit pictures. John, knowing how powerful visual images are to males, was saddened at how his son's young eyes came across the material due to a lack of security. He knew he should waste no time on installing an Internet filter and decided it would be best to move the computer to a more public place. John also knew he had to have a serious talk with Brian to undo some of the damage.

From pornography to predators, the dangers of the Internet are real for our families and for us. Jesus warned His disciples, "Look, I'm sending you out like sheep among wolves. Therefore be as shrewd as serpents and as harmless as doves" (Matt. 10:16). Type "Internet filter" into your search engine. You'll find plenty of easy-to-install software that will keep suggestive material off the screen, including risqué advertisements, and it will help protect children from predators. If you haven't already, don't waste a second on taking precautionary measures to safeguard your family's integrity today.

Surrendered and Single

The LORD is good to those who wait for Him, to the person who seeks Him. (Lam. 3:25)

Diane did not understand. All of her life she had assumed she would marry and have a family. She had looked forward to the opportunity to be a wife and a mother. But time was passing, and the possibility seemed to be slipping away. She expressed her frustration to Teresa, a single friend.

"I've tried to be patient, but sometimes the loneliness is so hard. I've watched as my friends married and their children came along. I realize now I may never know family life like that, and it hurts."

Teresa hugged her friend. "I understand. I wrestled a long time with that too. Finally, I asked God to give me whatever life would best serve His purposes for me and to help me be content with His will. Sometimes I still have the ache for a mate, but He has blessed me with an abundance of friendships of all ages and many opportunities to touch lives."

Being single when marriage is desired can become a consuming disappointment, and it requires a huge step of faith to surrender that desire to God. It means believing that "His way is perfect" (Ps. 18:30) and He "does not withhold the good" (Ps. 84:11) from His children.

In struggling with singleness, you may find help by seeking counsel and wisdom from other women who have been called to singleness either for a season or for a lifetime. Reading the perspective of other singles can also offer insight. Building strong relationships with a variety of age groups is a good way to experience family and community.

Patiently waiting does not require putting life on hold. It means living fully, productively, and remembering the truth that we are the bride of Christ with the ultimate wedding yet to come.

223

Sufficient Strength

He crowns you with faithful love and compassion. (Ps. 103:4)

Hesitantly, Mary shared her heart with her ladies' Bible study group. "My ex-husband has decided to pursue an alternate lifestyle. I'll be breaking the news to my two children this week. I need prayer for wisdom in responding to their questions and emotions. I also need peace as I face my own disappointment that our marriage will not be restored."

The group of single-again women silently gathered around their friend and sister in Christ. Their tears mingled with hers as they grieved and sought God for her tough circumstances. Each of them knew what it meant to face the end of a marriage. They also knew where to find the strength to move on.

Finally the leader prayed. "Lord, our eyes are on You because You are the Author and Finisher of our faith. You redeem our pain and losses, and You bring us hope. Be with Mary's family. Be her peace and their Counselor." As her friends provided the compassion of Christ, Mary went home encouraged. She would trust God to provide His power to face the sad days ahead.

No one emerges from the ending of a marriage without scars. Divorce is never God's perfect choice. But we also know that our greatest hurts and our greatest losses can be the seed for our greatest spiritual growth. A strong support system can help the victim of divorce move toward healing and begin a new life. Programs offered in many churches provide small-group encouragement and an accompanying program for children.

There can be life, even good life, after divorce because we have a God who gives "beauty instead of ashes" (Isa. 61:3) and "redeems [our lives] from the Pit" (Ps. 103:4). But we must let Him do His work of refining, restoring, and rebuilding.

On Their Own

*I will not die, but I will live and proclaim
what the LORD has done. (Ps. 118:17)*

Unlocking the apartment door, Allison stepped aside while her girls pushed past her, dropping backpacks, kicking off shoes, and heading for their bedroom. "Pick up your stuff and start your homework!" she called as she put her satchel on the table and keys on the counter. Halfway through the first week of school and she was already exhausted.

As she filled a pot with water, Sara called, "What's for dinner?"

"Your favorite: mac and cheese."

Kirsten called, "Mom, I'm tired of mac and cheese!"

Allison said, "We'll have something you like tomorrow."

Since Allison's divorce was final over the summer, she and the kids were on their own. Their father could not be counted on. She was grateful to be working again but had forgotten how draining teaching second-graders was.

After changing into shorts, Allison gathered dirty laundry and started the washing machine. While the macaroni was boiling, she made a salad, sliced apples, and checked her voice mail. One message: a mother from Sara's class asking Allison to bring cupcakes Friday. A party already? School just started!

Opening her satchel, she pulled out the papers she'd have to grade after dinner. Glancing at the clock, she realized she wouldn't get to bed before midnight again, and she'd have to squeeze in bill paying before work tomorrow. The school year stretched out before her like an eternity. *Lord, how will I ever make it?*

Yet God tells us His grace is sufficient for us, for His power is made perfect in weakness (2 Cor. 12:8–10). When you need strength to handle everything (and everyone) in your care, call on God. Put your trust in Him and just watch what He does.

Lunch Lady

Whatever you do, do it enthusiastically, as something done for the Lord and not for men. (Col. 3:23)

"Catherine," my manager, Dottie, asked, "would you mind cleaning off the lunchroom tables? The next group of kids will be here soon."

"Sure," I replied. I grabbed the cleaning cart and headed out into the lunchroom.

"Hey, lunch lady!" an eighth-grade boy shouted. "We can't eat at these gross tables!" My face grew hot as I held my temper in check at the student's lack of respect. Being a cafeteria worker wasn't a glamorous job, but it allowed me to work around my children's schedules, and it helped my family pay the bills. I finished the remaining tables and headed back toward the serving line. The kids were starting to line up for their lunches.

"Thanks, Catherine," Dottie said as she patted me on the back. "I'm glad you're on our team."

I smiled at Dottie and nodded. Somehow she always knew just what to say to make even the most common task seem worthwhile.

Just because you hold a job title that society doesn't swoon over doesn't mean that what you do isn't important. Not all of us are destined to be doctors, lawyers, and engineers. We all have different roles in life, yet each one of them is important in God's eyes.

We are reminded in Romans 12:4 that "we have many parts in one body, and all the parts do not have the same function." No matter what your job description, take pride in how you do your job. Whether you are a stay-at-home mom, a dog walker, or a cafeteria worker, job status is really not the issue. Your attitude and obedience are what matters to God. Although we may not always feel our jobs are significant, God has a plan for us and sees value in the work we do.

School Choice

He will guide you on the right paths. (Prov. 3:6)

"You're kidding, right?" my sister asked when I told her we'd decided to homeschool our daughters.

"No, we can't afford the tuition at the Christian school any longer. We've prayed about it, and this is where God is leading us," I said.

Several years ago when we first chose Christian school, we were criticized. One friend said, "They can't be salt and light at school if everyone looks like they do." Another friend, who had just done a major renovation on her home, commented that she just "couldn't afford Christian school." Others voiced concerns about academic excellence. So now that we've decided to homeschool, we know we'll hear even more comments. Comments like, "What about socialization? What will you do about math and science?"

But we know God has a plan for our daughters (Jer. 29:11), and after much prayer we feel that homeschooling them is part of His plan for now.

Today parents face so many choices in education—public school, private school, Christian school, and various forms of homeschooling. The most important thing we can do as Christian parents is to seek the Lord and His will for our children. If His will for your children is public school, He will help you guide them through it. If it's private school, He will provide the funds for you to keep them there. If it's homeschool, He will lead you to the resources that will help you.

Remember to pray first. And know that whatever option you choose, you may face opposition. God gives us our children as a trust, and with His guidance we must choose His best for them. So don't worry if others don't agree with your choice. It's really between you and the Lord.

Pride and Perfection

He has saved us and called us with a holy calling,
not according to our works. (2 Tim. 1:9)

My four-year-old was writing his letters when suddenly he let out an angry noise and sent a box of crayons crashing to the floor. "What's wrong, Jordan?"

"I messed up the 'D'! Now I have to start all over!"

"No, you don't. Pick up your crayons and try again."

"No, throw that paper away, Momma. It's no good!"

I wondered why he would be so hard on himself, but then I realized I often do the same thing. I hold most areas of my life to an unreasonably high standard. And if I don't use my time, energy, and money perfectly, I'm tempted to think I don't measure up. I get frustrated and discouraged.

I decided the best way to respond to Jordan's frustration was the same way God cares for me: with love and grace. "Here, Jordan," I said, "let's work on it together. I love you no matter what, even if you mess up, and I'll help you."

The struggle to be perfect is a losing battle. Because of sin, we live in a flawed and broken world. We strive to achieve the perfect body, the perfect job, the perfect marriage, the perfect children, and even the perfect relationship with God. But meeting those goals is more about our own pride than living a God-honoring life full of grace. The truth is that His love for us doesn't grow or shrink with our actions; it is constant and complete because it is established in Jesus, the only One who is perfect.

Take an honest look at your expectations for yourself, your relationships, and your responsibilities. Ask Him to show you areas where you can submit to His loving care, and thank Him that our salvation isn't dependent on what we do but on who Jesus is.

Seeking the Lost

Let your light shine before men, so that they may see your good works and give glory to your Father in heaven. (Matt. 5:16)

"So, Katie, what challenges have you faced lately?" Michelle was a good friend and mentor, and she didn't mince words when it came to our spiritual lives.

"Things have been really good lately. We love our church and our small-group Bible study."

"That's great! Are you reaching out to any non-Christians?"

"Well, I don't really cross paths with many non-Christians," I said hesitantly.

"Maybe you could start close to home," Michelle suggested. "Last Christmas I hosted a tea for the women on my street. That tea opened the door for me, and now I have a relationship with them and a place to start sharing the love of Jesus."

"That's a great idea. I could invite the young moms in my neighborhood over for a playdate. I know the wonderful things God has done for me through Jesus, and I don't want to keep that good news to myself."

God has called us to be salt and light to the world, and this means we must seek out those who don't know Him. Yes, we must not live like the world or embrace sin, but we are supposed to engage nonbelievers, be authentic with them, and share the goodness of God with them just as Jesus did in His life on earth. Sometimes we can unintentionally isolate ourselves by surrounding ourselves only with believers—working at Christian companies, attending Christian schools, using Christian-run businesses, and being involved in our churches.

Where could you get to know someone who needs the Lord? Consider your interests, responsibilities, and daily routine. You could take classes at the community center, jog with a neighbor, join the PTA at your child's school, or any number of other things. Touching the lives of others is an eternal investment.

I Will Be There

I will be with you when you pass through the waters,
and when you pass through the rivers, they will not overwhelm you.
You will not be scorched when you walk through the fire,
and the flame will not burn you. (Isa. 43:2)

When I saw Karen's number on the caller ID, I wondered how her daughter Amanda was doing after a trip to the emergency room. "She's OK," Karen told me. "The doctor said the cast will come off in a few weeks."

"That's good. But you sound kind of down."

"It just seems like I'm always going through some kind of crisis. Ever since Tim and I got divorced, I've had nothing but problems. I constantly struggle with finances, work is stressful, Dakota has been in trouble at school, Amanda has been sick, and now she has a broken arm." Her voice trailed off; then she continued. "I'm just exhausted trying to keep everything together."

"I know. I'm sorry you're going through such a rough stretch right now," I replied. "I can only imagine how difficult it is to be a single parent. But you're doing a great job even if you don't think so."

"Thanks for the encouragement," Karen sighed. "It just feels like I'm in motion 24–7. But you remind me that God hasn't forgotten us."

I smiled as I remembered the gift certificate for a pedicure, manicure, and a massage I hadn't used. "You definitely deserve a break, and I know just the thing. You're gonna love it!"

None of us is able to avoid having problems from time to time. Sometimes we go through periods where it feels like everything is caving in around us, and we wonder how we will survive. But God promised that He will be with us. Take comfort in His Word.

Paper or Plastic?

From Him the whole body, fitted and knit together by every
supporting ligament, promotes the growth of the body
for building up itself in love. (Eph. 4:16)

As the cashier scanned my groceries, the bagger asked, "Paper or plastic?" He quickly bagged up the contents of my shopping cart and began pushing it toward the door, but I intercepted him, smiled, and said, "That's OK. I'll take these out myself."

When the automatic doors opened and the ninety-degree temperature and high humidity hit me full force, I wished I had taken the young man up on his offer. I could have let him load my groceries while I started the car and got the air conditioner going.

But it wasn't just at the grocery store where I declared my independence. The Lord began convicting me that I was guilty of rejecting offers of help when I should be accepting. My good friend Donna had kindly offered to help with my family's garage sale, but I didn't want to inconvenience her. So I told her we had it covered. Another time after I'd had minor surgery, one of our neighbors asked if she could bring meals for a few days. "Thank you, but it's really not necessary," I insisted. I even found myself trying to do things on my own when God wanted to help me. *Thanks, God, but I can handle this all by myself.*

I began to realize that God wants us to obey when He calls us to do something, but He doesn't expect us to accomplish everything on our own.

Sometimes we need others' help. If we continually reject offers to assist us, we're depriving them and ourselves of a blessing. If you have trouble accepting help from others, ask the Lord if pride may be keeping you from accepting the gracious gestures of neighbors and friends. He has placed us in the body of Christ to help one another.

More Important Things

A greedy person provokes conflict, but whoever trusts in the LORD will prosper. (Prov. 28:25)

When my neighbor Marcia asked me to help with her son's birthday party, I gladly accepted. She was new in town, and her son, Trevor, was going to celebrate his tenth birthday. I thought it would be a good opportunity to get to know her a little better, and our sons were in the same grade.

From the moment my son, Josh, and I walked into their house, I was surprised to see all the things Trevor had. After the rest of his guests arrived, Trevor took them in the garage to show them his four-wheeler, his dirt bike, his hockey equipment, his bicycles, and other items. Inside Trevor showed the boys his electric guitar (which he didn't know how to play yet), his drums (ditto), his own computer, and his TV. I could tell Josh was impressed and so were the other boys.

When it was time to open the gifts, Trevor tore the wrapping paper off one present and said, "Aw, I already have one of these." He tossed it aside and proceeded to the next gift, unimpressed by each one. Marcia reminded him to thank his guests. I could tell she was embarrassed.

Most of us in the United States still have a high standard of living when compared to the rest of the world. But having plenty of things also has a downside. Many kids today have a sense of entitlement and think they should have the biggest, best, and most expensive everything. They aren't used to working or waiting for what they have, let alone doing without. Appreciation for things is sometimes practically nonexistent.

Pray that the Lord will help you to be wise in the purchases you make and that He will help you and your children be thankful for what you have.

Weathering the Storm

Whatever you want others to do for you, do also the same for them—this is the Law and the Prophets. (Matt. 7:12)

Stephanie swallowed the lump in her throat. "Marie, I need to take Gracie out of Good Shepherd's Academy. We just can't afford it anymore. My ex-husband isn't able to pay his share right now, or even child support, so things are extremely tight."

Marie held up her hands. "What do you mean he isn't able to pay? He's required by the court to pay child support."

Stephanie felt a strange need to protect her ex-husband's reputation, not wanting anyone to think of him as a deadbeat dad. "Greg lost his job."

"I hope you're keeping track of what he owes."

"I did at first. Then God helped me see that Greg isn't purposely holding out on us. He honestly can't pay. If we were still married, we would have to think of ways to cut back. So that's what I'm doing. I'm sorry, Marie. We don't want to leave, but if it's between school tuition and groceries . . ."

"I understand," Marie said. Then she opened a desk drawer and pulled out a folder. "Tell you what. Instead of leaving, fill out a scholarship application. When I explain your situation, I'm sure the board will approve it."

Many divorced couples find themselves in situations where a job loss makes child support payments difficult if not impossible. What is the correct thing to do when the situation is "he can't" instead of "he won't"? While it might be tempting to judge or offer advice on how to take action, perhaps the better question is how can you offer support without opening the door for long-term enabling? Ask God to help you plan in advance for how you will respond to such a crisis as well as how you will keep yourself reminded of His promises to provide.

Seeing What God Sees

Man does not see what the LORD sees, for man sees what is visible, but the LORD sees the heart. (1 Sam. 16:7)

Lloyd has worked as a greeter at our local discount store for as long as I've been shopping there. He is developmentally disabled, but he is well suited to welcoming customers and offering stickers to the children. He loves his job and his joy is contagious.

Martha works as a cashier in the same store. Well into her seventies, she has spent her life selflessly serving others. This might explain why everyone in our area who shops there knows about her. Amazingly, busy moms and teenagers show a surprising amount of patience as Martha meticulously scans and bags their items.

I marvel at how loved these two employees are. As much as I look forward to seeing them and have learned a lot from their model attitudes, I also know they could easily be targets for cruel remarks and behind-the-scenes jokes. Could it be that, like me, many customers see what God sees? Is it possible that God placed these two in that busy store to be lights for Him and reminders that He values a servant's humble heart?

In our image-driven culture it's easy to overlook or criticize those who look different due to age, disabilities, weight, or some other supposedly negative trait. We sometimes forget they are precious souls created and loved by God and made in His image. These traits might be the exact things that God purposed for His glory.

When God sent Samuel to find and anoint the future king of Israel, he was told to ignore the physical and remember what God sees—the heart. While we live in a world that values youth and beauty, God values inner beauty.

Shameless Prayer

Pray constantly. (1 Thess. 5:17)

Camille sat back with a sigh. "Ladies, do you really think our weekly prayer time is making a difference? It seems like nothing has changed, especially at the high school." Camille's fellow prayer partners looked at her with surprise. Was this the same faith-filled woman who began their prayer group just a year ago?

Realizing that even Camille occasionally needed encouragement, Lynn sat down beside her friend. "What's up?" she asked.

"Jake came home from football practice last night saying some of the coaches were using foul language again. I just thought that after all the time we spent last spring praying for a Christian coach, things would be different this year."

"We're not through praying," Lynn said. "We're going to keep asking God to build a strong, Christian influence in that coaching staff."

"You're right," Camille said. "And in God's perfect time He'll answer."

After Jesus supplied His disciples with a model prayer (Luke 11:2–4), He told them how to pray: with persistence or, more specifically, with shamelessness. While you might consider it rude to ask a friend for the same favor over and over, Jesus encourages His disciples, including us, to come before God's throne with the same requests as often as needed and without any embarrassment. He delights in our asking, and He promises to answer in His perfect timing.

Why do some prayers require persistence? Because sometimes He wants to accomplish even more in the meantime. He might change your heart and your requests, grow you in Christlikeness, teach someone else through your faith, or answer in a way you hadn't expected. Have you been praying about something for a long time? Keep praying and watch for God's hand in the meantime.

Tough Assignments

Do not grow weary in doing good. (2 Thess. 3:13)

Meg ran to answer the phone. She hoped whoever was on the line wouldn't hear three-year-old Jack screaming at her from his room.

"Hello, Meg. Are you OK? You sound winded." Thankfully it was her best friend, Jennifer, on the phone.

Meg sat down on the side of her bed. "I know Jack is just three, but I don't think I should let him tell me no or yell at me when I ask him to do things. What do you think?" Meg trusted Jennifer's advice.

"I think God has entrusted you with a strong-willed child," answered Jennifer with a chuckle. "But you're doing the right thing by insisting that Jack learn to obey. You'll just have to be consistent and stay on top of things."

"That's what I was afraid of," moaned Meg. "This is wearing me out."

"Hang in there. You're a good mom," said Jennifer. "Meanwhile, let's plan a girls' night out sometime soon so you can refortify!"

While we've all heard that parenting isn't for cowards, some of us are called to be braver and more fortified than others. Children come with myriad dispositions, and the strong-willed child will push any mother to her limits. But while God may allow your child to stretch you, He will not leave you without resources.

Proverbs 19:18 encourages, "Discipline your son while there is hope." The parent of the strong-willed child needs to be aware that every parenting moment counts, communicating to your child who is in charge and setting the tone for the remaining child-rearing years. If you are parenting a high-spirited child, pray for wisdom, grace, and fortitude, and commit to consistency. Remember, God has chosen you to train up this child, and He doesn't make mistakes.

Celebrate

Death has been swallowed up in victory. Death, where is your victory? Death, where is your sting? (1 Cor. 15:54–55)

My mother-in-law, Gayle, had been battling breast cancer, but she felt well enough to participate in a walkathon against the disease. She finished, exhausted but proud. A month later we learned the cancer had spread to her brain. Before we could grasp that news, she passed away.

We weren't ready to let her go. My husband had always been close to her; she was more of a mother to me than my own mom, and our kids adored her. How were we going to carry on?

A month later my friend Katy called. She knew how much I was grieving. She said gently, "Pam, you know Gayle was a believer, right?"

"Yes. She lived her life for the Lord."

"And you know Gayle is in heaven with the Lord Jesus, right?"

"Yes," I said.

"Then rejoice for her. This is what she has always wanted, deep inside her heart. To be with her Lord and Savior. To see His face, hear His voice, talk with Him. She is in the presence of the Love of her life, right where she wants to be."

I knew it was true. I still couldn't help saying, "But what about us?"

"You all miss her, I know, and you need to grieve. But focus on this: Gayle's greatest dream has finally come true. Her pain is gone; her deepest longing has been fulfilled. And you will see her again someday. But for now celebrate for her. It will ease your aching heart."

Yes, if the loved one is a believer, we can take comfort in knowing that she or he is now living forever with our God, and we will join them someday. It's what we've always truly longed for—the hope of heaven is a reality!

Never the Same

*Let us draw near with a true heart in full assurance of faith,
our hearts sprinkled clean from an evil conscience and our bodies
washed in pure water. (Heb. 10:22)*

My fifteen-year-old daughter, Jodi, needed to work on a school project, but our main computer had crashed. So I told her to use the computer in her dad's office. A few minutes later she walked into the kitchen. "Mom?" she asked, looking pale.

"What is it? Is something wrong with Dad's computer?"

"It's fine. I went to pull up the website I was on yesterday, and I saw several weird sites listed. I clicked one and a porn site came up. Do you think Dad is into porn?"

"What? No! Dad would never do anything like that!"

"But, Mom," she said, "go see for yourself."

After sending her to her room, I slowly walked into the office. What I saw on that computer screen was vile! I ran to the bedroom and wept, punching and screaming into the pillows so Jodi wouldn't hear. After a while Jodi knocked on the door. "Mom? Are you OK?"

"Just a minute," I said, blowing my nose and opening the door. She'd been crying too. "What's going to happen now?" she whispered, as I hugged her. "Do you think he's addicted?"

"I hope not. I'm so sorry you saw that, Jodi. I will pray that God will completely erase it from your mind and free you from it. And I want us to pray for your dad." She nodded. I hugged her again, knowing our lives would never be the same.

Pornography addiction destroys marriages, families, and lives. If your husband is viewing porn in any form, know that you are not the cause. He chose that sin, and he must repent from it. Resist the temptation to believe it will go away on its own. He needs counseling and firm accountability.

Losing It All

He alone is my rock and my salvation, my stronghold;
I will not be shaken. (Ps. 62:6)

I retrieved the mail from the mailbox and brought it inside. The box had been stuffed full of late notices from our credit card companies and even our mortgage company. After my husband, Kevin, lost his job, our son was in a serious automobile accident that required an extended stay in the hospital. We wound up owing a staggering amount to the hospital and various doctors. So Kevin and I began the painful process of bankruptcy.

Lord, I silently prayed. *It's bad enough that we're in this situation, but the worry I'm feeling is suffocating. I should feel relieved that we're finally going to have breathing room again with our finances. But instead I'm just stressing out that we couldn't meet our obligations to our creditors.*

I closed my eyes and tried to listen to anything God might be telling me. With all my heart I knew He wanted me to trust Him and believe He would be walking us through this tough time. I pictured giving my worry to God, laying it at the foot of the cross. I felt God telling me to give it all to Him. Not just my worry and stress but any other fears and doubts I was having as well. He was telling me to have faith. I knew God wanted me to live in freedom, despite my circumstances.

Worrying has a way of taking our focus off of God. One of His deepest desires is for us to know that no matter what we might face in our lives He is there for us. He wants us to trust in Him. When we worry, we're focusing on what could go wrong, not on God and His ability to walk us through our situation.

A Gift of Friendship

Oil and incense bring joy to the heart, and the sweetness
of a friend is better than self-counsel. (Prov. 27:9)

I walked down the hall of the nursing home and poked my head into Gladys's room. "Are you ready for me to read to you today?"

"Of course I am, Kathy," Gladys said as she waved me into the room.

"You got your hair done," I said. "It looks beautiful." I leaned over her to give her a careful hug, pulled a chair closer to the bed, and sat down. Gladys's brown eyes crinkled as she smiled again. "You're a blessing to me, and I thank God every day for you and your visits."

I leaned over and clasped her hand. "Gladys, you've been such a godly mentor, and I'm so honored that we're friends." I saw how hard it was for her to be all alone. Gladys never had children to look after her as she aged, and she'd been in the nursing home for almost three years. I was the only one besides the nurses and other residents she saw on a regular basis.

"We finished reading *The Hiding Place* last week," I said. "Did you have any particular book you wanted to start this week?"

"No, sweetheart. Whatever you've brought with you will be fine with me. I just enjoy listening to you and getting lost in a book."

Has God been tugging at your heart to reach out and help someone? Maybe He has given you a desire to help the elderly or the poor. Whatever He is prompting you to do, you can be assured that not only will you benefit from being sensitive to the Holy Spirit, but the person you'll be ministering to will be blessed as well. Mark 12:31 says, "Love your neighbor as yourself." Making time in your schedule for someone who needs your companionship is pleasing to God.

Suit Up!

This is why you must take up the full armor of God,
so that you may be able to resist in the evil day. (Eph. 6:13)

I asked Jesus to be my Savior when I was nine years old. I knew that I was a sinner, that I loved Jesus, and that I wanted to live in heaven with Him.

I did not, however, realize what a formidable enemy we have. The night I asked Jesus to be my Savior, my foe Satan began his attack on my baby Christian heart. He shot the "flaming arrows" (Eph. 6:16) of doubt into my faith, and I didn't know how to fight or defend myself. That's when I discovered the armor of God in Ephesians 6:10–17.

Today my nine-year-old daughter has some of the same insecurities I had so I'm teaching her about the armor. When Satan whispers lies to her, we put on the belt of truth, remembering all she knows about Jesus, the Truth. When the enemy tries to worm his way into her heart with sin, the armor of righteousness is Jesus' righteousness protecting her heart. The sandals of the "gospel of peace" will protect her soul from fear and doubt, just as shoes protect her feet. The "shield of faith" covers her entire life because she trusts God and knows He loves her. The "helmet of salvation" insulates her mind from lies, helping her remember what she knows about Jesus. The Bible is the "sword of the Spirit," our only offensive weapon. By reading and knowing God's Word, she'll be able to discern good from bad. The glue that holds it all together is prayer.

This battle isn't against people but against "spiritual forces of evil" (Eph. 6:12). The enemy's goal is to wound, even silence, God's children. Don't let him. Suit up. Put on the armor of God every day. Besides, you'll look good in bronze!

A Changed Life

He gave Himself for us to redeem us from all lawlessness and to cleanse for Himself a people for His own possession. (Titus 2:14)

At fourteen Jason was busted for selling marijuana at school. He was a frequent user and was trying to earn money to buy other drugs. He was promptly expelled from school and faced punishment from the law as well as discipline from his parents.

Although he was lonely and angry, Jason realized there were consequences for his bad choices. He began to truly regret his decision to use and sell drugs. Yet he remained lonely and angry.

One day out of the blue, Kellen, the youth minister at the church Jason sometimes visited with his grandparents, called Jason at home. He asked if Jason wanted to meet him for a burger. Kellen knew what had happened at school and that Jason was going through a tough time.

Kellen and Jason began spending time together every week. At first Jason was slow to open up so they just talked football. Gradually they started talking about God, forgiveness, and new mercies. After a few months Jason's heart was changed. God took a hardened young man and worked His miracle of salvation.

We often categorize people who struggle with addiction as "those people," and we think we either can't relate or don't know how to help. The first step is to remember that we are all sinners saved by grace. Next we must reach out and be a consistent, dependable friend. We must pray for wisdom and guidance, and we must be ready to seek professional help for those who are struggling so they can be rehabilitated and set free. God can redeem anyone in any situation; even more, He can use their trials for their good and His glory.

Silencing Shame

As far as the east is from the west, so far has He removed our transgressions from us. (Ps. 103:12)

"You seemed quiet at small group tonight, Amber. Is something bothering you?" Lily asked.

"To be honest, I just feel like I'm coming from a different place than most of you," Amber admitted. "You guys grew up in church, and you've lived good lives. I can't say that about myself. I just became a Christian a few months ago, and I look back on my wild life with a lot of regret. I was really promiscuous, and I don't want everyone to know about my past."

"Amber, you don't need to feel that way. We've all struggled with sin, and none of us is perfect. We all need Jesus desperately. And none of us is better than anyone else."

"But what do I do with my past? I mean, I'm ashamed of the things I did. I know now how wrong they were," Amber said.

"You confess them to God, and you trust that He forgives you completely. He is not a God of guilt and shame; He is a God of freedom and forgiveness. Who knows? He might bring someone across your path who is going through the same thing, and you can share about how Jesus set you free from your sin," Lily encouraged.

"I never thought about that," Amber reflected. "Thanks for not judging me, and thanks for reminding me of the truth."

Sexual sin often results in shame, alienation, and regret. However, all sin is serious—all sin leads to death, and we are all dead in our sins without the salvation of Jesus. If you or someone you know is struggling with the guilt of sexual sin, be encouraged that Christ's love can break those chains and lead you to true freedom. God promises that His forgiveness is unconditional and unending.

Living in Peace

Let the peace of the Messiah, to which you were also called in one body, control your hearts. (Col. 3:15)

Lord, please change my attitude about this visit with Denise, Carolyn prayed. *Help me honor You in my actions and show Your love to Denise.*

Carolyn's sister-in-law was coming to visit with her two children, and she and Carolyn usually disagreed about almost everything. However, Carolyn knew Denise was driving a long way and putting forth the effort to visit her family. She knew how important it was for her own children to have good relationships with their cousins and aunt, as well as what a good opportunity this was to live out the gospel and testify to what Jesus meant to her.

Within the first hour of her arrival, Denise criticized the way Carolyn had decorated the living room. But instead of firing back, Carolyn let the comments slide and asked Denise for suggestions about decorating.

Later Denise scorned the snacks Carolyn gave the kids, saying she was feeding them too much sugar. "You're welcome to whatever is in our kitchen, Denise. Make yourself at home. If what we have here doesn't work for you, we can go to the grocery." Carolyn continued this attitude of humility throughout their visit, keeping peace by refusing to engage in petty arguments. It wasn't easy, but by the end of the visit, Carolyn and Denise had several meaningful conversations and had made some fun memories with their kids. Denise actually thanked Carolyn for her hospitality and told her it was their best visit ever.

Living at peace with others doesn't come naturally to us. But we can overlook offenses and strive for unity. If you have an especially tense relationship that often involves conflict, cover it in prayer and ask the Spirit to bring His peace between you.

Part of the Family

He predestined us to be adopted through Jesus Christ for Himself . . . to the praise of His glorious grace. (Eph. 1:5–6)

Marcie squealed as she hung up the phone. "Clint, that was the social worker. They're placing a foster baby with us—tonight!" Clint grinned and said, "We better get some things ready. Is it a boy or a girl? How old?"

"A baby boy, just a few weeks old. I already have the crib set up, so let's get out the bottles and pull out Will's baby clothes. First, let's tell Will and Jamie we'll have a baby in the house tonight!"

A few hours later the family returned home with a baby boy named Jacob. His biological parents had drug problems, and he needed a safe place to stay for a while—maybe for good. Marcie knew their family had an amazing opportunity to shower Jesus' love on this little one for however long he would stay.

"Mom, when will we know if Jacob can stay with our family?" Will asked.

"It may be a couple of years before we could adopt him," Marcie explained. "But we're called to love him and care for him right now, and no matter what the future holds, God can use our time in this little boy's life to draw him close. We'll just love him one day at a time and pray that the Spirit will work in and through us to minister to his needs, physical and spiritual."

Foster care is a special calling for those who are willing to step into the life of a child to make a difference, whether for the short or long-term. If you are not in a position to take on that responsibility yourself, pray about supporting a ministry or a family who is looking after the needs of these children.

Today's Special

I plopped a laundry basket on the floor and sat down to fold a load of towels. Turning the TV to a home shopping channel, the picture on the screen caught my attention. *Microfiber cleaning cloths*, I read. *They're only $19.95 plus shipping and handling. Maybe I'll get those.*

While folding a load of jeans, I saw a beautiful necklace that would match my new blue dress perfectly. Then as I dusted, the show host convinced me that I simply *must* have the latest and greatest kitchen chopper-dicer. But before I could get to the phone to order, the host introduced Today's Special—a five-piece skin care kit that promised to reduce the appearance of fine lines and wrinkles in only ten days—and the shipping and handling were free!

Although I had made valid and useful purchases from shopping channels in the past, something wasn't right here. As I reached for the phone, the Holy Spirit interrupted my potential spending spree long enough for me to realize just how easily I had been influenced by the media that day.

Everywhere we go we are bombarded with billboards, magazines, music, newspapers—all kinds of ways for advertisers to convince us that we need whatever they're trying to sell. Sometimes various media are not only marketing a product but also selling a mind-set and their own values and agenda. Certain networks and newspapers are known for being liberal or conservative.

Be aware of the bias in what you are hearing and seeing. Pray for wisdom and ask God to help you filter through the smoke screen so you can see the truth.

Called to Kindness

See to it that no one repays evil for evil to anyone, but always pursue what is good for one another and for all. (1 Thess. 5:15)

Karen was devastated when her husband, Mike, died of cancer. They were supposed to grow old together, to hold their grandchildren, to travel. How could she face a future alone?

As Karen brought her grief and despair to God, He began to give her a new purpose. Mike had planned well and taken care of his family. She was comfortable and secure, but she knew other widows who weren't so blessed. As she started taking her eyes off her circumstances and reaching out to those around her, her own heart began to heal.

Karen began looking for opportunities to extend kindness to others, especially women alone. She visited, took them to lunch or on outings, sent cards, and even gave anonymous gifts of money. Her quiet acts of kindness blessed many lives, and her thoughtfulness provided a model for those around her. Karen's legacy would be not one of crippling loss but of lives touched for Christ.

God's Word calls us to be kind to the needy (Prov. 14:31), to speak kind words (Prov. 12:25), and to be kind to one another (Eph. 4:32). Choosing to be kind can be as simple as giving a smile or hug, holding a door, or helping with a grocery bag. Or it can require a sacrifice of money, time, and skills. Opportunities abound for those who let God give them direction. Lifestyle habits of kindness can open doors for building relationships, sharing our faith, or becoming a person of influence. It can become an ongoing adventure that brings double blessing to the obedient believer as well as the recipient. What can you do today to speak God's kindness to someone in your life?

Heart Health

The pure in heart are blessed, for they will see God. (Matt. 5:8)

Marla was torn. It had only been a week since she met Chris through a mutual friend, but she could tell she was opening herself up to him emotionally and thinking about him a lot more than she needed to be. He was a thoughtful, sweet, godly guy, and Marla enjoyed spending hours just messaging and chatting online. She could practically picture the ring on her finger, and she had already written out her new last name.

She called her best friend, Jenna, for a heart-to-heart. "I don't want to give my heart away so quickly, Jenna, but I don't want to miss my chance either!"

"I know you want a serious relationship with a godly guy, Marla, but you really need to guard your heart. Sit back and pray about this. If he's the right guy, God will open the door to a real relationship that's more than instant messages and e-mails. God has an awesome plan for you, so try to trust Him to make it happen."

We often talk about protecting our physical purity by preserving sexual activity for marriage, but we also need to consider protecting our emotional purity. Women are relational by nature, and we are drawn to intimacy with others. However, when considering marriage, it's important not to rely on feelings alone.

Many people approach marriage with unrealistic expectations, thinking their prospective spouse will be the answer to all their problems and will meet their every need. But because no person can do that—nor are they meant to—the end result is often disappointment and hurt feelings all around. Set smart limits in all aspects of your dating relationships, and realize that God alone is the keeper of your heart.

Beautiful Words

*A word spoken at the right time is
like gold apples on a silver tray. (Prov. 25:11)*

My husband, Will, was laid off a few months ago. He's been looking for a job, but still no interviews, no callbacks, no bites.

Encouraging others doesn't come easily for me; it's not my spiritual gift. I'm conscious of sounding forced or phony. But as I prayed about ways to encourage my husband during this rough time, God reminded me that encouragement is from one heart to another heart. It gives courage, helping someone to hang in there. Encouragement can be beautiful words or actions that uplift, support, and affirm someone.

So I wrote a letter to Will listing all the ways I love him. I made sure to thank him for a job well done on the home-improvement projects he's undertaken. I pointed out all his wonderful God-given gifts that any employer would be grateful to have in an employee. I reminded him of God's good plans for his life. I told him our daughters are getting to spend time with him they've never had before. I even made banana pudding and brownies with walnuts (his favorites).

A wise godly friend told me that a married man wants the admiration and respect of his wife above almost anything else. I realized my words and actions have great power over whether Will feels capable and respected or discouraged and beaten down. So I used truthful words and Scripture to reassure him that he is not alone and that he is deeply loved—by me and God!

In Scripture, God calls us to be encouragers. Why? Because we all need to be encouraged. Whether it's a sickness or a layoff, whether we know the person, whether we're gifted in that way, words and acts of encouragement are like water to a thirsty soul.

Learning to Trust

*He does not withhold the good from
those who live with integrity. (Ps. 84:11)*

Rachel emptied the last of the laundry detergent into the washer. *I guess I won't be doing any more laundry until payday*, she thought. Living paycheck to paycheck had become a monthly ordeal—a constant battle of trust to believe that God would provide.

She walked out to the mailbox for a breath of fresh air, cringing as she pulled the day's offerings. Another medical bill? *Lord, I am so overwhelmed by our financial situation. Please help me keep things in perspective. Thank You that my husband has a job and that we have a roof over our heads. Please help me not to stress.*

As she sifted through the rest of the mail, she laughed out loud. A sample of laundry detergent was among the letters. *Lord, thanks for reminding me that You know what we need, and You care for us lovingly and personally. I feel like You just reached down and gave me a hug through a little sample of detergent. Thank You!*

Sometimes we go through difficulties so that we will learn to trust Him more, so that we will put our faith in Him instead of ourselves or our bank accounts. We think we need many things, but the truth is we only need one thing: a Savior. And God has already provided His Son as a sacrifice for our sins. He has taken care of our greatest spiritual need, so how much more will He take care of our material needs!

When life weighs you down, remember that He is Lord. When you have Him, you have a Protector and Provider who loves and cares for you.

That's Just Perfect

God is my strong refuge; He makes my way perfect. (2 Sam. 22:33)

Jenny unplugged the vacuum cleaner, wound up the cord, and put it away. She had been cleaning all day and was ready to start dinner.

Eight-year-old Jared and six-year-old Trent burst through the front door, tracking dirt onto the family room carpet. "Take off your shoes!" Jenny shouted. "I just cleaned in here. Now I'm going to have to do it all over again." Fuming, she dragged out the vacuum again and began shoving it vigorously back and forth across the carpet.

Later that evening after the boys were in bed, Jenny sheepishly told her husband, Todd, about her outburst earlier that day. "Will you pray that the Lord will help me control my temper?"

"Honey," Todd began, "I will, but I think the root of the problem may be perfectionism. I know you like to have things looking nice, and I do too, but the house doesn't have to look perfect all the time. We have two healthy, active boys, and things are going to get messed up sometimes. We just have to accept that and deal with it."

Jenny sighed. "I see your point."

"Just have some fun with the boys and learn to let things go once in a while," Todd said. "Our relationships are much more important than keeping a perfect house."

We're constantly being exposed to images of perfectly decorated homes that are always ready for a white-glove inspection. But most of us live in the real world with other people, pets, and problems. While it's good to do our best to clean and organize our homes, we should not let perfectionism take precedence over relationships.

Perfectionists are bound to be disappointed in others and in themselves. The only perfect One is Jesus. Trust Him to make your way perfect.

Not Helpless

*You Yourself made the heavens and earth by
Your great power and with Your outstretched arm.
Nothing is too difficult for You! (Jer. 32:17)*

I prayed along silently at church as my pastor was going over the church's prayer requests. The needs were so many, so staggering.

There's the couple who just filed for divorce; a man with a wife, three children, and a baby on the way who just lost his job; my precious mentor's husband who was just diagnosed with lymphoma; a teenager who needs a heart transplant. As I listened, I also thought of the problems our nation is facing: job loss, financial scandal, foreclosures, political corruption. I added my own family's needs to the list: needs for physical healing, for employment, for reconciliation.

The pastor began to preach, and guess what? It was about peace—Jesus' peace—not the kind the world gives (John 14:27) but peace in Him and through Him (John 16:33). Jesus tells us not to be fearful or anxious, no matter how hopeless it seems.

Silently I thanked the Lord that I could offer up these hurting souls with huge needs to Him. My shoulders are not big enough to carry these situations, but the compassion He has placed in my heart can be lived out. I will do what I can to come alongside my brothers and sisters, helping in practical ways, and I will lay each need at the throne of the King who can mend bodies, hearts, and lives.

It's so easy to feel overwhelmed with all the needs around us every day. But our God is never overwhelmed, never helpless, never defeated. He is mighty to save, and that means not just our spiritual salvation, but marriages, financial catastrophes, health issues. Remember, you can cast all your cares upon Him because He loves you (1 Pet. 5:7).

Light in the Dark

The Son of Man has come to seek and to save the lost. (Luke 19:10)

"We're over here," Amy called to my husband through her car window when he arrived to pick me up from work.

Amy and I took breaks, ate lunch, and left work at the same time. Hanging out with Amy meant dealing with the smoke, a colorful vocabulary, and stories from her tumultuous life. I was one of the only women at work who didn't smoke, go to bars, or talk like Amy.

"How can you stand it?" my husband asked as we drove home.

"I like Amy. I think she needs a Christian friend." I didn't like the fact that she smoked and used foul language, but how could I expect clean-cut behavior from someone with her background? God had helped me see Amy as a woman who desperately needed Him. I'd decided early on that instead of feeling contaminated by all I had to put up with in my secular workplace, I would seek opportunities to encourage my coworkers, pray for them, and share what God had done in my life. When Amy started asking questions about God, I saw what He could do when I chose to be a friend instead of grumbling about their worldly lifestyles.

Working outside the home typically means working alongside nonbelievers. The language, offensive jokes, and destructive life choices can be hard to deal with. At the same time we have daily opportunities to reflect the light of Christ.

When questioned about His choice of company (namely tax collectors and women with questionable backgrounds), Jesus reminded His critics that He came for those who needed Him most—sinners. He loved them yet spoke the truth, and in the process many were changed. He can be our example of how to shine in a dark world.

Good Intentions

*If you live according to the flesh, you are going to die.
But if by the Spirit you put to death
the deeds of the body, you will live. (Rom. 8:13)*

"I have a confession," said Emily, picking up her menu. "The reason I asked you to such a late lunch is to keep me away from the television at one o'clock. That's when the soap opera comes on that I'm trying to quit watching."

Julie admitted, "I can relate."

Emily asked, "You're addicted to soaps too?"

"No," Julie laughed, "but I've struggled with similar temptations. When I became a Christian, the Holy Spirit began to show me some of the sins in my life. I wanted to clean up my act, but it was hard."

"How did you do it?" asked Emily.

"A wise mentor told me the Bible promises God will do the cleaning up. I just need to cooperate. So I make sure I spend quiet time in prayer and reading my Bible every day. As I find Scriptures that give me strength and hope, I write them on index cards. Occasionally, I've told some trusted friends about my struggles and asked them to pray for me."

Emily asked, "Will you pray for me to lose my fascination with this show?"

"I'll even show you some verses to stick on your TV!" said Julie.

The Bible says in 1 Thessalonians 5:23 that God will sanctify us. He alone can truly change lives from the inside out so the change is permanent and true. Without His help, our attempts to loosen the grips of habitual sins are just exhausting walks down a road paved with nothing more than good intentions. And we all know how far good intentions take us.

If God has pointed out a destructive habit or attitude in your life, commit to turning completely away from it. Do your part and trust God to do His.

Globally Minded

*Whatever you did for one of the least of these brothers of Mine,
you did for Me. (Matt. 25:40)*

When Mandy became a Christian, she thought that being saved was all there was to it. But as she plugged into a church and began to grow through hearing the Word, being discipled by godly women, and getting involved in a Bible study, she realized there was more to the Christian walk than just being saved. She began asking God to give her compassion for the needy.

Mandy saw that many Christians had a heart for various types of mission work around the globe. Several of her friends were involved with child sponsorship through Christian organizations, and some donated to mission work through their local church.

Mandy asked God to show her how He wanted her to help. One evening while researching charitable Christian organizations online, she prayed, *Father, the needs are so great, and I'm only one person. Please show me how I can serve You by serving others. Give me wisdom.*

Mandy saw opportunities to help children who needed surgery, feed the hungry, educate girls in China, and many others. When she began reading about women and children who had been sold into prostitution, it broke her heart. She decided that she would contribute to an organization that helps to rescue and rehabilitate women and children who have been exploited.

When we look at all the people in need around the world, it's positively staggering. People drink contaminated water, die from hunger, suffer in brutal wars, live in unspeakable poverty, are victims of human trafficking—the list is practically endless. But we serve a big God, and He doesn't ask us to solve all the world's problems. He just asks us to do our part. So if you feel that God wants you to become more globally minded, pray for discernment. And watch God work.

Preparing for Flight

*I know the plans I have for you . . . plans for your welfare,
not for disaster, to give you a future and a hope. (Jer. 29:11)*

As my son, Jake, approaches high school graduation, many have asked if he will follow the career paths of his father and grandfather. I know Jake could be a great doctor, but he needs to chart his own course. More precisely, he needs to follow God's plan for his life.

When Jake approached me a few nights ago—concerned about college, his major, and a future career—I tried to reassure him and help him sort through everything. I let him bounce ideas off me, even some that sounded far-fetched. I'll admit I had to hold my tongue a few times, but in the end I know Jake must make his own decisions. I'm excited to see where God takes my son in life and to see what kind of man he becomes on the journey.

Parents should provide their children a safe and nurturing nest and then give them strong and able wings to leave that nest. As the time approaches for your children to leave home, you can prepare them for the uncertainties ahead by helping them understand that God loves them and has a purpose for their lives.

While most teens are not interested in lectures about God's sovereignty and perfect will, they will allow you to encourage them with Scripture and prayer if you do one crucial thing first: listen to them. You may be tempted to point out how outlandish your child's dreams are, but choose instead to listen with interest and an open mind. Then challenge your teen to seek God, His will, and His provisions. Assure him that God is interested in their dreams, passions, and plans. Finally, express confidence that God has great things in store for your child.

Surprised by Servanthood

Whoever wants to become great among
you must be your servant. (Matt. 20:26)

Liz and Judy were stunned when, after prayer and a brief intro, the conference speaker walked to the platform. Surprised, Judy turned to her friend: "Liz, I never for one minute suspected that the lady we were talking with in the dining hall was our guest speaker. She seemed so concerned about everyone else, and she certainly didn't promote herself in any way."

Liz said, "I didn't have any idea either. She was so busy doing the menial stuff like moving chairs, setting up tables, and opening boxes, I just assumed she was a conference assistant. But I was impressed with her friendliness and gentle spirit."

Judy commented, "Well, I'm certainly going to listen closely to her presentation. Her humility and servant's heart have impacted me already."

We live in a culture that nurtures the celebrity syndrome. Even in Christian circles people are often placed on pedestals whether they want to be or not.

When Jesus' disciples aspired to greatness or a prominent place in His kingdom, He assured them that whoever wanted to become great must become a servant. Then He reminded them that He came not to be served but to serve (Matt. 20:26–28).

Many times our flesh resists the humility of servanthood. But through the self-denial of quiet service, we grow in Christ and find favor with God. Jesus reminds us in John 12:26, "If anyone serves Me, the Father will honor him."

If you find yourself resisting the work of a servant, ask God to give you joy so that the "slave whose master finds him working . . . will be rewarded" (Luke 12:43).

Forgive

Forgive, and you will be forgiven. (Luke 6:37)

My sister Heather was barely eighteen when she married Brad, a young man she thought was her Prince Charming. But not long after their wedding, he began cheating on her.

When one of Heather's friends spotted Brad getting cozy with another woman in a corner booth at a restaurant, she reluctantly decided to tell Heather. Brad seemed repentant and promised her it would never happen again, so she gave him another chance.

Over the next several years, Heather and Brad had two daughters. He also had several girlfriends during that time, including one who was pregnant with his child. "I just can't take it anymore," Heather cried to me one evening. "Some people say I should stay with Brad for the sake of the girls, but what kind of a message does that send them about staying with a man who refuses to be faithful? How can I teach them to value themselves if I don't respect myself enough to care how he treats me?"

Since Brad refused to go to counseling with Heather, she had to face the fact that her marriage was over. She began seeing a Christian counselor who helped her deal with her anger, rejection, and insecurity. It's been a long ordeal for her, but as she forgives, she also heals.

Whether we feel a person deserves our forgiveness, it is in our best interest to forgive them. Harboring bitterness and unforgiveness puts a barrier between God and us.

Peter probably thought he was being generous when he asked Jesus if he should forgive someone who had wronged him seven times (Matt. 18:21). But the Lord gave Peter a surprising answer: "70 times seven" (v. 22). In other words, keep forgiving. But be aware that forgiving the offender doesn't mean you must reconcile. Behavior that is abusive and unacceptable should not be tolerated.

Never Too Late

The ants are not a strong people,
yet they store up their food in the summer. (Prov. 30:25)

I can't remember a time when my husband and I were not living from paycheck to paycheck. Hoping to get ahead, we moved to an area with a lower cost of living. But instead of getting on top of things, we faced years of job losses, health problems, and broken promises of career advancement.

After our second son was born, I managed to set some money aside to open an IRA so I could start saving a portion of my freelancing income. Although I opened it with a small amount and haven't been able to contribute much over the past few years, I keep the account open and leave the money alone. Not that I haven't asked myself, *Why bother? What difference will it make?* But I know that a little savings, even an account opened years ago, is better than no savings at all. It's never too late to start.

I've listened to stories from people who began saving early in life only to lose large chunks to an unstable economy, forcing them to start over. But I've learned to trust that God blesses our efforts to save, no matter what age we are when we begin or begin again. My quarterly statements remind me that I may not reach retirement with enough to travel the world, but I will have something.

According to Proverbs the ant, one of the tiniest creatures on the planet, stores for the future. Warnings of when it's "too late" to start stocking up don't seem to come into play. Scripture also provides evidence that God can multiply the efforts and provide beyond expectations for those who obey. The key is to do our part by being responsible, obedient stewards of all God entrusts us with.

The Most Toys

That's how it is with the one who stores up treasure for himself and is not rich toward God. (Luke 12:21)

Michelle ignored the guilt twisting away at her stomach and added the pink jacket to her online cart. Her daughter Justine didn't need it, but at 30 percent off she couldn't pass it up.

"Honey," Jim called to her as he entered the computer room, clutching the checkbook. "Why all these debit purchases in one day?"

"Lindsay and I went to the outlet mall on our way home from the women's retreat. I got some great deals."

"Your great deals added up to almost five hundred bucks."

"Most of it was for the kids—school clothes, winter items. If you knew what I would have paid in a regular store . . ."

Jim sank into a chair. "I don't care, honey. We have enough stuff in this house to clothe a small village. Have you seen our credit card statement?"

"What do you mean? Last month I only . . ." Before she could finish, Jim held out the statement. Had she really spent that much?

With no words to justify her spending, she moved the computer mouse to her shopping cart and emptied it.

A popular 1980s bumper sticker claimed, "Whoever has the most toys wins." Those who bought into it would probably say they won debt, strained relationships, and daily stress to their lives. Jesus told a parable about a rich landowner who accumulated more grain than he knew what to do with, only to die and leave his wealth behind. What do we gain by buying more than our closets can hold? Then again, how much more do we benefit from hungering after the true riches of God?

Never a Zero Balance

Don't worry about tomorrow, because tomorrow will worry about itself. Each day has enough trouble of its own. (Matt. 6:34)

"We did it!" I waved the envelope containing my husband's cardiologist's bill in the air. "We have officially paid off your heart attack. It took five years but we did it. We need to celebrate."

Less than a week later Norm went to the hospital with chest pain; scar tissue blocked the stent he'd received after his heart attack. Two more ER trips followed, both involving chest pain, meaning overnight stays and expensive tests. A large bill arrived as a sobering reminder that we may never see an end to heart-related expenses. While I thanked God for payment plans, I couldn't help feeling let down and discouraged.

Soon afterward a friend updated me on her serious health issues. As she described her experimental treatments and battles between her doctors and the insurance company, I waited for her to mention the mounting financial burden. Surely hers far surpassed ours. She not only had a chronic illness, but she also suffered ongoing complications that stemmed from it. This didn't even count the times when her husband needed surgery and her kids got sick. Yet money woes never came up. She clearly had faith that, if God allowed her to struggle with health problems, He would provide.

I want to be like her, I prayed. *Help me to trust You with our medical bills even if we never see a zero balance again.*

Even Jesus lived without financial security so He could speak from experience when He said, "Don't worry about tomorrow." God always provided for men and women in Scripture, whether they were ill, widowed, or serving Him full-time. His constant provision continues to teach me to trust His ability to cover the cost of any illness, emergency, or ongoing health crisis.

Root of the Problem

Make sure that no one falls short of the grace of God and that no root of bitterness springs up. (Heb. 12:15)

Everyone else seemed completely engaged in the pastor's words, but Ella couldn't even focus on the message. Ever since Pastor Randy had neglected to visit her daughter in the hospital during her tonsillectomy, Ella had struggled with her attitude toward him. But while she continued to feel justified in her anger, she also longed to hear a word from God again.

Unable to concentrate, Ella thumbed through her Bible and landed on a familiar story. She began to read about Joseph in the book of Genesis. She remembered that Joseph had forgiven his brothers much greater offenses. Reading through chapter 45, she understood that Joseph had kept from growing bitter by looking at his circumstances from God's perspective.

During the closing prayer Ella asked God to forgive her for harboring anger toward her pastor. She recalled the many times he had been faithful and the personal sacrifices he made to serve his flock. As she walked by him after the service, Ella extended her hand, smiled, and said with sincerity, "I'm looking forward to next week's sermon."

We all get our feelings hurt, and sometimes we become angry. But the Bible tells us in Ephesians 4:26–27 to deal with our anger quickly so it doesn't fester and become a tool of Satan. He can use our bitterness to sever relationships, put distance between us and God, damage our testimony, drown out the voice of the Holy Spirit, and steal our joy.

When someone or something hurts or angers you, resist the temptation to nurse that wound. Instead, ask God to help you see things from His vantage point and bring healing to your broken heart. Keep your heart soft and offer genuine forgiveness.

Exhausted

*Get up and eat, or the journey will
be too much for you. (1 Kings 19:7)*

"I don't know what's wrong with me," said Jan as she gently bounced her ten-month-old son on her hip and spoke to her sister on the phone. "I'm just exhausted."

Mandy giggled and said, "You're supposed to be exhausted! You have three preschoolers." But as she listened to her sister's attempt to soothe her crying son and settle his two squealing siblings, she remembered what those days were like and rethought her response.

"Are you getting enough sleep?" Mandy asked gently.

"No," Jan replied. "Like you said, I'm supposed to be exhausted."

"I'm sorry for teasing you," Mandy apologized. "I know when my two were little, I lived for nap time. Do you rest when they rest?"

"I feel guilty if I lie down in the middle of the day. There's so much to be done before Jack gets home."

Mandy understood her sister's dilemma, but she also knew that physical and emotional exhaustion makes us vulnerable to Satan's attacks. "Listen, you're no good to anyone if you're exhausted. Take a nap today, OK? Your family will benefit from having a well-rested wife and mom."

Jesus knows what it is to grow weary. He spent His days traveling by foot, teaching His hungry disciples, confronting skeptics, and meeting the needs of hurting people. He also knows the importance of rest. Not only did God establish a day of rest for His people (Exod. 20:9–11), but Jesus also took time to rest from the activity of His day as He needed it (John 4:6).

Depending on the demands of your day, you may have difficulty getting the sleep your body requires. Ask God how you can change your schedule to get the amount of sleep you need, and commit to making rest a priority.

Known by Heart

I am fully known. (1 Cor. 13:12)

As my daughter, Katie, got in the car after school, she was crying. "Mama, Ashley called me 'weird' today, and Madison said my hair is too frizzy," she sobbed.

I was instantly transported back to my own painful middle-school days when I never fit in, wasn't pretty enough, didn't say and do the "right" things. *Lord, how can I teach her to navigate these turbulent, confidence-killing waters?*

"Katie, you have to understand what you mean to Jesus. You have to find your worth in Him," I said.

"But what does that mean?" she asked.

"That means what Jesus says about you is true. The Bible says that you are loved with an eternal love, bought with a high price, and you're valuable. He knows what you're all about because you belong to Him and He has handcrafted you for something special. Satan and the world will always try to tell you that you're not enough."

"But they all think I'm a nerd because I'm good at math and I play the clarinet."

"Sweetie, do you remember when I told you that the president of my high school class called recently to invite me to our class reunion? She was one of the most popular girls in the school. But after she called, I realized I couldn't remember anything about her. The point is, many of these people you go to school with are only in your life for a short time. Don't put too much importance on what they say about you. Instead, remember that you are worth much to God."

God knows all about us: our strengths, weaknesses, talents, doubts, insecurities, capabilities, sins. And yet knowing all that, He died for us and has an important, eternal plan for our lives. We are loved and known by heart, by the Great Heart.

Take Courage

*The fear of man is a snare, but the one
who trusts in the LORD is protected. (Prov. 29:25)*

Several years out of college, I felt called to join an organization that helped children in the metro area, and I moved into a low-income apartment complex. It didn't take long, however, for my fears to begin to cause me to doubt God's calling. I was fearful about raising enough money to live on. I was also fearful about my safety in a crime-ridden neighborhood where alcoholism, drugs, prostitution, and violence were prevalent. I began having panic attacks and didn't last more than a year there.

Though many might empathize with my fear in that situation, I've found that I continue to struggle with anxiety even as a stay-at-home mom in an upscale neighborhood. Many of my current worries center around fearing man, placing too much importance on what others think of me.

Lately, however, I have determined to put off fear and put on faith, getting serious and intentional in praying about my fear and learning what God says about it. Here's what I'm learning:

The Bible addresses fear more than 260 times, and God encourages His people not to fear. He warns us to remember what He has done for us so we'll be faithful. Fear is often at the root of sin. We choose what is not pleasing to God, particularly when we're afraid of what others might think of us. Many people get into debt trying to keep up with others' lifestyles.

Envision how different your life might be if you made all of your decisions free from worry, if you didn't care what others thought, and if you didn't play the "what-if" game. If you want victory over fear, begin memorizing, meditating on, and speaking aloud Scriptures about faith as you take every fearful thought captive and let God transform you.

A Bigger Boss

He stores up success for the upright; He is a shield for those who live with integrity. (Prov. 2:7)

Every time Paula opened her home office drawer and caught sight of the small gadget, her conscience was pricked. It had been several years since she had "borrowed" the item from work. It seemed so insignificant among her employer's office supplies. She knew others who helped themselves to much bigger items. Still, Paula was pursuing a deeper relationship with God. She was learning to listen for His voice and obey in big and small things.

Finally, one day as she spotted the gadget and sensed the nudge, she responded. "Lord, I know it was wrong for me to bring this home, and it's wrong to keep it. Peace with You is more important than saving myself the embarrassment of admitting I took something that didn't belong to me."

As Paula sat quietly before the Lord, she sensed Him prompting her to act. She placed the item in an envelope and included a note of confession and apology. She also explained that her faith called for her to live a life of integrity and honesty. Writing the name of her boss on the envelope, she put the package with her computer bag.

The workplace provides potential temptation for many subtle sins such as fudging on time cards and mileage forms, taking extended coffee and lunch breaks, missing work for questionable sick leave, "borrowing" office supplies, and goofing off on company time, as well as participating in office gossip.

Psalm 51:6 says, "Surely You desire integrity in the inner self." Jesus taught that we are called to be salt and light to the watching world, that "everyone who names the name of the Lord must turn away from unrighteousness" (2 Tim. 2:19)—of any kind. The workplace offers unique forms of stress and temptation, but we are called to live out our faith in a winsome way.

Unscheduled Appointment

We who are strong have an obligation to bear the weaknesses of those without strength, and not to please ourselves. (Rom. 15:1)

It was one of those encounters God clearly initiated. The day was cold and windy as Cathy and her friend set up their book and photo booth at the festival. When one of the displays toppled over, the young woman beside them reached over to help. As she picked up one of Cathy's books, she introduced herself. Her name was Tonya. She was a young mom with two children.

Through casual conversations during the day, Cathy discovered that Tonya was a new Christian who was struggling in her marriage. Tonya confided, "We've separated, but we're trying to work it out."

Cathy encouraged Tonya. "It's important to pursue your relationship with God, stay connected to a church family, and seek Christian counseling. Remember your husband is just a man, and he will fail you. God will not."

After the festival Cathy and Tonya stayed in touch. She also arranged for Tonya and her husband to attend a marriage retreat where they received a fresh vision for their marriage.

Statistics indicate that the state of marriage in the church is not much different from the state of marriage in the world. Young couples need to see good marriages up close. They also need mentors who are transparent about their own struggles in marriage. They need to see husbands and wives holding on to faith through the tough places, learning to extend grace and rejecting unrealistic expectations. If couples in the church can safely share their struggles and receive encouragement as they are held accountable, they will be more likely to persevere.

Would God have you mentor someone within your sphere of influence? Or do you need to seek a mentor?

The Classroom

Teach a youth about the way he should go;
even when he is old he will not depart from it. (Prov. 22:6)

When Jack was in kindergarten, he came home with a flyer announcing Winter Fest in December. Christmas was not mentioned. Over coffee I asked advice from two friends with older kids.

Cindy said, "After Tommy was born, I heard a Christian educator speaking on worldview. A child's worldview is shaped as early as six years of age. We have to be diligent to teach them about God."

"I'm not even sure what *worldview* means," I said.

"Worldview is what you believe about certain things, like God, Jesus, life after death," Valerie said. Cindy nodded. "We need to know how a Christian worldview differs from other beliefs." Valerie added, "You've already given Jack a good foundation, Joan. You talk to him about the Lord; you tell him Bible stories."

"Yes, but how can I know what he's being taught in school?"

"Volunteer in the classroom," Cindy said. "Stay in touch with his teacher. Look through notebooks and textbooks he brings home to see what he's studying." Valerie added, "See if it's undermining your values or trying to prove that God doesn't exist."

One of our most important jobs as parents is being involved in our children's education. We need to know what they're being taught in school. We also need to be supportive of our kids and an advocate for them when trouble comes along, remembering to honor Christ in our dealings with our children's school. Even more critical is teaching our children at home about the Lord, equipping them with knowledge of the faith, giving them the tools they need when confronted with other beliefs. Where our kids are involved, we never stop studying!

Torn

*The God of all grace . . . will personally restore, establish,
strengthen, and support you. (1 Pet. 5:10)*

"Being a working mom is harder than I ever thought it
would be," I told my sister. I was driving home from work, stuck
in traffic, wondering what to fix for dinner. "I miss the girls, I
miss my clean house, I miss being able to help at church," I said,
sniffling into the phone.

My husband lost his job recently, and God gave me the perfect job, tailor-made for me. I hadn't worked outside the home
for ten years, except for freelancing. So for now the entire financial responsibility for our family is squarely on my shoulders.
And for now my husband's full-time job is finding a job.

At first I was elated to be working. I felt so loved by the
Lord because He provided exactly what we needed at the precise
moment we needed it. But oh, how I miss the way things were!
I miss waking my daughters up in the morning and fixing them
breakfast. My husband helps out at home, but he doesn't notice
things that I notice. There's always laundry that needs attention.
We're always out of milk and bread. And lately, my time with
God has been hurried or nonexistent.

I feel so torn. On the one hand, I'm so grateful to the Lord
for the work He's given. On the other, I feel like I'm falling
behind in the nonwork parts of my life. But I know God put
me where I am for such a time as this. I will trust Him to make
my rough places smooth, my crooked places straight, as we work
together on my schedule and my to-do list.

If you are a working mom and the main breadwinner, the
stress can sometimes be unbearable. But take heart, sweet sister!
There is One who knows your struggles, joys, and fears, who is
ready to step in with love, comfort, and encouragement.

All about Countertops

*I have learned to be content in
whatever circumstances I am. (Phil. 4:11)*

I want new countertops. Actually, I've wanted them for
some time. It seems like everyone I know has these beautiful
new countertops in their beautiful new kitchens. Mine are the
same old, original-to-the-house laminate countertops.

I've tried to be patient, but some days I feel like a grown-
up two-year-old, alternately pitching a fit and whining at God
about a hunk of stone to sit on top of my cabinets. Oh, of course,
I don't voice those things out loud. But I want it! And I want it
now!

My husband and I have always tried to be good stewards of
what God has given us. We've tithed. We've paid off our house.
We've saved. But one bad career decision and a series of unfortu-
nate circumstances, and now we just get by.

Those countertops have become a symbol for all the things
I feel I cannot have in life, now or ever. But I don't think God
appreciates my tantrums about it. He reminds me about all the
good things He's done in my life. Salvation. A job. A home. A
husband who loves me. Children who love me.

So maybe that hunk of stone isn't so important. Maybe
the Lord wants me to revel in the goodness I already have since
it's all from Him anyway. Maybe He's after growth in patience
or rearrangement of priorities or contentment in my heart or
refinement of my character.

Whatever He's after, I want to honor and glorify Him. I'm
going to wait on Him and His answer, peacefully, contentedly,
quieting my inner two-year-old.

So what do *you* want?

Balancing Generations

I will proclaim Your faithfulness to
all generations with my mouth. (Ps. 89:1)

Susanna looked at her watch as she heard her daughter's car pull in the driveway.

"Hi, Mom. Are the kids doing OK?" Jill asked as she pushed open the door.

"They're in the kitchen having a snack." Susanna smiled. "We had fun today."

Jill took a deep breath and raised her eyebrows hopefully. "Would you mind watching them a couple more hours then? I need to shop for the party next week."

Susanna glanced at her watch. "I need to visit Grandma this afternoon. It's getting late. She looks forward to my coming, and I don't want to disappoint her."

"Oh, Mom, you can see her tomorrow."

But Susanna knew her presence was the highlight of her mother's day. She'd missed yesterday too.

"Honey, I love being with the kids, and I want to help, but Grandma needs me. Tomorrow I can watch the children while you shop. Then maybe you could stop and see Grandma afterwards too."

Sandwiched between younger and older generations, it's difficult to find balance. While we recognize the importance of pouring our lives into a future generation to shape their minds and hearts, we sometimes fail to appreciate how older parents thrive on attention from their family. Our busyness shouldn't crowd out those who once poured themselves into our own lives.

Some people, on the other hand, feel overly obligated to their parents. The playfulness of young children seems frivolous by comparison. Consequently, they neglect to do Jesus' bidding to "let the little children come" (Mark 10:14). Pray for balance in showing faithfulness to each generation, and don't forget to nurture your husband and yourself as well.

Tempting Texts

Whatever is true, whatever is honorable . . . whatever is pure, whatever is lovely . . . dwell on these things. (Phil. 4:8)

"Anything interesting happen at school today, hon?" Gail asked sixteen-year-old Ellie.

"We had an assembly during sixth period. It was about sexting and stuff."

"Sexting?" Gail asked.

"It's when you send sexy pictures or text messages on your cell. The main point of the talk was that you can go to jail if you do it because it's considered pornography," Ellie explained.

Gail asked, "Do you understand why sexting is wrong—not just legally?"

"Well, I know God made me and He made sex, and I don't want to share either with just anyone, much less everyone," Ellie said.

"Your dad and I have taught you God's way because He knows what's best for us. If you ever doubt that, will you please talk to me about it?"

Sexual sin is nothing new, but today's advanced communication and graphic technology allow sexual messages to spread quickly and with a degree of separation that tricks people into feeling safe from consequences. As you help your own teen or those in your church or community navigate the challenges of adolescence, emphasize the value of sex as God designed it. Keep the conversation about sex ongoing and open. Explain the benefits of sexual purity and the dangers of promiscuity of any kind. Help them see the long-term effects of not just creating images and texts that don't go away but of giving part of their hearts away permanently. Finally, set boundaries on media time and be involved in their media world. Sit down together regularly to go over their online presence and history. You are your child's God-ordained guide and protector, and you have the privilege of pointing their hearts toward Him in all things.

272

Small Things

Never let loyalty and faithfulness leave you. Tie them around your neck; write them on the tablet of your heart. (Prov. 3:3)

The chocolate cake melted in my mouth. "Want some?" I asked Janet, who shook her head. I grinned. "I blame my sweet tooth on my dad."

She laughed. "I blame my thighs on my mother."

"So do I! I mean—on *my* mother, not yours."

We both laughed, and I said, "Maybe I should cut down on sweets. You're never tempted by dessert. Look how strong you're being right now!"

She shrugged. "For me, resisting sweets is easy. Spending money is my weakness. Lately I've been buying stuff on impulse—little things like funky nail polishes, froufrou shower gels, expensive coffees. I always rationalize it, but I don't actually need any of these things, and the Lord has been speaking to me about it."

"Really?" I asked, slowing down to listen.

She nodded. "It's a waste of money and it adds up. I want to start being more obedient, more faithful with the small things."

Her words echoed in my mind long after dinner. Faithful with small things? Like cake, cookies, and candy?

In the parable of the talents (Matt. 25:14–30), the servants who were faithful with little pleased their master very much. He then put them in charge of more. When we decide we want to please the Lord and be effective servants for Him, we often start out taking small steps. As we show faithfulness, we are given more responsibility, some other work that lines up with the gifts He gave us. Then we begin to look forward to hearing those longed-for words: "Well done" (Matt. 25:21).

Balancing Act

Delight yourself in the LORD, and I will make you ride over the heights of the land, and let you enjoy the heritage of your father Jacob. (Isa. 58:14)

"I wish I could work from home like you do," Lucy said.

"I'm really blessed, but it's not always easy getting things done," I replied. "Jack works at home too, so if I want to get anything done, he has to watch the baby and vice versa. It can really be a balancing act. Sometimes I feel like I work all day because of the way I have to work—an hour or so at a time."

"Hmm," Lucy said, "I hadn't thought about that."

"But on the positive side, we don't have to pay for gas getting to and from work or day care."

"That is such a blessing," Lucy replied. "My commute has become so expensive."

"I really wanted to be a stay-at-home mom after Isabel was born," I said, "but we were having trouble paying all the bills. God answered my prayer by providing a job I can do from home. It can get crazy sometimes, but I know I'm fortunate."

Lucy nodded. "I can relate to that too. Raising a family and working is certainly a challenge. I'm so glad you found a way to make it work for your family."

Learning how to balance your time between your family and your job is a learning experience. Seek the Lord's guidance on how He wants you to schedule your days and how to make everything happen. He knows what is most important, and He's aware of everything on your plate. As Paul stated in Romans 8:28, "We know that all things work together for the good of those who love God: those who are called according to His purpose."

Easing the Pain

You satisfy me as with rich food; my mouth will praise
You with joyful lips. (Ps. 63:5)

It was a brisk fall morning when Bob decided to place the divorce papers in my briefcase. He didn't even have the decency to give me any warning.

That night when I got home from work, I confronted him. "Bob, let's at least go to a counselor or our pastor to see if we can work things out."

"There's really no point." Bob stated with no emotion. "I fell out of love with you a long time ago."

His words were like a slap in the face. They stung my heart and I felt betrayed and abandoned. *How could he do this to me?* We'd been together almost twenty-one years.

When he left, I started eating to soothe myself. I knew better, but at the time I really didn't think about the consequences. I just wanted to dull the pain of his rejection. But in the following months, food became my only source of happiness, and I began to eat whenever I needed a pick-me-up.

After several months of moping around, I felt God telling me to stop turning to food and start turning back to Him. At the same time I felt the Holy Spirit telling me that even if Bob didn't love me anymore, God always would. Now was the time to turn my hurt over to Him and rely on Him as my true source of joy and comfort.

If you think you may be an emotional eater, or if you turn to some other distraction when you're stressed or upset, it's time for a change. God's deepest desire is to be our number-one love, and He is always there to help us through the hard times. "For since He Himself was tested and has suffered, He is able to help those who are tested" (Heb. 2:18).

Truth for Teens

Whether you eat or drink, or whatever you do,
do everything for God's glory. (1 Cor. 10:31)

Every week I meet with a freshman in high school named Julia. We talk about life, and I encourage her to pursue a relationship with the Lord.

Recently several teenagers from our community were in a tragic car accident. All three high school students in the car had been drinking, took a turn too fast, and their car flipped and hit a tree. A seventeen-year-old named Kevin died in the crash.

After Kevin's death Julia surprised me with her reaction. "I didn't even know Kevin that well, but I can't stop thinking about what happened. It made me realize that we don't know when the end will be. This accident made me see that living weekend to weekend, party to party, is not really living at all. It's made me ask what I'm living for."

The reality of Kevin's death has been difficult for our small town. But God is using the circumstances to open people's eyes to the reality of life, death, and eternity.

Many times we take the attitude that kids need to get that wild streak out of their system, which often takes the form of underage drinking. But this behavior is illegal, dangerous, and habit-forming, and it is our responsibility as the church to equip students to make godly choices for their own spiritual and physical benefit.

One of the best ways we can teach students about godly choices is by living out those choices in relationships with them. If you demonstrate your love through action, they will see God's love in you and understand His dependability as well. If you don't have a teenager at home, reach out to a teen in your church or neighborhood. In this way you will be pointing the younger generation toward the life-saving love of the Savior.

Better Off Blessed

Commit your activities to the LORD,
and your plans will be achieved. (Prov. 16:3)

"But we told the kids we would spend fall break in Florida," Grace lamented. Since transferring the children to the Christian school at their church, Grace had looked forward to the extra break they took in October. She'd heard endless stories from other moms about short lines at tourist spots and off-season hotel prices.

"That was before my company cut out our bonuses," Troy reminded her.

Grace tried to stuff her deep disappointment. These days it seemed like tight finances were butting into every area of life.

Two weeks later, as Grace watched her son and daughter playing behind the mountain cabin that a couple from church allowed them to use free of charge, gratitude filled her. Sure the kids had been upset about the change of plans, but it dissolved as soon as they saw the fishing boat and the tree house. They enjoyed nature walks and other forms of simple fun that no theme park could have touched. *Thank You, Lord, for preventing us from taking that expensive trip. We would have missed this!*

In our uncertain economy cutting corners has become commonplace. Sometimes it's fun to compare the deals we get on kids' clothes, household items, and groceries. But what about those days when the numbers in the checking account scream for a major change of plans?

Proverbs 16:9 reminds us that while we make plans, the Lord determines our steps. We can apply this to finances too, trusting that God has His own plans. Often they are far better than any that we could devise. But even if He doesn't replace a theme park with a peaceful mountain cabin, we know in our hearts that He gives us what we need and holds back what we don't.

Girls with Class

The holy women who put their hope in God also beautified themselves in this way. (1 Pet. 3:5)

My eight-year-old daughter, Anna, went to a birthday party for a friend from school. When I picked her up from the party, she exclaimed, "I like Britney Spirits! She's so fashiony!"

My mommy antennae immediately went up because Anna had never even heard of Britney Spears. "Why is she 'fashiony,' baby?" I asked.

"Well, my friends said her clothes are cool," Anna replied.

"Anna, the way you dress sends a message," I said. That exchange began a new application of Deuteronomy 6 to the raising of Anna, especially where God tells us to teach His words to our children. We began teaching Anna about dressing modestly.

Anna is now twelve, and we still talk about dressing modestly. We've talked about how girls and women dress now. Her dad talked to her about how guys view girls who show too much skin. We've also filled her mind with God's Word, and we remind her that her worth is not based on her clothes, her looks, or what the world says about her. Instead her worth is based on her inner beauty in Jesus. Our culture teaches girls that to be liked, admired, and viewed as cool, they should wear skimpy clothes. But God calls believers to a better way.

It is never too early for Christian parents to begin teaching our children about modesty and purity. If you have a daughter who is showing interest in fashion, begin now to teach her that she can wear cute clothes and still be modest. As she grows older, find examples of teens who dress appropriately but are admired for their fashion sense and style. Show her that dressing modestly does not equal frumpy!

Noteworthy Sacrifice

If anyone wants to come with Me, he must deny himself,
take up his cross, and follow Me. (Matt. 16:24)

As Lydia and Melanie shared lunch with their new pastor's wife, they encouraged Dana to join them for their girls' day out—shopping, eating out, and taking in a chick flick. "I'd love to," Dana said, appreciating the invitation, "but Jack is leading a workshop at church that day. I won't have anyone to keep the boys."

Melanie remarked, "I always just get my mom or sister to keep mine."

Dana said, "Unfortunately all our family lives in other states. Babysitters are not easy for us to come by, especially with four active boys!"

"I hadn't thought about that," confessed Lydia. She thought a minute then added, "I guess being in the ministry requires a lot of sacrifice."

"It's tough at times," agreed Dana. "I miss my family terribly. But God has always supplied surrogate grandparents wherever we've ministered. I'm sure in time we'll find people here who will love and care for our active crew as well."

Each of us who choose to submit to Christ's lordship in our lives must often sacrifice time, money, dreams, possessions, or relationships in order to obey Him. Still, those who heed the call to full-time ministry often sacrifice even more.

The woman who supports her husband in church ministry, evangelism, or missions often finds herself far from family and friends. She also sacrifices time with her husband so he can minister to others. She often sits alone in church, finds it difficult to make deep and trustworthy friendships, and forgoes her own career plans to follow her husband wherever God leads. While most ministry wives consider the blessings to far outweigh the sacrifices, they still deserve our understanding, support, and prayers. Take time to show a ministry wife that you also notice and appreciate the sacrifices she makes.

Minister with Joy

*Now we ask you, brothers, to give recognition to those
who labor among you and lead you
in the Lord and admonish you. (1 Thess. 5:12)*

People often complain to my husband about the pastors in our church. You see, my husband is a deacon and is on the church's personnel committee, so members feel free to call and complain about what isn't going their way. The sermon's too long. The music isn't contemporary enough, traditional enough, reverent enough, loud enough. The family minister doesn't offer a full-blown children's church. The youth minister isn't having enough socials for the students.

My husband was on the phone today with a particularly rude member, one who calls to complain often, and I heard my husband say: "Paul, God has called this man to be our pastor. I'm sorry he doesn't do everything to your liking, but this is God's church. I would advise you to pray about it, and then talk to Pastor Joe face-to-face to discuss any suggestions you have. But remember, God says our pastor has been appointed by the Holy Spirit to shepherd His flock."

His words prompted me to renew my commitment to encourage and stand by the shepherds God has appointed to labor among us, to admonish us, and to lead us in the Lord. The pastors at our church spend their lives serving their congregation, and I want to encourage them so they can minister with joy.

An imperfect shepherd leading an imperfect flock. Sounds odd, doesn't it? But because we live in a fallen, imperfect world, our pastors are fallen, imperfect people (just like their fallen, imperfect congregations). God has placed the responsibility of shepherding His flock, His church, in the hands of pastors who are called and appointed by the Holy Spirit (Acts 20:28). So let's support and encourage them.

Tempted

Gina and Ryan had been assigned to work on a project together, and they had made a big impression on our boss. When Gina and I had lunch together, I congratulated her. "I couldn't have done it without Ryan," she said, smiling. But something in her smile gave away her feelings for Ryan.

"Gina, you're not thinking about getting involved with him, are you?" I asked. "He's married."

"He said that he and his wife are separated, and it's only a matter of time before they get a divorce." I stabbed my salad with my fork and said, "He told you that?" Color rose in her cheeks, and she said defensively, "His wife is a real shrew. All she cares about is his paycheck."

Gina was young, single, and naive, and I didn't want to see this sweet friend wind up in a messy situation. Knowing she had grown up in a Christian home, I said: "God gives us rules and boundaries to protect us. Don't allow this temptation to ruin your life. You could wind up really regretting it, and I don't want to see you hurt."

As part of the fallen human race, we all face temptation, and the enemy will hit each one of us in the area in which we are most vulnerable. When we work outside the home, for example, we need to be vigilant. In some cases we may spend more time with our coworkers than we do with our spouse, family, and friends. It can seem natural to bond with someone who understands our work situation, but we must be careful not to form an emotional attachment that's off-limits.

First Peter 1:14–15 says, "As obedient children, do not be conformed to the desires of your former ignorance. But as the One who called you is holy, you also are to be holy in all your conduct."

The Truth

In the latter times some will depart from the faith, paying attention to deceitful spirits and the teaching of demons. (1 Tim. 4:1)

Tracy and Alicia finished packing up the shoe boxes containing Christmas gifts to send overseas and collapsed on the sofa. The TV was on, and a popular afternoon talk show was just beginning.

"Have you noticed how she has really gotten into New Age thinking and philosophy lately?" Alicia asked. Tracy nodded. "She has some programs that give great information, but I don't know. It seems a little weird to me."

"She's done a lot of good, and she influences a tremendous number of people, but you need to separate the truth from the lies. On one of her programs she even denied that Jesus Christ is the only way to heaven."

"No way!" Tracy said. "I thought she was a Christian."

Alicia shrugged. "We have to be careful of anything or anyone—no matter how famous they are or how much good they do—that would lead us away from God's truth. He doesn't want us to be deceived."

Today there are many messages out there—messages telling us that we are little gods, that if we're good enough we can get into heaven, that a good God would not send people to hell, or that all roads lead to Him. As Christians we need to know the truth—the real truth, not outright error or partial truth. Jesus is the way, the only way. In John 14:6, He said, "I am the way, the truth, and the life. No one comes to the Father except through Me." And Paul said in Galatians 1:8, "If we or an angel from heaven should preach to you a gospel other than what we have preached to you, a curse be on him!" If what they're saying doesn't line up with Scripture, don't buy it.

Find the Time

He went up on the mountain by Himself to pray.
When evening came, He was there alone. (Matt. 14:23)

"I want to spend time with God, but I just can't seem to find the time," said Leslie to her mentor, Jane.

"I struggled with the same thing when I was in your stage of life," said Jane, "but if you're ever going to get to know Him and His heart, you will have to make some adjustments. First, you have to find the time to spend with Him and then show up just as you would for an appointment with your doctor.

"Leslie, tell the Lord of your desire to meet with Him. Ask Him to help you find the right time of day to spend with Him, and then make it a priority. If your best time to be with Him is in the morning, you may have to get up a little earlier and drink a whole pot of coffee before you can even see to read your Bible," Jane said with a smile. "But if you consistently meet with Him, it becomes a holy habit so that if you skip a day, you miss Him like a friend who has moved away."

"But what about interruptions?" said Leslie.

"You'll always have interruptions," Jane replied. "But most interruptions can be ignored. God will bless your efforts to spend time with Him."

To grow in our relationship with God, we need to spend time with Him. But sometimes we can't seem to find the time. Evaluate your schedule. If you're overwhelmed with all you have to do, maybe some things need to go. Then determine the best time for you to be with the Lord. Make it a priority to protect that time with Him! It is the most important calendar item of the day.

Sleeping Duty

Which is the way to what is good?
Then take it and find rest for yourselves. (Jer. 6:16)

Nine months of preparation and I was still surprised by all of the things I needed to learn when my daughter Stephanie was born. I'd read books on childbirth and what to do the first year, but nothing could truly prepare me for becoming a new mom.

God answered our prayers for a healthy baby, and I was grateful. But I was completely and utterly exhausted. My body had taken those nine months to grow and nurture my baby, and I'd hoped to snap back within a couple of weeks. Who was I kidding? I look back on it now and laugh at my expectations.

Changing diapers or giving her a bath weren't the hardest part; it was the lack of sleep. I was so exhausted from the sleepless nights that I could barely function during the day. I thank God for my husband, Zach, who pitched in when he wasn't at work. It took months before I was able to get the proper amount of sleep my body needed.

One of the biggest challenges of becoming a new mom is getting the right amount of rest. When your body is fatigued, life seems to go in slow motion. You might feel less alert and more irritable. But losing sleep isn't just aggravating; it can actually delay losing some of the baby weight you might have put on during your pregnancy.

If you find you're exhausted, cut yourself some slack. Give yourself permission to be less than perfect, and ask those around you for help.

Maybe you have a friend who could help you with the laundry. Or maybe your mom could come over once a week and pitch in. Most important, seek God's guidance (James 1:5) and trust Him to strengthen you and help you.

Creation Clues

His invisible attributes . . . have been clearly seen . . . ,
being understood through what He has made. (Rom. 1:20)

My husband and I were so excited. The kids were with my mother-in-law, and we were spending a week in Colorado. Our flight arrived at night, and we drove north of the airport for about forty-five minutes to reach our rural cabin. As the road began to twist and turn, I wondered what was around us. The city lights were far behind us, and the headlights of our little rental car didn't give us much of a glimpse into the surrounding canyon.

The next morning we walked outside our cabin, and what we saw took our breath away. On every side we were surrounded by jagged mountains. The sky was a brilliant blue, and the aspen trees next to us in the canyon were bright yellow with fall color. Most surprising was the rushing river close to our cabin. We heard the water when we arrived the night before, but we had no idea that such powerful rapids were right outside our door.

Seeing God's beauty come to light after the darkness of the night reminded us of the miracle He works in our hearts, bringing us out of darkness and into His marvelous light. Creation brings glory to its Maker, and when we immerse ourselves in its beauty, creation can be a tool God uses to draw us closer to Himself.

So try to spend some time outdoors soon in the world God created. Take a walk through the woods, visit a flourishing garden, or even study the intricate detail of a spiderweb. Allow new aspects of His creation to remind you of what a big God He is. It will make you even more grateful that He loves you personally and intimately.

Building Up

Life and death are in the power of the tongue,
and those who love it will eat its fruit. (Prov. 18:21)

"Late again," I muttered. Dinner was cold and the kids were in bed. Dan had another big deadline that kept him working late. I lugged a laundry basket into the den and started folding clothes. Soon the back door opened. Dan came in, giving me a half smile and a kiss. He looked exhausted.

After warming his dinner, I caught him up on our preschoolers' latest antics and how much I was looking forward to our plans for tomorrow night. "The sitter is confirmed," I said.

Dan didn't say a word; he just looked at his plate and chewed. Suspicious, I asked, "We're going to the party, right?" He looked at me sadly. "I can't, Tara. We have a last-minute meeting that will go late."

"But, Dan, Friday night?"

"We've got to get this project finished. I may even have to work Saturday too. I'm sorry. I'll make it up to you."

I stood up, suddenly seething. "I've heard that a hundred times before, Dan. You won't ever make it up to me—you're too far in the hole. I'm so sick of this. You always disappoint me!"

Stomping to our room, I punched my pillow and flopped onto the bed. I lay there a long time, thinking it over. I had torn into him over something he couldn't control when what I really wanted was to shore him up. I began to pray for help to mend the hurt I'd caused.

The pressure men feel to perform at work can be overwhelming. The world tells them they've got to work harder and longer to be successful—or even to keep their jobs. At home our careless words make it worse. We can honor our husbands by encouraging and building them up (1 Thess. 5:11).

So Different

God created man in His own image; He created him in the image of God; He created them male and female. (Gen. 1:27)

Lauren, my thirty-year-old daughter, sighed into the phone. "I don't get it," she said. "Why did God make men and women so different?"

I smiled, even though she couldn't see me, and said, "It might seem like it would be easier if we could marry someone who is just like we are. But by creating men and women to think, feel, respond, and act differently, God gives us opportunities to balance each other out. If you're having an emotional day, you don't want Carson in exactly the same mood."

Lauren chuckled. "Yeah, I see what you mean."

"And being married to someone who is different allows us to grow in ways we couldn't with our clone. In order to get along, we have to learn to do things like get to the bottom line instead of talking our man's ear off and sit through an action movie instead of a chick flick.

"If we each married someone who was exactly like we are and we always got our own way, we would be selfish people who wouldn't know how to give and take. But instead we learn to compromise and to see things from another point of view. And there's something I've learned after thirty-two years of marriage: I'm not always right, and my way isn't the only way."

If you are married, you have an opportunity to grow and mature through being in an intimate relationship with someone who is hardwired differently from you. Celebrate his uniqueness, and instead of being frustrated because he doesn't think, feel, respond, and act just like you, learn to appreciate the unique way God created him.

Pray as You Go

The urgent request of a righteous person is very powerful.
(James 5:16)

Janine, a Christian friend at work, has become my spiritual mentor. One day I told her I wanted to teach Amelia, my seven-year-old, more about prayer. "But how, with all these single-mom responsibilities?" I asked.

"When my kids were little, I prayed with them throughout the day," Janine said. "You may have more time than you think. Ask God to show you."

He did. I realized that we spend valuable time in the car. One morning on the way to school, I told Amelia, "I'm going to pray for you every day before I drop you off." I thanked God for her teacher and friends and asked that she learn a lot. She asked me to pray about her spelling test too. When I picked her up at the day-care center, she said, "God helped me, Mom! I got every word right!" We thanked Him immediately for helping her remember what she had studied.

One night before bedtime, I asked Amelia some questions Janine had suggested: "Is anything bothering you? Are you sad or worried?" A moment later Amelia said, "I'm sad because Brooke and I had a fight on the playground." We asked God to forgive her for her part in the argument and to help her and Brooke make up. Amelia said, "I feel a lot better."

A vital part of parenting is teaching kids about prayer. We've all seen, sometimes to our dismay, that kids model parents' behavior. If we don't pray with and for them, how will they ever learn to do it themselves? Children can be powerful and effective prayer warriors. Explaining that prayer is "talking with God" and keeping our prayers simple and fresh (Matt. 6:7–8) will help them understand He is our ever-present Friend. Let's remember to pray for them in our own prayer times as well.

Tell Someone

*I acknowledged my sin to You and
did not conceal my iniquity. (Ps. 32:5)*

Tonya had tried to handle this problem on her own, but to no avail. Finally, desperate to talk with someone who would help and not judge her, she had decided to confide in her Bible study teacher, Joyce.

"I didn't mean to get hooked on pornography," explained Tonya. "I just stumbled across a television show one night while I was up late by myself. The show was pretty explicit, but it captured my attention."

"Unfortunately your story is not uncommon," Joyce assured Tonya. "Did you find that the images stayed in your mind long past that evening?"

"Yes," admitted Tonya, relieved to find someone who understood her dilemma. "Since then I've stayed up late a few nights by myself just so I can watch more. It's so embarrassing to tell you this, but I need help."

Joyce said, "We're going to pray about this right now, and then I'm going to find you the help you need. You're not alone in this struggle."

Some sins, especially sexual ones, seem to have more sticking power than others. Satan knows this and uses them to ensnare us in feelings of hopelessness. Pornography, because it is a visual stimulant, is one such highly addictive temptation. According to one research center, approximately 17 percent of all women struggle with an addiction to pornography. You or a close friend could be one of them.

Addictions are strongholds that require more than just wishful thinking to overcome. Thankfully resources are available to women who are willing to be open about their struggle with pornography. The most important step, as with any stronghold, is to tell someone so the grip can be loosened.

In the Stars

Do not turn to mediums or consult spiritists, or you will be defiled by them; I am the Yahweh your God. (Lev. 19:31)

"There's a gas station. Let's fill up," Laurie said, pulling into the parking lot. "Sounds good," said her college roommate, Val.

Back on the interstate a few minutes later, Val unwrapped her candy bar and flipped through the magazine she'd just bought. "Hey, look! Here's the horoscope page. What's your sign?" Laurie frowned, sipping her soda. "My sign?"

"Yeah, you know—Virgo, Sagittarius, Leo. Your birthday is in May, right?"

"Yes, it's May 8, but . . ."

"Here it is." Val started reading aloud the description for Taurus.

"I'm not interested, Val," Laurie said, her voice full of warning.

"Why? Don't tell me you think it's bad to read your horoscope!"

Laurie said, "Didn't you listen to T. J.'s message at the campus Bible study a few weeks ago? He said astrology, Ouija boards, and stuff like that are offensive to God."

"Oh, please. God is the God of the universe, the Most High! Why would He be offended by something silly like astrology? Nobody actually believes that stuff."

"Whether you believe it or not, reading your horoscope can give the enemy a foothold in your life. Instead of going to God with concerns about the future, you're consulting the enemy. That's when 'silly' becomes dangerous."

Astrology and horoscopes, though seemingly harmless, are part of the occult. And when we dabble in them, we are inviting evil influences into our minds and hearts. We are showing that we don't trust God with the future, and we don't want to go to the Bible for answers. No wonder He's so offended by the occult!

Healing and Hope

Godly grief produces a repentance not to be regretted. (2 Cor. 7:10)

I'd long admired Rex and Sandy's marriage. Both in their sixties, they have energy and passion to go on numerous overseas mission trips each year and assist in our church's youth department. They obviously love each other deeply and enjoy ministering to others side by side.

That's why I was so surprised to find out that their marriage had faced the storm of infidelity and survived. One night I had the opportunity to hear Rex share his testimony. He humbly told his audience that he had sinned against his wife by having an affair fifteen years earlier. Though he ultimately returned to his wife and the Lord, his family paid a price for his sin.

I asked Sandy how she had been able to reconcile with Rex when unfaithfulness ends so many marriages. She said when Rex demonstrated genuine repentance through his words, actions, counseling, and accountability, she sensed God prompting her to give their marriage another chance.

Infidelity places unimaginable stress on a marriage. The spouse who commits adultery often loses the trust and respect of their mate. The offended marriage partner sometimes loses his or her self-esteem and the desire to stay committed. Some assume the only solution is divorce when the marriage has been so wounded. But some couples do reconcile with God's help, allowing Him to do a redemptive work in them and in their marriage.

God has mourned the unfaithfulness of His beloved throughout the generations, but He has always shown compassion and mercy to those who will return to Him. Reconciliation is His desire, and love is His motive. If you or someone you know has suffered from a broken trust, seek God's best. Ask Him to give the grace needed for healing and hope.

Doctor's Orders

You were bought at a price.
Therefore glorify God in your body. (1 Cor. 6:20)

As I lay in the room at the outpatient surgery center waiting for my gastroenterologist, I tried to relax. This was going to be my second colonoscopy. I had already made it through the dreaded "prep" the day before, following a liquid diet and drinking a huge quantity of an awful-tasting liquid designed to cleanse the intestines and colon before the procedure.

Although I was supposed to schedule my second colonoscopy three to five years after the first one, I put it off for various reasons: *I'm so busy with work. The prep is horrible. I'll do it later. I want to switch doctors, or do I?* Now it was seven years after the first procedure. The previous doctor had found several polyps, and it had certainly crossed my mind that my new doctor might find more polyps—or worse. *Have I waited too long?*

When the doctor finished, I heard the words, "Everything is fine," and breathed a sigh of relief. Next time I would follow the doctor's orders and return at the recommended time.

Americans currently have access to the best medical care in the world. We can visit top-notch doctors who use the latest technology to diagnose and treat their patients. Many diseases can be prevented or are treatable if they are caught in the early stages. But in order to make full use of that medical care, it's important to take the time to visit our health practitioners for regular checkups.

While God can heal miraculously, He frequently uses modern medicine. So follow your doctor's instructions about the frequency of visits and scheduling diagnostic tests. Take good care of the body God has given you through proper diet, exercise, rest, and medical care.

Called

Will not God grant justice to His elect who cry out to Him day and night? Will He delay to help them? (Luke 18:7)

My daughter-in-law, Sheryl, graduated college last December with a degree in early childhood education and certification in special education. While the end of the year is not the ideal time to get a teaching position, she hoped something would open up for her. In the meantime she accepted substitute teaching assignments, but there were no phone calls from school districts about permanent positions.

When the economy took a nosedive, school districts began cutting budgets and enlarging class sizes instead of hiring new teachers. August came and went, and there was still no teaching job.

Sheryl's student loans were coming due, and it was putting a big strain on their budget. Substitute teaching didn't pay much, and they couldn't count on a regular paycheck with sporadic assignments. We all continued to pray.

Then a couple of months later, Sheryl received an offer to teach special-education students, and she accepted. "I love what I'm doing now," she says, "and I know this is what God has called me to do." When she tells me what her day is like, I don't know how she does it. The kids are needy, but the Lord gives her the grace to minister to them. She loves her students, and they love her.

In the past college graduates were in high demand, but now a degree is no longer an automatic ticket to finding a career. People from many walks of life are unemployed or underemployed, forcing many recent grads to move back home.

If you know someone who is out of work or trying to find his or her first full-time job, pray. Ask the Lord to give them wisdom as they search for employment. Remember the persistent widow in Luke 18:1–8. God is faithful.

Wrong Timing

A man's heart plans his way,
but the LORD determines his steps. (Prov. 16:9)

"Please let the test be negative," Terry prayed aloud. But a bright pink line on the test strip screamed positive. Terry groaned. "Oh, no." With two daughters in high school and a son in seventh grade, she had just traded stay-at-home-mom status for a part-time job she loved. She and her husband had plans—plans that did not include reliving the diaper and tantrum years.

"I'm too old to have another baby," Terry cried over the phone to her friend Leslie.

Leslie said, "Not according to that pregnancy test."

"But I'm at high risk for Down Syndrome at my age. And we don't have room for one more body in this house. Leslie, I can't have this baby. John won't even have to know."

Leslie cut Terry off. "Do you hear yourself? God obviously wants this child in your family. My sister had a perfectly healthy baby at forty-six. My college roommate had a child with Down Syndrome at thirty-two. But they both consider their boys to be the best surprise blessings of their lives."

Terry reached for a tissue, too embarrassed to speak. She had just considered an act that she'd claimed she could never commit, all because a baby would mess up her plans. Could this shock really be a surprise blessing?

While some pregnancies are carefully planned, others arrive when a couple least expects it. The joy of a precious life is overshadowed by fear, disappointment, and frustration. Suddenly the unthinkable choice becomes, even if for a moment, thinkable. But as many mothers of unplanned pregnancies will confirm, surprise babies bless our lives in unimaginable ways once we choose to embrace the life God created. Prayers of "Why now, Lord?" turn to praises for how beautifully He upsets our plans.

Unique Purpose

My grace is sufficient for you, for power is perfected in weakness. (2 Cor. 12:9)

"Would you like to try the flute?" Mom asked as she filled out the form. I eagerly said yes. As a fourth-grader, I knew it was time to try out a band instrument. But I was the first visually impaired student in the school district, so I'm sure my mom wasn't shocked to receive the disappointing news that I couldn't participate in band.

Instead of fighting the system, she signed me up for piano lessons, along with my younger sister, Sherry, who also had low vision. She'd heard enough "can't" messages. What about the things we *could* do?

Whatever my parents' original dream was for us, the only disappointment we heard was how hard it was for them to watch us struggle. While they were protective and realistic, they chose to focus on our strengths, encouraging us to participate in activities and excel in school, constantly reminding us that God had a unique purpose for our lives. I have grown to thank God for my low vision, knowing it allowed Him to take me far beyond anyone's expectations.

As parents await the birth of a child, how many plan with disabilities in mind? We hope for athletes, musicians, and honor students. How crushing it must be when those plans are flattened with news of a physical or mental limitation.

Surely the mother of the blind man Jesus healed anxiously awaited a strong son who would do great things and care for her in her old age. Instead the man's blindness provoked questions about who sinned. Jesus' response reveals that God had a dream for this man too—to display His glory through him.

Parents like mine model the benefits of laying disappointments at the Creator's feet, then asking Him to display His power and reveal His plan.

Healthy Boundaries

A sensible person sees danger and takes cover, but the inexperienced keep going and are punished. (Prov. 22:3)

Maggie took a deep breath and prayed for courage. Her ex-husband, Dave, had crossed the line when he became abusive toward her during their marriage, and she was forced to keep the boundaries in place. "The judge ruled that you can visit the children every other weekend with supervision," Maggie reminded him.

"You know that ruling is too stiff, Maggie. And it's not fair that both kids have a birthday in the same month."

"I understand, but you'll have to celebrate Jacob's birthday next month." Maggie wanted to extend grace to Dave, but she knew the time for that had passed. Because of his unpredictable anger she could no longer give mercy where her children were concerned. She would show Dave respect, but she would not let him push her when it came to the kids.

"The kids will see you in a couple of weeks," Maggie said.

Healthy and well-established boundaries are necessary for any relationship but all the more important in relationships with dangerous or difficult people. Jesus' parable of the wheat and tares in Matthew 13:24–30 states that all of us must live and work side by side with people who live contrary to God's ways. Sometimes we don't even have the option of distancing ourselves from them because we are irreversibly linked. But we can establish appropriate boundaries for our safety.

Many people feel guilty about enforcing boundaries. But in Paul's second letter to the Thessalonians, he urged them to insist on proper behavior from one another (3:6–15). If you are in a relationship with a difficult person, seek godly guidance or professional help in establishing proper boundaries. If abuse is involved, get help as soon as possible.

Partners in the Gospel

*After they had fasted, prayed, and laid hands on them,
they sent them off. (Acts 13:3)*

Denise walked around the missions market, excited and encouraged by all of the different ministries represented. It amazed her how sacrificially people could live.

Denise loved hearing their incredible stories of how God worked on the mission field, stories that often told of God's miraculous interventions in difficult circumstances and how people came to accept Christ. Some of those stories were about how God provided for the missionaries' needs just as He had provided manna from heaven to the Israelites day by day. The theme of financial need was consistent among all of the missionaries.

Denise, however, was barely able to provide for herself on her Social Security and pension money. After tithing, she didn't know how she could give any more money and still pay the bills. Prompted by the Holy Spirit, however, she asked one of the missionaries if his family had any needs other than money. She was pleasantly surprised to learn there were many creative ways she could support them.

Though we may not feel called to the mission field, we are still part of what missionaries do and are responsible for sending them out and encouraging and aiding them in their work—God's work. People often think there are only two ways to be involved in missions: either move to a foreign country or give money to missionaries who serve there. But missionaries have many needs. They need consistent, committed prayer warriors who are willing to pray regularly for them. They desperately need encouragement such as letters, care packages filled with little familiar things from home, Christmas cards, even short phone calls. Maybe you can't give money, but you can still give a lot. Pray today about how God wants you to partner with His workers in the field.

Lost and Found

Anyone finding his life will lose it, and anyone losing his life because of Me will find it. (Matt. 10:39)

The news shook the rural Southern town where the missionaries grew up. Drew, Shara, and their children had been serving in West Africa for several years, helping the community with small business development. But their Christian faith was a threat to terrorists in the area. The terrorists made plans to abduct Drew, but their abduction attempt was thwarted when he resisted. They murdered him instead.

Shara and the children came back to the United States to grieve and regroup. As their families came alongside, Shara took her story of God's grace and provision to the community of believers. Not only did she express forgiveness for those who took Drew's life, but she prayerfully made plans to return to the area and continue sharing the love of Christ when the time was right.

Shara expressed her heart to a friend. "We understand how these people think. They believed that taking Drew's life was the right thing to do. They still need to hear truth, and our family is still called to go. But we desperately need the prayers of God's people to go with us."

According to Open Doors Ministry, 70 percent of the world's population experiences some kind of religious persecution. Stories abound in Christian news sources of those dying or being brutalized for their faith. We may sometimes be tempted to "hide out" in the safety of our freedom, but our brothers and sisters in Christ who make up the persecuted church and those called to go to them need our prayers.

Believers in North Korea, China, India, Africa, Iran, Vietnam, and many other areas of the world should have the faithful prayers and support of the free church. And those who risk everything to serve them should have both faithful prayer support and financial provision.

Lies and Truth

*Those who look to Him are radiant with joy;
their faces will never be ashamed. (Ps. 34:5)*

To the nurse it probably seemed like an innocent remark. To the teenager it was the beginning of a spiraling battle with weight, shame, and loss of self-esteem.

Darla was tall and had a large frame. Although not excessively heavy, she still had a young girl's pudgy features. As the nurse weighed her, prior to a doctor's visit, she said, "If you're ever going to get your weight under control, you must do it now."

Haunted by that voice, Darla's food and exercise issues bordered on compulsions for the next ten years. She hid her weight loss with layered clothing. She disguised her meager food intake with deceptive skills. But God finally exposed Darla's poor physical condition, and eventually she found the road to recovery through medical intervention and the prayers of her family.

Being a Christ follower does not exclude us from battles with body image. Our minds and eyes are continually bombarded with images of perfection in looks, size, and style. The pursuit is perfection and the end result is . . . beauty and happiness? Who believes that lie?

Sadly, too many women and girls do buy the lies. They develop discontentment and make constant comparisons of themselves to others where they often fall short. Unless we are able to combat the lies of the world with the truth of God's Word, we are vulnerable to clever marketing.

God's truth declares that we are His daughters (2 Cor. 6:18). He sees us as chosen and valuable (1 Pet. 2:4), redeemed (Isa. 43:1), and greatly loved (Eph. 2:4). The cure for struggles with shame and body image is to transfer our longing for the approval of others into a longing for the One who has made us "remarkably and wonderfully" (Ps. 139:14).

Just One

Who can separate us from the love of Christ? (Rom. 8:35)

Walking through the restaurant lobby filled with families, I said to the hostess, "Table for one."

"Just one?" she asked, eyebrows up. "In that case I can seat you now."

She showed me to a tiny table wedged into a corner near the kitchen. All around me sat couples and families. I scanned the menu but already knew what I wanted. On Sundays my singles group often came here, but today I was alone.

The server came by. "Just one today?" she asked, perky, annoying. Plastering on a smile, I said, "Yes. Just one. And I'm ready to order." As I waited for the food, I pulled out my journal and started writing. *God, I get so tired of being single. Loneliness is always just below the surface. And on days like today, it bubbles over.*

"Bridget?" came a voice beside me. I looked into the smiling face of Andrea, a former coworker and friend I hadn't seen in months. Jumping up, I hugged her. "It's great to see you!" she said. "Can I sit for a minute?"

"Of course," I said, offering her the other chair. "Isn't Tim with you?"

"Yes, but we just ordered so I have time to catch up with you before the food comes." Andrea's presence and caring attitude turned my mood around. After she left, I wrote, *Lord, thank You for reminding me that You see me. Thank You for sending a friend to lift my spirit.*

Singleness can sometimes mean loneliness at work, at church, at home. If you're single, know that the Lord God sees you and loves you. He has a plan for your life that only you can fulfill. He wants you to seek Him first.

And regardless of your marital status, you probably know someone who is lonely. Invite her over for a meal. Be a friend. You'll both be blessed.

Priority

I belong to my love, and his desire is for me. (Song of Sol. 7:10)

After Bible study my friend Lynn asked me, "Have you ever heard that we're supposed to put our husbands before our children?" When I nodded, she said, "I don't get it. Our children need us. We're their mothers, after all."

"Our husbands do too, even if they don't show it."

"But Mike is an adult! He can handle it if I'm not always available. My kids can't."

"Here's my take on this. When my kids see that Bill is my highest priority after God, they understand that they're not the center of the world. They see that their parents love and value each other and the marriage. It gives them a strong sense of security, which kids desperately need."

"But how can I make Mike my priority when I'm so busy with the kids? If we're actually home when he gets home, I'm either helping with homework, making dinner, or doing laundry."

"Here's what I do. When Bill comes home, I greet him with a kiss. At dinner he and I talk for a minute or two before the kids chime in. If he's late, I sit with him while he eats dinner. The kids know not to interrupt my time with him. I also regularly ask myself: *When was the last time I gave Bill my undivided attention?* That includes physical intimacy."

Lynn sighed and said, "I'm so exhausted I can't even think about that. I need to pray about all this."

Nurturing our marriages is a gift we can give our children as well as ourselves. In Scripture God makes clear that we are to value and cherish our marriages and our mates. You may need to make some tough decisions, like cutting back on kids' activities. Pray for guidance on how to proceed.

The Voice of God

*When you pray, go into your private room, shut your door,
and pray to your Father who is in secret. (Matt. 6:6)*

One day while on the phone with my friend Beth, I said, "A lady at church says she hears God's 'still, small voice' all the time. Other women say that God told them to do something. I pray, and I love the Lord, but apparently I'm not plugged in like they are. I've never heard His voice. Have you?"

"No, but God doesn't always speak audibly."

"What do you mean?" I asked.

"Sometimes with Scripture I sense Him showing me what it means and how to apply it to my life. Sometimes I feel a prompting to reach out to or pray for someone."

"How do you know it's from God and not yourself?" I asked.

"With the insights from Scripture, the thoughts that come are way beyond me spiritually. If a thought or feeling I have doesn't contradict Scripture, it could be Him. If it would bring Him glory or further His kingdom, it probably is Him."

"And if I feel prompted to pray, it's probably God," I said.

"Right. These are not things Satan would want you to do because they honor God. And of course, if you feel an urge to sin, that's definitely not from God."

"I think I'm beginning to understand this a little better."

God speaks in different ways. But most often—maybe every single time—He will impress upon our hearts an internal prompting or insight that we know couldn't have come from us. He will speak through Scripture, through the words of a sermon, through prayer, through quiet times alone with Him. If you aren't sure, talk with a mature Christian friend about your impressions.

The Karma Trap

Since we have been declared righteous by faith, we have peace with God through our Lord Jesus Christ. (Rom. 5:1)

One night at a family dinner, Linda pulled her sister aside. "Patricia, I'm concerned about some e-mails you sent me recently. The messages seem very New Age—like you're buying into this philosophy of karma and good deeds as the solution for the world's problems rather than trusting in God and His grace."

"But Christianity holds to many of the same principles. Jesus said that you reap what you sow, right? That's karma."

"Jesus was talking about the consequences of your choices," Linda said, "not a principle of the universe. God is in control, not us. He loves us so much, and He knows that we could never be good enough to save ourselves by our works. Our only hope is in a God who can forgive and save us from our sin and its consequences. He gives us much better than we deserve."

New Age thinking is subtle and can sound similar to some of the truths of Christianity. But Christianity holds out a hope the New Age movement can't offer—the peace, assurance, and hope found in Jesus, not in ourselves. As you encounter New Age philosophies, beware of the nuances that say we can control our lives and eternities and that sin isn't serious. Sin is a reality, and it is so serious that God sent His only Son to die in our place to take away sin's power. "He made the One who did not know sin to be sin for us, so that we might become the righteousness of God in Him" (2 Cor. 5:21). Praise God that He has given us a personal relationship with Him through Jesus, and be mindful of ways you can use the truth of Scripture to break down the lies of New Age thinking.

Involved

Grandchildren are the crowning glory of the aged. (Prov. 17:6 NLT)

When my husband, Bill, and I were raising our three children, our parents weren't very involved with their grandchildren. While the grandparents remembered birthdays and gave Christmas gifts, there were no offers to babysit—no respite for an occasionally beleaguered stay-at-home mom, and little help or encouragement was given. Our parents probably felt they had raised their kids and shouldn't be saddled with the responsibility of being called upon to pinch-hit once in a while.

But Bill and I want to be involved in the lives of our grown children and grandchildren. And for the ones who live far away, it requires extra effort. While it can be expensive to travel, I'm always on the lookout for cheap airfare.

When Bill and I can't be there in person to read a story, put a bandage on a skinned knee, give big hugs, or help with homework, we pray for wisdom about how we can stay connected. We make frequent phone calls, send e-mails, and drop cute cards in the mail—just to let the kids know we love them. They know they can call us and we'll take the time to listen.

We always pray that God will use us to impact the lives of our children and grandchildren for God's kingdom. We want to be a blessing to them and to be available to help when it's needed. It takes extra effort, but it's so worth it!

When families live far apart, the cost of travel can limit the frequency of visits. But thanks to technology, communication can be easier. If you live far away from your family, make frequent phone calls and send letters or e-mails. Digital photography makes it easy to share photos and videos. Ask God to help you be a positive influence in the lives of your loved ones.

Did You Vote?

Government is God's servant for your good. (Rom. 13:4)

"Did you vote this morning?" asked Dawn as she and Amanda jogged their second lap around the park's running trail.

"Oh, I didn't even know there was an election today," Amanda admitted. She wrinkled her nose in embarrassment. "I used to be so involved in the political scene, but ever since the kids came along, I just haven't kept up. It's embarrassing really."

Dawn shook her head. "I can totally relate. When my twins started school, I realized I didn't even know who was on the school board making all those important decisions about my children's education." She paused to take a few steady breaths, then added, "That's when God showed me that part of being a responsible parent and a godly influence on our world is being an involved citizen and educated voter."

"Wow!" said Amanda. "I'd never thought of it that way. But I wouldn't even know whom to vote for."

"I tell you what," said Dawn. "I have a voter's guide in my car. I'll give it to you to study this afternoon and then you can pray about it and go vote while I watch your kids. How does that sound?"

With all the other responsibilities we juggle, it can be difficult to stay informed about government policies, leaders, and elections. But if Christ followers want to impact our world positively, we must make the effort to stay informed and involved.

Romans 13:1–7 reminds us that governments are established by God for the good of the people. Therefore, it only stands to reason that godly people should be involved in government—holding office, giving input, voting, volunteering, and praying.

Kids in Crisis

We have redemption in Him through His blood, the forgiveness of our trespasses, according to the riches of His grace. (Eph. 1:7)

As my older sister's confidante, I knew her secret before anyone else did—she was pregnant. Although she was only a senior in high school, Shari and her boyfriend wanted to marry. But when my parents found out, Dad went ballistic. In his usual fashion he yelled, ranted, cursed, and threatened. Teen pregnancy was scandalous in 1964, and Dad was big on not doing anything to embarrass the family—especially him.

We didn't know the Lord back then, and Dad demanded that Shari get an abortion—never mind that it wasn't even legal at the time. He said he would find a doctor who would perform the procedure. Fortunately Mom talked him out of it, and a small, hasty wedding was planned.

When classmates began noticing Shari's expanding waistline, she dropped out of school. Whispers of her swift departure followed me to my first year at the same high school the following year. A month before her due date, Shari went into labor. Due to placenta previa, a condition in which the placenta is close to or covering the cervix, little Jill was stillborn.

Dad stated flatly that it was all for the best, but Shari was heartbroken. All before the age of eighteen, she had grown up in a dysfunctional family, become pregnant out of wedlock, married a man who would later turn out to be unfaithful and abusive, missed her prom and graduation, and buried her firstborn.

When kids are in crisis, families are in crisis. Whether it's an unplanned pregnancy, drugs, alcohol, or some other tragedy, it affects parents, children, and even extended family and friends. If you have a child in crisis or know of a family who does, pray and don't give up. God never does.

On a Roll

*When pride comes, disgrace follows,
but with humility comes wisdom. (Prov. 11:2)*

My husband, Nick, had just become a Christian. Soon we joined one of our church's small groups that met at Don and Audrey's house.

One evening Nick wanted to join in the discussion about creation, and he started to mention his interest in astronomy. But one small slip of the tongue—he said "astrology" rather than "astronomy"—and I thought Audrey would come unglued.

Nick tried to explain his mistake, but Audrey was on a roll. She let us know in no uncertain terms that she had been a Christian for a long time—much longer than Nick, of course—and that he should renounce his interest in astrology and the occult immediately. Audrey's spiritual pride was clearly on display, and she wanted everyone to know that she was much farther along on her journey than any of the rest of us.

I'd like to say that Audrey and Nick were able to clear up the misunderstanding quickly, but unfortunately that wasn't the case. Nick was deeply offended and didn't want to go back. We were able to find another small group where we felt welcome and where we've both grown spiritually and relationally. Audrey eventually apologized. Nick forgave her but has avoided being in a group with her.

Sometimes a competitive nature is good. If an athlete is competitive, that's good. Their innate drive can help them push themselves to excel and win. But if that same competitive nature is carried over into a person's spiritual life, it can result in spiritual pride. The "I'm further along than you" or "let me set you straight" attitude is not so good.

God values humility (see Phil. 2:3), and no one should boast. "The one who boasts must boast in the Lord" (1 Cor. 1:31).

Prayer Request?

Be gracious to me, God, according to Your faithful love; according to Your abundant compassion, blot out my rebellion. (Ps. 51:1)

"Will you pray for me?" I asked my friend Diane. I went on to tell her about a hurtful situation with a mutual friend. "I need to get over this before I see her again." My call for prayer and advice quickly turned into a rant.

"She's so pushy and intense. She had no right to say what she did. I hate it when she . . ."

Later I struggled to fall asleep or even pray. I felt convicted. I had desired prayer support, but I'd also called on a friend I knew would agree with me when the first opportunity to gossip arrived. Whether I had a right to be angry, I realized I'd handled it incorrectly.

Forgive me, God, I prayed. *I confess: I asked for prayer hoping it would open the door to dump my frustrations.* As soon as I made things right with God, He showed me the solution. I did need to voice my hurt—to the friend who had offended me.

Choosing to live for Christ does not mean we never sin. When we succumb to temptations to lie, cheat, hate, or gossip, our poor choices often seem justified at first. Then later, when God shines a light on our true motives, we see the darkness that lurks in our hearts.

Scripture reminds us repeatedly that sin, no matter how we rationalize it, builds a wall between us and God. David offers many examples of how we can break that wall down through confession. While admitting we were wrong isn't easy, it brings relief and a fresh start. Sometimes we even get the answers we were looking for when we made that regretful error in the first place.

You Can Do This

Rest in God alone, my soul, for my hope comes from Him. (Ps. 62:5)

I couldn't believe we were in the ER again. It was our fifth visit to the hospital in seven months—two surgeries for my husband, two for me—followed by more hospital bills then we'd expected to pile up in a lifetime, let alone in less than a year. Now my husband had chest pain and shortness of breath. Since Norm had a heart attack five years before, I knew it needed to be taken seriously. Still, a tiny voice inside me wailed, *I can't be here again! And God, we can't afford this!*

Tears threatened, so I made an excuse to leave Norm's room. As I hid in the bathroom trying to regain control, I asked God to help me deal with whatever results came up. *But I can't do this*, continued to echo inside.

Yes you can, My Father whispered. *You aren't here alone. Just hang on to Me.* I walked out feeling stronger and less consumed by the stress of the situation. Whatever happened, with God's help, I could deal with it.

When everyday struggles with kids, our husbands, work, and maintaining a home are compounded with unexpected events, we are often tempted to scream, "God, I can't do this!" But we tend to forget that He is waiting to lighten the load. He may not remove the problem, but He can help us find answers, give us peace, and catch us when we crash from the exhaustion of it all. It's reassuring to know that many of the psalms were written in the heat of major stress. They remind us of the power of staying tuned into Him through it all—listening for His voice, calling on His strength, and praying for His peace.

Honoring God's Plan

Wives, submit to your own husbands as to the Lord. (Eph. 5:22)

When my husband decided our family would not attend his grandparents' sixty-fifth wedding anniversary party in another state, I felt strongly that Matt had made the wrong decision. Not only was I certain his extended family would question our absence, but our own children had also looked forward to seeing their grandparents and cousins. I couldn't see how Matt's decision could possibly be best.

Knowing what the Bible says about marriage, I wanted to honor God's plan for authority in my home. Still, it was difficult when I feared Matt's decision could wound feelings and damage family unity. Even so, after briefly and respectfully expressing to Matt why I felt we should attend the party, I chose to support his decision. We did not attend the party; and, indeed, we faced some resentment from Matt's family.

Almost three months after the party, Matt admitted he had learned a lesson from his mistake. He assured me we would never again miss another significant family event if at all possible. I was so thankful I hadn't nagged him about his decision so he could hear the Holy Spirit instead.

Ephesians 5:23 says, "The husband is the head of the wife as Christ is the head of the church." He has been placed in a position of leadership over his household. His model for leadership is Christ Himself. Ephesians 5:25 says the husband is to love his wife as Christ loved the church and gave Himself for her.

Submission does not mean wives cannot voice their opinions or must endure abuse. In a healthy Christian marriage, husbands value the opinions of their wives and then prayerfully act as the Lord leads.

A Party in Heaven

There will be more joy in heaven over one sinner who repents than over 99 righteous people who don't need repentance. (Luke 15:7)

When I invited my coworker to a concert at my church, she laughed and told me, "Lightning would strike the church if I walked in." But her *eyes* weren't laughing. Immediately after her sarcastic quip, she looked as if she might cry.

"What's wrong, Paula?" I asked. "Why would it be so shocking for you to come to church with me?"

Paula fidgeted a bit then said: "I went to church when I was growing up, but I just got away from it somehow. I've lived a pretty rebellious life since I left home. Bottom line is I don't think God would let me come back now." I knew Paula's lifestyle wasn't godly, but I had no idea she felt as if God had written her off.

"You can always come back to God, Paula," I assured her. "It's never too late."

Paula looked uncertain, but she went to that concert with me, and there wasn't even the slightest hint of lightning. But I'm sure there was one lively party in heaven.

Jesus assures us in Luke 15:7 that heaven rejoices when a wandering soul returns to God. Unfortunately many people who have drifted away or rebelled against Him assume He has given up on them or is angry with them. But this notion is simply a lie from the enemy. Satan wants to keep straying believers from returning to their God and the sweet fellowship He offers.

The truth is, God is saddened by our rebellion, but He never gives up on us. And while our fellowship with Him is strained by our sin, our Father-child relationship with Him remains the same. Don't let the lies of the enemy keep you from returning to your heavenly Father. He loves you and celebrates your return.

Never Alone

This is my comfort in my affliction:
Your promise has given me life. (Ps. 119:50)

Debra had spent the last year almost in a fog while grieving, taking care of paperwork, and making tough decisions. Her husband's death had changed her world and her future. She knew God had promised to be a husband to her (Isa. 54:5), but sometimes He had seemed far away too. When the phone rang with a lunch invitation from someone who had "been there," Debra gladly accepted.

At the restaurant Jan hugged Debra, saying, "I remember how I missed hugs after my Don died. Now tell me how you're really doing."

Debra confessed to Jan: "Sometimes I'm mad at God. I don't even want to get out of bed on gloomy days. And I can't imagine life ever being good again."

Jan nodded. "I understand and I remember those dark days. But you'll begin to have better days. Your life is not over. God will lead you forward, and one day He will use you to encourage someone else."

Debra looked at Jan's peaceful, joyful expression. Somehow, she knew, she would build a new life and that she had made a new friend.

The Bible is filled with stories about God's care for widows. There is Elijah and the widow in Zarephath (1 Kings 17:9–16), Elisha and the widow in debt (2 Kings 4:1–7), and Jesus raising a widow's son to life (Luke 7:11–17). How hopeful to know that He is compassionate and kind—a husband to those facing life after the loss of a partner. We also see widows with powerful ministries. As painful as it is, the loss of a mate does not mean a life without purpose.

Closet Full of Blessings

*Each person should do as he has decided
in his heart—not reluctantly or out of necessity,
for God loves a cheerful giver. (2 Cor. 9:7)*

"What did you talk about in your class tonight?" I asked my eight-year-old son, Liam, as we drove home from our Wednesday night program at church.

"We learned that each one of us has a closet full of blessings," Liam said proudly.

"That sounds interesting," I said. "What exactly is a closet full of blessings?"

"The teachers asked us to look in our closets for things we don't need. Then they said maybe we could donate those things to the poor."

I love it when Liam gets excited about helping others.

"Mom, could we go through our closets this weekend and clear out the things we don't use anymore?"

"Great idea! I know my closet needs to be cleaned and organized too," I said, as I smiled and silently thanked God for giving my sweet son a generous heart.

God deeply desires for us to bless others. Have you taken the time recently to ask God how He can use you to bless those around you? Maybe you're someone who has a "closet full of blessings" that could be sorted out and donated. Maybe there are extra blankets, clothes, or other useful items at home. Perhaps instead of waiting until spring for some closet cleaning, you can clean out the items you no longer need now. Then pray and ask God where He would like for you to donate those items. You never know who you might be blessing when you listen to the voice of God.

Matthew 25:40 reminds us that whenever we do something to bless others, we are really blessing God Himself. "I assure you: Whatever you did for one of the least of these brothers of Mine, you did for Me."

A Life of Love

You were called to be free, brothers; only don't use this freedom as an opportunity for the flesh, but serve one another through love. (Gal. 5:13)

When I became my mother-in-law's caretaker, I felt as if I didn't have a personal life anymore. I no longer had time for last-minute lunches with friends or leisurely shopping trips. Now wherever I went, Gail and her wheelchair went too.

After a while I began to feel bitterness and resentment toward her for my unwanted and untimely responsibility. Sometimes I'd think, *If she'd only gone to the doctor when she knew there was something wrong, maybe she could have avoided having a stroke.*

But when my father-in-law asked me to help, I couldn't turn him down. Gail could no longer be left alone while Wade went to work. She'd fallen one too many times while he was away from home for him to feel she was safe by herself. Even though my husband and I prayed about it and knew it was what God wanted me to do, it was not an easy decision to make. I begged God to help me become more selfless. Eventually I began to understand that a life of sacrifice is a life flowing with God's love.

Loving another person is not about what we can get from the relationship. Living a selfless life is about making conscious choices to do the right thing for others. After all, your life is not just about you. Maybe you've been in a position where you needed to make a life-altering sacrifice. Did you obey God, or did you tune out His voice and do what you wanted to do?

John 15:13 says, "No one has greater love than this, that someone would lay down his life for his friends." Sometimes obeying the Lord is difficult, but God knows just what you're capable of doing with His help.

In His Eyes

Who is wise and has understanding among you? He should show his works by good conduct with wisdom's gentleness. (James 3:13)

My boss asked for my input on a project that a team of coworkers had been wrestling with for a while. I sat in on their meetings and made a few suggestions about how to resolve the issues they were having in implementing the new program. I also offered some new ideas that could help make certain phases of the project run smoother.

Janet, one of my coworkers, immediately jumped on one of my ideas, telling the group how it wouldn't work. In fact, in the days that followed, Janet was quick to voice opposition, no matter what I said.

Baffled and hurt by her response, I talked to my husband about Janet's anger. "Kay, you know that anger is usually a response for something that's deeper inside the heart. Janet may be feeling threatened by your ideas and suggestions because this is her job," he said.

"But our boss put me on the project," I said.

"Yes, but Janet might feel afraid for her job. She might be hurt because she couldn't pull her part of the project together."

Over the next few weeks, I prayed for Janet every day. I did all I could to be gracious and kind to her. I continued to do my job with integrity. And although I don't know what God is doing in her heart, I know He's drawing my heart closer to His. I know He's doing a work in me.

Anger is a normal, God-given emotion, but its cause is usually deeper than the surface issue. If you are feeling angry, ask God to show you the root cause of your anger. And if you are the brunt of someone's anger, talk to the Lord about that too.

Valuable Discussions

We have conducted ourselves in the world, and especially toward you, with God-given sincerity and purity, not by fleshly wisdom but by God's grace. (2 Cor. 1:12)

"Mom, what is sex?" asked my seven-year-old son, Grayson. I was taking Grayson and his friend Carter to soccer practice. They were in the backseat, and I was glad they couldn't see my red face. Before I could speak, Carter said, "Oh, you know, it's where you check the box on the soccer form that says you're a boy or a girl."

"Oh," Grayson said. And that was it. They went on to something else. I slowly exhaled.

That evening I discussed the incident with my husband. We both knew that Grayson didn't know much about sex; he is our oldest child, so he hadn't heard things from an older sibling. But we also didn't know how to talk with him about it. We wanted to teach him God's view of sexuality—not the world's.

First we prayed and asked the Lord for direction. We researched Christian resources and learned that talking with our children about sexuality is not a one-time "talk" but an ongoing dialogue using age-appropriate language and teachable moments, never giving them more details than they can handle at one time.

When we think about talking to our children about sexuality, we can feel embarrassed and overwhelmed. Where do we start? Yet we know if we don't do it, someone else will. But remember, as Christians we have the Architect of the plan and His Word on our side. By being open, honest, and positive, we can give them a healthy view—God's view—of a sexual relationship: the integration of physical, spiritual, and emotional intimacy between a husband and wife. Teach them that they can talk to you about anything, anytime.

Working Wisely

Holy brothers and companions in a heavenly calling, consider Jesus, the apostle and high priest of our confession; He was faithful to the One who appointed Him. (Heb. 3:1–2)

"Come watch the end of the match!" my coworker and fellow tennis fan Alicia said. "I have it streaming live on my desktop. *I have* to see who wins this tournament."

It was a slow workday, and I really wanted to watch my favorite player defend her championship title. "OK," I agreed.

But later that afternoon the Holy Spirit prodded my conscience. It wasn't right to spend time at work watching a tennis match. Even if I did have some downtime, there were plenty of ways I could spend my time constructively benefiting my employer, not myself. For example, I could do some extra reading to further my knowledge of my field, organize an area of the office that needs work, or touch base with some of my contacts. I am called to be a good steward of my employer's time and resources, serving the authorities out of respect for the God who has gifted me and called me to my position.

It's easy to allow personal distractions to take up our time at work. Surfing the Web, sending personal e-mails, scanning social networking sites, and even making personal calls use the time our employers are paying us for. It may not seem like a big deal in our culture—after all, many of our coworkers do it throughout the day, and many of our employers either don't know or don't care. But we answer to a holy God who sent His perfect Son to die for our sins. He loves us and calls us to obey Him in response to that love. Even if it means you stand alone, work with integrity, knowing that you are working as unto the Lord.

Dream House

I trust in You, LORD; I say, "You are my God." (Ps. 31:14)

Our next-door neighbors recently moved but not because they wanted to or because of a job transfer. Joe and Diane's house—the one she had once told me was their dream house—is now in foreclosure.

Like many Americans, Joe and Diane thought the price of real estate would continue to climb as it had historically. So they stretched to put a down payment on the house next door. They worked hard to improve the property—landscaping, installing granite countertops and new appliances, and finishing the basement. They financed their improvements by taking out a second mortgage.

But when the economy tanked, Joe lost his job. He's been unemployed for nearly two years now. As a last resort Joe and Diane wanted to sell their home and move into something less expensive. But the real estate market had already taken a nosedive, and the price of homes plummeted. Now they were upside down on their mortgage—owing far more than their house was worth. They received help from their church for a while, but eventually they got so far behind on their payments they felt there was no way they could ever catch up.

We all shed tears the day they packed up a rental truck with their belongings. We prayed for God's blessing on them, but I know they face a difficult path. Many people today have had to resort to bankruptcy—some because they bought too much house for their income, others because their circumstances changed.

But while we can't trust in our finances or the changing economy, we can trust in God. He is the same yesterday, today, and forever (Heb. 13:8), and He will be there for us day after day—more dependable than the sunrise. Trust in Him.

Bowing Out

Wisdom resides in the heart of the discerning. (Prov. 14:33)

I had been looking forward to teaching at the writers' conference for months, but it meant covering my own travel expenses. However, back surgery had put my husband out of work for longer than expected. Other costly health issues had followed, making it harder for me to justify flying out of state for an opportunity that required spending as much as I got paid.

"I can write off the plane ticket as a business expense," I argued. "If I bow out, they might never ask me again. This is a great conference to add to my résumé." But our credit card statement declared the sad reality: we were in too much debt to justify the trip. With a lump of disappointment in my throat, I e-mailed the conference coordinator and explained the situation.

"You didn't have to do that," my husband said after I received a reply, solidifying that I wouldn't be teaching at the conference.

"I can always apply next year. Paying our bills is more important right now." And I truly meant it.

Careers can offer exciting opportunities, whether we work outside the home or from the house. Yet our dreams tug at one sleeve while the needs of our husband and kids tug on the other. Our will dukes it out against God's. We make plans only to have them complicated by an illness or emergency. On these occasions it helps to remember that God is in control.

Often there is no easy answer, other than what Scripture says about obeying God's will and putting others before ourselves. As hard as this can be sometimes, we know that God blesses our willingness to sacrifice. Our obedience will bring a sense of peace and often a fatherly affirmation, *You did the right thing.*

A Quiet Place

Very early in the morning, while it was still dark,
He got up, went out, and made His way to a deserted place.
And He was praying there. (Mark 1:35)

I sneaked into my home office early with a long to-do list running through my head. My Bible, journal, and devotional called to me from the bookshelf, but the clock screamed louder. In thirty minutes I had to get my youngest up for school. If I expected to get a head start, I needed to begin now. Pausing to pray and read my Bible would only suck away valuable time.

My day continued at its frenzied pace until I tucked my seven-year-old in for the night, leaving me too exhausted to do anything but fall into bed. Had I really accomplished more by diving headfirst into my day? What happened to following Jesus' example of taking time to commune with the Father?

The next day I tried the opposite approach. I ignored the tug of my laptop and my list, reaching instead for my Bible and journal. As I spent time with God, I savored the difference in my mood and my idea of what I needed to accomplish. If the Son of God spent time in prayer, who was I to think I could get by without it?

Jesus had a busy schedule—teaching, preparing His disciples for ministry, and meeting the needs of others. He knew that He had a short time to accomplish what He came to do. Yet how often do we see Him bolting upright in the morning and tackling a long list of tasks? He was fully God, yet in His humanity He knew where to draw His strength. He offered us an example for how to go into a purpose-filled, productive day. Sometimes an exhausting ending reminds us that reflecting and honoring Christ includes starting our days as He did.

What He Doesn't Know

Don't let your mouth speak dishonestly,
and don't let your lips talk deviously. (Prov. 4:24)

"What did Jim say about those Facebook messages from Brian?" Candice asked Lena as they crossed the parking lot to the coffee shop.

"Nothing. I haven't told him."

"Lena, you need to tell him."

"Why? So he can make a bigger deal about it than it is? It's not like I plan to get back together with my first boyfriend. He just wants to catch up, like my other friends from high school."

Candice stopped in front of the entrance. "Sorry, I know I sound like a nag. It's just that Mike and I are working through some problems in our marriage, and they all started with us being dishonest."

"I'm not being dishonest. I'm just not telling him about a friendship I know would upset him."

Candice offered her friend one bit of advice. "I keep myself in check by thinking of situations this way—if I feel the need to hide it from my husband, then I shouldn't be doing it."

Proverbs 4:24 says, "Don't let your mouth speak dishonestly." Withholding certain kinds of information can be a form of dishonesty. You're right, your husband probably doesn't want to hear every detail of your day, but he deserves to know if you've connected with an old boyfriend on Facebook or you've racked up a large credit card bill. Anything you would want him to share with you probably qualifies as something to disclose.

When we're tempted to let small deceptions creep into our marriage, perhaps we should consider how the sins that tear so many couples apart begin. Adultery, addictions to gambling and pornography, compulsive spending—all begin and feed off deception. And face it—you can't have a healthy marriage without a foundation of mutual trust.

For Your Child's Sake

The father of a righteous son will rejoice greatly, and one who fathers a wise son will delight in him. (Prov. 23:24)

Julie's husband, Jeff, had just told twelve-year-old Mandy she couldn't attend the slumber party she had anticipated all week because she'd lied about a situation at school. But Julie wondered if the punishment wasn't too extreme.

"Do you really think that was necessary?" Julie asked.

"Julie, I know you're softhearted and I appreciate that. I think God meant for us to balance each other as we raise Mandy and Jason together." Jeff took Julie's hand gently. "But the way we discipline our children now will undoubtedly help determine their future. Don't you want Mandy to understand the consequences of lying once and for all? Don't you think it needs to hurt a little when she does the wrong thing?"

Julie knew Jeff was right. She had watched other parents fail to discipline their children and reap the consequences.

It's difficult to discipline our children appropriately and consistently. Naturally we don't want our children to suffer because of their bad choices. We want to protect, bless, and enjoy them. But the Bible teaches parents to discipline their children "while there is hope" (Prov. 19:18), while there is still an opportunity for them to learn from their mistakes so they choose more wisely in the future. If we neglect to discipline our children because we don't want a fuss or dread their tears, we're not doing them any favors. In fact, we could do great damage by sending them into the world as undisciplined adults who disregard the consequences of their actions.

Ask God to help you evaluate your style of discipline. Are you too soft, too harsh, or appropriately firm and loving? Do you need to be more consistent, raise the bar of expectations, or make the penalties of wrong behavior more fittingly painful?

A New Day

*I am about to do something new; even now it is coming.
Do you not see it? Indeed, I will make a way
in the wilderness, rivers in the desert. (Isa. 43:19)*

The surprise party Mary's husband had planned was drawing to a close. Moms and dads were gathering their children, helping them pack coloring books into their backpacks. Mary was glad her friends had brought their little ones with them.

Mary and Jack had finally come to terms with the fact that they would not have children of their own. The disappointment had hung heavy over their marriage for months. But during the summer the couple, both teachers, volunteered to assist in an inner-city kids' club while the regular workers rotated through much-needed vacations. Jack and Mary had quickly fallen in love with the children, and God opened their eyes to the many children all around them who needed love and attention from Christian adults like themselves.

She didn't know if they would adopt or just find other ways to engage with children, but Mary knew God had a plan for her and Jack to invest in children in the classroom and beyond. And while the scene of parents and their children would have caused her to sink just months ago, Mary took a deep breath, thanked God for the well-loved children in her midst, and reached for a tiny pink jacket. It was a new day.

We all face myriad disappointments in life—a lost job, the end of a dream, the death of a relationship, the ache of infertility, a failure, a broken promise. But Isaiah 43:19 tells us to pay attention to God in our times of disappointment because He may be up to something new and amazing. How are you handling your disappointments today?

A Life of Integrity

He knows the way I have taken;
when He has tested me, I will emerge as pure gold.
My feet have followed in His tracks. (Job 23:10–11)

My husband started a financial services business a few years ago with the mission of helping people grow their money. His heart was to take care of his clients. But the worldwide financial crisis hit, engulfing our little family with it, and consequently, my husband had to close his business. He's been looking for a job ever since.

In the meantime we took our daughters out of the Christian school they were attending, and my husband began to home-school them. While this road has been difficult for him as a man—men are wired to work and be breadwinners—I am constantly amazed at the way he works with our daughters, day after day, on math, language arts, science, and history.

Even though he could be bitter at the apparent "no man's" land he lives in, he puts aside his heartaches and lives each day with integrity. The adult Sunday school class he teaches is growing. People at church seek him out with questions about their portfolios. He is a trusted confidant for several men who are facing life challenges. And he is a deacon and a sounding board for our pastor. And what he is in public, he is in private: trustworthy, honest, faithful, true.

Only God and I see the hurt that lives in his heart, but he continues to hold on to the Lord and to what He has called him to do. His life exudes integrity in the midst of suffering.

Integrity. We've heard it defined as the way you live when no one is looking. Even when it seems like God isn't doing anything about our pain, we must continue to do what we know to do—living honestly, with integrity, for Him.

My Reflection

Everyone should look out not only for his own interests,
but also for the interests of others. (Phil. 2:4)

Recently at our church's women's retreat, the main speaker was a missionary to women in war-torn Uganda. Most of these women had inadequate food, shelter, and clothing, and many were HIV positive. They had been raped during the war, or their husbands had been unfaithful while serving as soldiers and brought the disease back to them. Yet they smiled, danced, and sang at the church services they attended. When asked what made them so joyful, they simply said, "Jesus!"

The speaker asked us to donate small toiletry items for her to take back to Uganda—things like toothpaste, soap, lotion, and especially small mirrors, which the women could use to see themselves. She told us most of these women had never seen their own reflections.

This reality spoke to my heart. How much time do I spend in front of the mirror each day? How much money do I spend on my appearance? And how much energy do I waste worrying about how I look? These women had far greater concerns than their physical appearance: whether they would be able to feed their children that day, how they would get medicine to treat their deadly disease. My self-centeredness not only saddened me, but it also drove me to the cross. These women understood what mattered in life—Jesus and nothing else. They put their hope in Him, not in the things of this world.

When we focus on ourselves and our own comforts, we push out the needs of others. Jesus gave up His life for us, and He calls us to die to ourselves by putting others first. No, taking care of ourselves and our families isn't evil, but leaving nothing for others in need is. Seek to live a life that reflects who Jesus is.

Heart of Gratitude

*Give thanks in everything, for this is God's will for you
in Christ Jesus. (1 Thess. 5:18)*

Last year my parents invited a big crowd to their house
for Thanksgiving. During dinner the discussion turned to who
would host the Thanksgiving dinner the following year. Since
Mike and I had just bought our first home, we were drafted. I
had never cooked a turkey or hosted a large get-together in any
setting—let alone in our small home.

Sixteen people confirmed their attendance. *Great,* I thought.
*How are they all going to fit around our tiny table? I'll have people
spread out all over the house.*

Then I realized I was being grumpy instead of grateful. I
prayed, *Father, please help me quit grumbling and remember that
Thanksgiving isn't about the food or where everyone sits, but it's a day
to focus on all of the blessings You've given us.*

We're all tempted to have a grumpy, negative attitude from
time to time. But viewing situations with a heart of gratitude is a
deliberate act of the will and takes practice. Through the study of
God's Word, we can learn to see our circumstances from God's
point of view. Then when we begin to focus on all the Lord has
done for us, we can serve Him and others with genuine gratitude.

Keeping things in perspective when we have such busy
schedules can be difficult. We need to remind ourselves what
special occasions like Thanksgiving are all about. Rather than
focusing on how frazzled we are, we should give thanks to God
for all the blessings we have. Spend time resting in Him, and He
will help us take care of the rest.

"Whatever you do, in word or in deed, do everything in
the name of the Lord Jesus, giving thanks to God the Father
through Him" (Col. 3:17).

Gratitude

*I will praise God's name with song
and exalt Him with thanksgiving. (Ps. 69:30)*

Never in a million years would I have thought my husband and I would lose our home, but we did. When Jake handed the keys over to the mortgage company's representative, I had to fight back tears. I felt a deep sense of sadness about life not going the way we'd planned.

Even so, I knew we were luckier than most people in our situation. We had a place to stay with family, and my husband still had his job. So although I certainly didn't feel cheerful about what was happening, I knew that God hadn't abandoned us.

As I sat in the passenger's seat crying, I felt God's gentle whisper that He still held us in the palm of His hand. In a way this was a new beginning. I silently pleaded with God to give me an attitude of gratitude in the midst of difficult circumstances.

Over the next few weeks, I made an effort to look for the best in all circumstances. I searched for and read Scripture that was positive and uplifting. Although our situation hadn't changed, my faith had grown, and I knew God was working for our good.

Do you have something in your life that you're having a hard time being grateful for? Maybe you've lost a job, your home, or even a loved one. If you have experienced something so devastating that you just can't see anything positive, God can still help you be grateful for what you do have. First Thessalonians 5:16–18 reminds us to "rejoice always! Pray constantly. Give thanks in everything, for this is God's will for you in Christ Jesus." And Romans 8:28 promises, "We know that all things work together for the good of those who love God: those who are called according to His purpose."

Thanksgiving Blessings

He who plows ought to plow in hope, and he who threshes should do so in hope of sharing the crop. (1 Cor. 9:10)

Megan opened the e-mail from Susan. She hadn't heard from her in forever. To her dismay Susan's e-mail told the story of her husband's multiple infidelities and their subsequent divorce. Now, Susan, who had been a stay-at-home mom and homeschooler of three, was living in her friend Lisa's basement rent-free. She had lost her home in foreclosure, and she and the kids had nowhere else to go.

Susan knew that believers who were able looked "after orphans and widows in their distress" (James 1:27), so, for the sake of her children, she included a list of basic needs such as pantry items, babysitting, and school supplies.

Megan knew she needed to connect with her hurting friend. She asked God to show her how to love Susan during this time and to give her wise and understanding words to say as she picked up the phone. During the conversation Megan learned that Susan and her children would celebrate Thanksgiving by themselves. She had no family in state, and Lisa was going out of town. Without hesitation Megan invited Susan to come to her house for Thanksgiving. Susan hesitated at first, not wanting to inconvenience Megan but soon agreed it would be nice.

Perhaps you have so much to be thankful for this year, you've run out of fingers and toes to count your blessings on. Maybe, instead, this is a tough year for you. You've experienced the loss of a loved one, a financial difficulty, or some other challenging circumstance. Ask the Giver of all good things how to reach out and connect, especially at times like Thanksgiving, either to bless someone out of your abundance or to receive during a time of need.

Costly Little Mistakes

He opens their ears to correction and insists they repent
from iniquity. (Job 36:10)

On the first night of our vacation, I learned we had been double-billed at the hotel. What I thought had been a smooth process of making reservations online had resulted in a mistake on the part of the booking agency and a costly extra charge on my credit card. Though the hotel clerk assured me the situation would be easily rectified, I wanted it addressed quickly.

As I lay in bed listening to the ocean waves crash against the shore that night, I was thankful all had been set straight. The booking agency had willingly acknowledged the mistake and credited my card. My trust in their services had been restored.

I ended my day in conversation with my heavenly Father, and I realized afresh why I should acknowledge my mistakes quickly too. Not that God would stew over my unconfessed sin as I had fretted over the faulty charges. But if I want Him to trust me with more spiritual insight, new challenges, and opportunities for serving Him, I need quickly to acknowledge when I've blown it. I was glad I didn't have to argue with the agency that had double-billed me, and I definitely don't want my Father to have to "argue" with me over my sins and mistakes.

Psalm 103:14 says, "For He knows what we are made of, remembering that we are dust." But He also does not take even our smallest sins lightly. Sins left unconfessed grow into bad habits, and before we know it, we are blinded to the seriousness of the offense and try to rationalize it.

Honor your relationship with your heavenly Father by acknowledging your mistakes quickly, calling them what He calls them, accepting His gracious forgiveness, and turning around to head in the right direction.

Humble Heart

*The result of humility is fear of the LORD,
along with wealth, honor, and life. (Prov. 22:4)*

My dad, a quiet, kind, and humble man, retired from middle management twenty years ago. He now works behind the scenes making coffee for the weekly prayer breakfast, serving ice cream to disabled kids, counting money at church. He has never sought the limelight.

When I was in college, a position opened up at his company that would have been a promotion for him. He told his boss he was interested and told him why he was the one for the job. The other two men being considered lobbied hard, even pulling strings in upper management, but Dad refused to go overboard in tooting his own horn. In my college know-it-all-ness, I said, "Dad, you are too humble! If you don't sell yourself, you'll get overlooked in this world."

"They know I'm interested in the job. My record and commitment are solid," he said. "If this is part of God's plan for me, I will trust Him for it. If not, He must have something else in mind."

Dad didn't get the promotion. I was angry at his company and frustrated with him. But Dad was fine, reiterating his faith in God, continually thankful for his job which allowed us to live comfortably. I was grateful, too, but still wished he had played by the world's rules. Now, years later, having grown in my walk with the Lord by watching his, I'm so glad he didn't.

People who don't think they have a problem with pride are the worst offenders because they are blind to it. Yet despite what the world says, we have nothing to be proud of. All we have and are, even the air we breathe, comes from God. A truly humble person focuses on God and others. Jesus, the perfect model of humility, made Himself nothing because He considered us worth saving.

God's Grace

We have all received grace after grace from His fullness. (John 1:16)

Linda and I have been friends for a few years. We go to the same church, we've served on some of the same committees, we're in the same Sunday school class . . .

And she told me she is being baptized this Sunday.

"As a child, I walked the aisle at my church, was baptized, and that was it. I've always felt unsettled about my salvation experience though, and about a month ago the Holy Spirit showed me why. During Pastor Brett's sermon I realized I was trying to save myself," she said.

"What do you mean?" I asked.

"I've tried to make it on my own goodness. I thought if I was good, God would be pleased with me. I never understood grace until that day," she said. "He said Jesus plus anything else does not equal salvation. He said that God's grace is a free gift we cannot earn but can only accept."

That Sunday I watched as Linda was baptized the second time, for all time. And we rejoiced. Heaven rejoiced over Linda that day!

God's grace is a difficult concept to understand because we've been taught that no one gets a free lunch. But Jesus is the only One who can save us from our deep abyss of sin. We don't deserve His grace, and yet He gives it to any of us who will accept it. Completely. Perfectly. Permanently. Salvation is not Jesus plus our church membership. Not Jesus plus our good works. Not Jesus plus our offerings or our service or our prayers. If salvation could be earned, if grace is something we deserve, if we could save ourselves, then we are serving a man-made god, bringing Him down to our level. There would be no reason for Jesus to have died.

Single-minded Service

. . . so that you may be devoted to the Lord without distraction.
(1 Cor. 7:35)

Two years after her divorce, Becky still struggled with loneliness. She kept busy with work, but she still had difficulty making friends at her new church, especially since she wasn't the most outgoing person. She often felt like a fifth wheel, the only single person in a world of married couples.

She had tried a singles Sunday school class but felt awkward. She had even joined a community book club but felt like she didn't fit in. Besides, her job took so much out of her, she only wanted to veg out in front of the TV in the evenings. Still, she did wish she were more connected and not so lonely.

Father, what should I do to connect more with others? Becky prayed. She immediately remembered overhearing a conversation as she walked to the sanctuary last Sunday about how there weren't enough workers in the nursery on Sunday mornings. Serving in the nursery would be something she could do well and a way to get to know others.

If we're honest, many of us think singleness is a curse, not a blessing. Paul, however, had something different to say. He said, "God gives the gift of single life to some. . . . When you're unmarried, you're free to concentrate on simply pleasing the Master" (1 Cor. 7:7, 32 MSG). Regardless of the reason, being single is an opportunity to use your time to serve as God leads you.

Perhaps He is leading you to teach a class, commit to being a prayer warrior, volunteer with a local ministry, or go on a short-term mission trip. Looked at with the right perspective, singleness can be an open door, a state of freedom that offers new opportunities. Ask God to show you how to make the most of it.

A Heavy Heart

He will yet fill your mouth with laughter and your lips
with a shout of joy. (Job 8:21)

When my family first realized I was depressed, I think they were in shock. They had never known me as a person who seemed down. My father would lovingly tell me to stay occupied to "keep your mind off of things," and my mother would patiently listen as I cried to her over the phone. But nothing seemed to help.

I should be able to get over this by myself, I'd think. But I couldn't shake the despair. Even when I took my father's advice and tried to keep myself busy with work and school, I felt dead inside. The only thing that seemed to ease my pain was sleep. So I began to do that—a lot.

My real breakthrough came when I finally realized I needed to see a professional. I sought the help of two different doctors: One was a Christian psychologist who worked with me to get to the root of my problems, and the other was a physician who prescribed medication that helped me feel normal again. I finally found real hope for me.

Depression does not discriminate by race, sex, or religious affiliation. It can be brought on by a stressful event, or it can begin for no apparent reason. Sometimes genetics can even play a role. But let's face it—no one wants to be depressed or suffer from the stigma associated with it. It's a serious illness that doesn't always go away on its own. The symptoms of depression can range from feeling downhearted or despondent to feeling suicidal. If you realize you are depressed, you need to seek help.

Also, remember to call on God. No matter how you may feel, He is with you and wants you to trust in Him. You are not alone.

Dark Secrets

My disgrace is before me all day long,
and shame has covered my face. (Ps. 44:15)

Allison finally gathered the courage to visit a Christian counselor. Once there, she didn't know where to start. The sexual abuse of her childhood, ugly as it was, seemed to belong in a different lifetime. She sometimes even felt as though she had dreamed it. But other times the shame of those dark secrets raised its ugly head with paralyzing ferocity. She was ready to deal with the past once and for all.

"Don't feel you have to tell me everything today," the counselor said when Allison seemed to be searching for where to start. "We're beginning a process that may take us a while, but eventually you'll gain victory over your past." Allison hadn't really considered victory a manageable goal; she had just hoped for coping skills.

"You really think I can get to the point where this doesn't hang over me like a dark cloud?" asked Allison.

"Absolutely," the counselor answered with an encouraging smile. "When you bring what happened in secret out into the open, examine it for what it really was, and allow God to bring healing, Satan can no longer use it to shame and victimize you."

Many of us have things in our past that we hide from others because they bring us such shame. While we don't need to broadcast them, we also don't need to allow those dark secrets to pull us into the shameful shadows they cast. Whether we are victims of another person's sin or responsible for our own rebellion, we can live in the light without fear of condemnation. No matter what you have gone through, God knows and has put all your tears in His bottle (Ps. 56:8).

Hogging the Piggy Bank

My God will supply all your needs according to His riches in glory in Christ Jesus. (Phil. 4:19)

When my son, Bennett, turned six, we started giving him an allowance each week. We soon found out we had a little miser on our hands. Bennett never spent a dime. At first, I was proud of his self-control. But when I asked Bennett what he was saving for, he said, "Nothing. I just want to have a lot of money in my bank." I realized he saw money not as a means to an end but as an end in itself.

"Bennett, remember that God gives us money so we can use it for His glory. He is the One who provides for us, and although saving can be a smart thing to do, having lots of money isn't the most important thing."

Bennett looked thoughtful. "If I spend my money or give it away, I may not get any more."

"Well, that might be," I said. "But we can trust that God will always provide for us. He takes care of us inside and out."

Bennett seemed OK with that. "How 'bout if I use some money to make a shoe box for Operation Christmas Child?"

I smiled. "Tell you what: I'll match however much money you want to spend. Then you can really fill up that shoebox for a child in need."

When we're living and working just for a paycheck, we're not really living the abundant life God promises and desires for us. Money is not for our own personal benefit or satisfaction but to use for God's glory and to help those in need. We must spend and save wisely, making sure our material abundance is also a blessing to others. God is in control, and He promises to meet all our needs according to His glorious riches in Christ Jesus.

I Want

A greedy man is in a hurry for wealth;
he doesn't know that poverty will come to him. (Prov. 28:22)

As a divorced working mom, I try to stick to a budget. But recently when my kids saw all the commercials on TV touting the latest toys and gadgets, they thought they were entitled to whatever their little hearts desired. At ages ten and eight, strong-willed Sarah and master-negotiator Adam were not about to give up one item on their Christmas list without a fight.

Later when I strolled through the mall, I began to feel the same materialism I saw in my kids. *Oh, what a gorgeous purse,* I thought. *And look at that cute pair of peep-toe shoes. I want . . . I want . . .* When I realized that I had been bitten by the greed bug as well, I knew I needed to make some changes.

As a family we decided to give up TV for a while. Instead, we listened to Christmas music, read Bible stories, and talked about the significance of Jesus' birth. We also played board games and invited neighbors over for hot cider and a family-friendly holiday movie. The turning point came when we, along with other members of our church, served Thanksgiving dinner at a homeless shelter. We all began to realize how blessed we are.

Sarah and Adam were shocked to see children their own age in old, worn-out clothing. And when they realized these children would most likely have no gifts for Christmas, they offered to shorten their lists and do extra chores to earn money to buy presents for them.

God's Word says we are to worship Him alone, not stuff made by man. If materialism has reared its ugly head in your life, confess it to God. Then ask Him what steps you need to take to become wholly devoted to Him.

Attitude Check

Those who promote peace have joy. (Prov. 12:20)

Last year when we visited my in-laws for Christmas, my mother-in-law was critical of everything I did. She didn't like the Christmas gifts I chose for her. I didn't prepare the gravy in the correct way. And when our three-year-old daughter had a tiny accident on the carpet, I thought we were going to have to rip it up and rush out to the home center store to replace it.

Since then I've nursed a grudge against my mother-in-law. I feel that I can't do anything right in her eyes. But is my "baditude" right? I know what God would say: He would gently, mercifully say no.

I began spending time on my knees with God about the real heart of the issue. He impressed upon me that my bad attitude—my resentment—toward my mother-in-law could be turned around with His help. He reminded me that we have much in common: the love we share for my husband and for our children. And maybe we are both being sensitive when what we really want is to be friends.

So this Christmas I will be visiting with my in-laws. I'm prayed up, and with God's help I will be kind and loving. I will leave the attitude behind and seek friendship with her in the name of Jesus.

Paul says in Philippians 2:5 to "make your own attitude that of Christ Jesus." But how can we do that when we have an attitude of resentment, bitterness, or just plain grumpiness? We do it by remembering how much Jesus loves us, what He's done for us, and how far He's brought us. And when we ask Him each day to fill our hearts with His love, we can leave the attitude behind.

The Red Purse

Which of you, wanting to build a tower, doesn't first sit down and calculate the cost? (Luke 14:28)

An $80 purse isn't in the budget, Clarissa's conscience nagged as she moved the mouse toward the check-out button. *You and Jeff agreed—no unnecessary purchases.*

"Why did the economy have to turn him into such a tight-wad?" Clarissa whispered to the computer screen. "I work hard for my money. I'll just put this on the credit card and pay the bill before he sees it. I'll let him think I bought the purse with my personal cash. It'll be an early Christmas gift to me from me."

Then she remembered Brenda, whose husband just lost his job unexpectedly. Brenda regretted using her credit card unwisely—the one her husband repeatedly asked her to use for emergencies only. She tearfully admitted at Bible study that her "emergencies" usually involved clothes and lunches with friends.

Clarissa stared at the pretty red purse that matched her Christmas dress perfectly. "God, I'm sorry," she whispered. "Help me be more frugal and respectful of my husband."

Then she smiled. She moved the purse from her Shopping Cart to her Wish List and e-mailed it to Jeff—in case he hadn't bought her Christmas gift yet!

Sins have a way of coming back to bite us. How many times must we be caught in a lie, have our insensitive words get back to the one person who wasn't supposed to hear them, or live to regret going against our spouse's wishes before we learn? Let's not wait until we get ourselves into a mess we can't clean up—a damaged relationship, broken trust, or major consequence—before we see the importance of making the right choice when we get the chance.

A Deadly Affair

The one who commits adultery lacks sense;
whoever does so destroys himself. (Prov. 6:32)

As Karen told her daughter, Jasmine, good-bye and hung up the phone, she couldn't help but feel the heaviness of her past mistake bearing down on her tired shoulders. Could her own adulterous affair, confessed and forgiven sixteen years ago, somehow have made it easier for her adult daughter to choose the same destructive path?

Stirring her coffee absentmindedly and turning the pages of her Bible in search of some sort of comfort, Karen thought about the myriad effects of her forsaken sin. She and Thomas had struggled several years to rebuild their marriage. Her children had heard stories of their mother's infidelity at school and church. And while her pastor had refrained from showing shock or judgment, he had asked her to step down from her leadership roles for a while. Other people in the church had mixed reactions to her confession; and, although most of their friendships had been restored in the years that followed, a few old friends still kept their distance.

Karen located the model in Psalm 51 she had used for confessing her adultery those many years ago. She read the words aloud and prayed that her daughter would soon repent from her own adulterous relationship.

Adultery in particular brings on many deaths—the death of trust, a marriage, children's innocence, reputation, opportunities for ministry, and more. Commit anew to keeping your marriage bed sacred and pure. No new fling, no budding romance, no "interesting and attentive man" is worth so many deaths.

If you are struggling over a sin you have committed, confess it to God, repent, and accept His forgiveness (1 John 1:9).

Missions and More

The Lord has commanded that those who preach the gospel should earn their living by the gospel. (1 Cor. 9:14)

Recently I saw in our church program that the annual missions conference was approaching, and people were needed to host home meetings for individual missionaries. I immediately contacted the missions department to let them know I was willing to help. I figured it would be easy enough to offer hospitality by simply opening my home as a place where missionaries could tell others about their work, but I was dismayed to find out that I would have to do much more than I thought.

Rather than just open my home, I would be responsible for getting the word out, inviting as many people as I could, and educating them about what the missionaries (whom I didn't even know) did. I hadn't counted on such a sacrifice of my time, and I wondered if it was too late to back out. As I talked to God about my predicament, He reminded me that these missionaries needed advocates, and the little I would do to prepare was nothing compared to the sacrifices they made daily.

Later, after the successful home meeting, I was glad I had said yes to God. The missionaries were encouraged, and I learned so much about their ministry and the miracles God was doing through their work around the world. Best of all, I was able to be a part of their work without ever leaving my hometown!

Missionaries rely on the body of Christ to make their work possible. Though supporting them might mean giving up time or money, we're joining God's work in unreached places when we do. Make an effort to find out what God is doing outside your world. You might be surprised by what He asks of you.

Family First

*Don't work only while being watched, in order to please men,
but as slaves of Christ, do God's will from your heart. (Eph. 6:6)*

"I don't know how you do it, Anne," came Marla's voice on the phone. "If I were at home with kids all day, I would go nuts. If I had any kids, that is."

Anne laughed at her old friend. "I do get stressed out sometimes, but I enjoy it too. I believe the Lord wants me to be home with them. And watching them grow and develop is rewarding."

"But what about that ambitious woman I knew in college? Didn't you say you'd always have a career, that you wouldn't let kids slow you down?"

"I didn't know then that being a stay-at-home mom would be the best career move I could ever make."

"Do you think every mom should do that?" Marla asked. "What about moms who have to work to survive?"

"I know a lot of moms have to work. I know others just want a career. And I believe God honors that," Anne said. "All I'm saying is that even if a mom works, she needs to figure out how to keep her family her top priority. She needs to ask the Lord for help with that." She paused, listening to tiny voices rising in the den. "Gotta go. Jeffrey and Katelyn are fighting."

"And you'd rather referee them than climb the corporate ladder?"

"Any day of the week!"

A mother's role is unique and important. Her love, training, and guidance can make her house a home. The way to accomplish that is to put her family at the top of her priorities, right after the Lord. He can give her the discernment she needs to make wise choices customized to fit her particular situation and the needs of her family.

Honor

*Listen to your father who gave you life, and don't
despise your mother when she is old. (Prov. 23:22)*

As Shelly was getting ready to leave, the phone rang. It was her parents' number. "Hi honey," her mom said. "How are you?"

"I'm fine, Mom." Shelly's voice sounded impatient even to her own ears. "I'm on my way out."

"Oh, I'm sorry. It's just that I haven't heard from you lately so I thought I'd call." Shelly rolled her eyes. "We talked yesterday, remember?"

"Oh, that's right. I forgot. So how are you today?"

"Well, I'm busy now," she said, gathering her purse and keys. "I'm going to pick Sam up from school and take him to soccer practice."

"Sam is playing soccer?"

Shelly squeezed the phone in frustration. "We talked about it last week."

Her mom paused before saying, "I'm sorry. I'm getting so forgetful."

Her mom's memory had always been so sharp, but lately it was starting to go. Deep down Shelly was afraid of what these memory lapses could mean, but she was having a hard time being patient with her. As she drove, she prayed, *Lord, she deserves better treatment than what I'm giving her. Forgive me for not trying to understand.*

What does "honor your parents" look like when you are an adult and they are getting older? According to Proverbs, it means listening to them. Being patient when they tell you that story you've heard a hundred times already. Living your life wisely, not making foolish decisions that will bring them heartache. Helping them as they grow older. When we honor our parents, we honor God. He sees and knows and is pleased.

Let Go of Regret

His mercy is from generation to generation on those who fear Him. (Luke 1:50)

One evening my temper got the best of me. "Would you two be quiet? I just can't take your fighting any longer!" I tried to take a deep breath and relax. But my twins' constant bickering was driving me up a wall.

"But it wasn't me," both of them whined.

"STOP!" I yelled. "Just go get ready for bed." My face felt hot, and I could feel my blood pressure rising. I just needed to be alone.

As soon as they left the room, I collapsed into an armchair and started crying. I knew I was letting my anger take over when I tried to discipline my kids, and I regretted the fact that I yelled so often. *Lord,* I quietly prayed, *You know I've been struggling with anger issues. Please help me stop taking out my frustration on the kids. Please help them forgive me for speaking so harshly.*

I opened my Bible to Luke 6:36: "Be merciful, just as your Father also is merciful." Then suddenly something clicked. I realized God was not only telling me to be merciful to my kids but also to receive His mercy for my sin. When we don't focus on anything except what we've done wrong, we aren't focusing on God and His grace, which is never deserved no matter how good we are. The regret we feel can steal the joy that God intended for us to have.

No matter what the sin is, God forgives if you are repentant. "Though your sins are like scarlet, they will be as white as snow; though they are as red as crimson, they will be like wool" (Isa. 1:18). We need to remember that once we repent, God wipes away our sin. He no longer remembers it. We can move on with a clean slate.

Grace for the Broken

The LORD of Hosts says this: Make fair decisions. Show faithful love and compassion to one another. (Zech. 7:9)

Monica tried to focus on the worship leader and think about the lyrics of the hymn, but her eyes continued to stray to the woman at the end of the pew. Monica was certain some of the men around her were also struggling to keep their eyes off the exotic redhead with a plunging neckline, tight, hip-hugging pants, and too much makeup who was swaying to the music. Monica looked at her husband and rolled her eyes.

At the altar call Monica made her way to the front to pray with those who came forward. To her surprise the redhead walked up to her with tears rolling down her cheeks. Monica swallowed hard and took her hand. As she prayed with this new believer and heard about the pain of her father's abandonment, her alcoholic mother, and abuse from her mother's lovers, Monica wept with shame and compassion. This woman needed Jesus' love, not her judgment.

The people who offend us the most are sometimes the most broken and wounded, but often our first reaction is to regard them with disapproval and judgment. The Pharisees did this too when a sinful woman interrupted their dinner with Jesus to cry and anoint His feet with oil. They condemned her, but Jesus had compassion. He saw her heart, not merely her outward looks and actions (Luke 7:36-48).

When someone provokes us, God would have us look beneath the outward offense to the person's heart and pray for them, knowing they are in a battle common to us all. We are all sinful creatures, needing God's forgiveness and grace to find victory over the brokenness in our lives. The next time someone offends you, give them grace just as Jesus would.

We Are Family

If we walk in the light as He Himself is in the light, we have fellowship with one another. (1 John 1:7)

After my husband passed away, I sold our farmhouse and moved into a nearby town. I felt like I was starting out on my own again, alone and a little anxious.

When I visited a church nearby for the first time, I felt like I had come home. The music lifted my spirits, the people were warm and friendly, and the pastor preached the truth of the Word. After the service a sweet, young couple invited me to eat lunch in their home. Over a simple spaghetti lunch, I shared my story with Kelly and Brent and their two young children. Kelly then shared that they had moved to the area just two years prior, and they missed their own families. Before I left, Jamie, the six-year-old, gave me a picture to hang on my refrigerator. It said, "To my new friend!" and had a picture of a rainbow underneath.

Since that first lunch I have shared many meals with my new friends. Brent and Kelly have become like my own children, and they say I'm an "adopted" grandma to their dear children. God provided loved ones nearby when I needed them most, and God is also using me to make a difference in their lives.

God has a special place in His heart for the lonely. Jesus knows the heartache of loneliness and despair—He felt it Himself during His life on earth (John 16:32–33). He understands the depths of our sorrow and doesn't leave us in the midst of it. He is always with us, and He is always for us.

Ask God for eyes to see those who are lonely. Reach out to them with companionship and the love of Christ.

New in Town

The local people showed us extraordinary kindness. (Acts 28:2)

Leaving our home in the Midwest was difficult. We were active in our church and had made a lot of friends there. But my husband, Kevin, had been transferred by his employer, so we made yet another move.

When we arrived at our new location, we quickly found a church that seemed a good fit for our family. The preaching was scriptural and inspiring, and the worship was amazing. After attending for a few weeks, the pastor announced that they were having a monthly fellowship meal after the Sunday morning worship service. We gathered our three children from their respective classes and the nursery and joined several people at a large, round table to eat lunch.

During the meal Kevin and I tried to engage the other people in conversation, but apparently they didn't care to socialize outside their own little group. We felt like intruders. Chalking it up to a random event, we attended the next fellowship meal the following month. This time we sat next to two couples who must have been best friends forever because once again we weren't included in their conversation. Once we introduced ourselves, the couples turned their attention to each other. We felt invisible.

After praying about it, we decided to look for another place to worship. We're pleased with our new church, whose members warmly welcomed us. Because of our previous experience, we're involved in a ministry to newcomers. We know how we felt when we were ignored, and we want people to feel included in the body of Christ.

Next Sunday make a point to reach out to visitors and new members at your church. Make them feel welcome. Ask the Lord to help you notice when someone needs a friend, and be one.

Undivided Attention

*Know that the LORD has set apart the faithful for Himself;
the LORD will hear when I call to Him. (Ps. 4:3)*

My five-year-old grandson and I held hands as we walked toward the park. I treasured these precious moments with him, so I had taken the day off work. When we arrived at the playground, Joey ran toward the slides. He began to climb the ladder, and I stood nearby watching him play.

I overheard a young father who was sitting on a bench. His little girl was twirling around on the jungle gym saying, "Look, Daddy, look!" But he ignored her; he was busy talking on his cell phone.

The little girl continued to try to get her daddy's attention—twirling, running around the playground, and calling, "Look, Daddy, look!" Finally, the man put his hand over his cell phone and snapped, "Be quiet! Can't you see I'm busy?" The girl's head drooped, and she looked down at her shoes. My heart broke for her.

I recalled times when my children were young and I lost my patience because I just wanted some peace and quiet. I prayed for the man and his daughter, that the Lord would heal the hurt and remind the young father how precious and fleeting those moments are.

Today we lead busy lives. We've grown impatient when our children or loved ones seem to continually demand our undivided attention. After all, we're only human. But our loving heavenly Father has all the time in the world to listen to us, whether we're just telling Him about our day or pouring out our hearts to Him over a difficult trial we're going through.

Thank God for loving to hear from us without becoming impatient. And thank God for His ability to listen to all of us at the same time—still giving us His undivided attention.

Worth the Risk

Peter and the apostles replied,
"We must obey God rather than men." (Acts 5:29)

For the second time that weekend, Kelly heard the medicine cabinet open and shut before her daughter RaeAnne's friend Bekka emerged from the bathroom. Bekka's sheepish expression intensified Kelly's concern. Kelly slipped into the bathroom and opened the cabinet. What could Bekka be looking for among the floss, cosmetics, and skin cleansers? Then she spotted a small prescription bottle. *Oh no, I never threw away the pain killers from RaeAnne's appendicitis attack.*

Kelly grabbed the bottle and opened it, recalling the few that RaeAnne had actually taken after her surgery. The bottle was half empty. Had Bekka taken them?

God, what should I do? Kelly knew she needed to confront Bekka and possibly even RaeAnne, then talk to Bekka's parents. Kelly thought, *Whether I'm right or wrong, this could tear a friendship apart. Not to mention how this will affect my relationship with RaeAnne.* But if something happened and she'd kept quiet . . .

Several minutes later she knocked on her daughter's bedroom door. "Bekka, can I talk with you privately please?"

Why can't doing the right thing guarantee a storybook ending where everyone involved is grateful for our wisdom and courage? Instead it often involves confrontation and unpopular decisions that cost us treasured relationships. So we keep quiet instead of speaking up, cover up the truth, and do whatever is needed to keep peace.

Scripture is filled with men and women who chose the difficult road regardless of the cost. Their examples reveal that our choices often reflect the loyalty of our hearts. Are we more concerned with what people think or what God wants from us?

Redeeming the Pain

Let your widows trust in Me. (Jer. 49:11)

As Cheryl listened to the young mother's story, her heart went out to her. Her church was sponsoring a women's event, and she had decided to attend the workshop called "When Life Hurts." The leader asked attendees for brief responses to the question, How has life hurt you? A young mom tearfully answered, "A few weeks ago my husband was killed on the job. We have three children, and I don't understand why God allowed this to happen."

Cheryl knew immediately why God had led her to this class. Her own past loss and circumstances mirrored this young mother's current trial. As soon as the class ended, she approached her and introduced herself. The widow's name was Tammy.

"Tammy, my husband also died unexpectedly when my children were young. I'd love to spend some time with you and find out how you're doing. I can also share how God carried me through those sad, hard days. Maybe we can get together sometime soon."

The death of a spouse is a shattering loss. When young children are also left fatherless, a mother's healthy grieving is often complicated by increased responsibilities, urgent decisions, and the need to cope with parenting under pressure. Wrestling with God's will and purposes is a normal part of the process.

For a young widow the gift of loving friendships and a supportive family can make all the difference in a gradual and healthy recovery toward a hope-filled future. But the greatest resource of all is knowing that widows have God's attention. He is not offended by their questions and will bring comfort in the pain. And when the healing has happened, God can use us to speak His hope to others.

Church Matters

Let us be concerned about one another in order to promote love and good works, not staying away from our worship meetings. (Heb. 10:24–25)

When Tina was young, her entire family attended church faithfully until the death of her uncle. Because he took his own life, some church members responded with condemnation instead of comfort, and her mom left the church. Eventually her dad also left the church, and alcohol became the drug of choice in their home.

She had trusted Christ as a young girl and sometimes attended church alone, but it was difficult. Sibling relationships became more dysfunctional through the years also. She eventually married, but that relationship, too, became rocky. Finally, when her daughters were born, she knew she needed God and a church family if she was to parent well and build a strong marriage.

"Since returning to church," she says, "God is growing me and using me. He has even brought healing to some of my childhood hurts. I am so thankful for the body of Christ."

While we are all flawed and in need of grace, God established the church for His purposes to encourage one another and to share Jesus with the world. For our maturity and His service, we are to function together, not alone.

Consider these truths about the church: (1) Following his conversion, Paul spent his entire life establishing, equipping, and encouraging churches. (2) Revelation is a book of letters to the churches. (3) Jesus "loved the church and gave Himself for her" (Eph. 5:25).

No one denies that the church, made up of fallible people, can be a source of hurt and failure. It can also be a place of great growth, healing, and redemption. It is never wise to separate from our brothers and sisters in Christ. We are family.

The Invisible Ones

The eye of the LORD is on those who fear Him—
those who depend on His faithful love. (Ps. 33:18)

Last year Sam and I divorced after I discovered his affairs. He wasn't honest with people at church, either, about his adultery and instead placed the blame on me. Suddenly I was the bad guy. People who didn't even know me—or the truth—told me I should take Sam back. They said hurtful things. They didn't see my pain.

Before the divorce we sometimes went to lunch after church with other couples. But now I felt that those friends acted like my toddler, Bella, and I didn't exist. When I picked her up from class, I heard other families making plans together. *Lord, am I invisible? Don't they see me?*

When I needed them most, my church let me down. If I had not had a strong faith in Jesus, I might have left the Christian faith. But I found a new church where I'm now involved in the divorce-recovery/single-parent ministry. God is using me to comfort those who are hurting and abandoned by their spouses to help them see that they are not invisible.

With divorce the layers of loss go deep. One of these losses is a sense of identity. No longer are you a married person—and in church culture, if you aren't married, you are often an afterthought. When you're excluded even at church, the pain and loss you already feel are intensified.

Reach out to single parents and divorced people at your church. Ask them to sit with you and your family. Invite them to lunch. Show the love of Christ by your actions.

No matter who we are or what we've been through, we are not invisible to God. He sees and knows all we deal with. He shares our pain and wipes our tears. His love never fails.

Contentment at Christmas

If we have food and clothing,
we will be content with these. (1 Tim. 6:8)

I have always loved the beauty of the Christmas season. As a child, I was a little disappointed that our house didn't look like the gorgeously decorated homes in magazines. We didn't have big, fluffy garlands with gold accents. Our tree was small, and all the ornaments that had been collected over the years were mismatched. When I grew up and started my own traditions with my family, I was determined to have *Southern Living* Christmases. Containers full of decorations soon lined our garage wall.

Last Christmas, however, was different. Service commitments along with raising a strong-willed toddler were maxing out my time and energy. Just looking at the containers in the garage exhausted me. So I decided just to decorate the tree and put up our nativity set. No garland on the banister. No lights on the columns. No knickknacks scattered around the house. Then my in-laws suggested that we not exchange gifts with them, drastically reducing my shopping time and budget.

Once my commitments ended in mid-December, I used the time I would have spent shopping and decorating to focus on celebrating Christ's birth. Christmas was made lovely with prayer and drawing near to the God who drew near to us. It was made bright by attending special worship services with my family, reading the Christmas story, and rejoicing in song. I found I didn't need all the decorations and gifts. I did less; yet it was the most meaningful Christmas I can remember.

Contentment is never a more elusive state in our culture than at Christmas. There's nothing wrong with decorating and giving gifts during the holidays. But if your well-meaning holiday to-do list has worn you down, you may want to simplify.

The Carousel

I am churning within and cannot rest. (Job 30:27)

One Saturday while I was Christmas shopping at the mall, I paused briefly to watch the children on the carousel near the food court. Most of them seemed to be having a good time, but one young girl began to cry. "Make it stop, Mommy! It's too fast!" Frightened by the movement and speed of the carousel, the little girl clung to her mother until both could safely exit the ride.

As I continued my quest for the perfect gifts, throngs of shoppers clogged the aisles, and I grew impatient trying to pass everyone who wasn't in as much of a hurry as I was. Couldn't they speed up their pace? As a single working mom, I only had evenings and weekends to shop.

Then as I fumed over a slow-moving elderly woman and her younger companion, the Lord spoke to me. *Why are you always in such a hurry? I give you twenty-four hours in each day, just like I give everyone else. Trust Me with your schedule. I can meet your needs.*

Suddenly I felt like the little girl on the carousel that was spinning too fast to get off. Between working full-time, being a single mom, and trying to hold everything together, I was exhausted. A typical dinner consisted of burgers and fries we wolfed down on the way home from sports practices at night. I realized that my life was out of control, and I knew the only solution was to submit to the Lord and follow His lead.

The pace of life today can be hectic for all of us, and sometimes it gets out of balance. But Jesus wants us to have peace. In John 14:27, He said, "Peace I leave with you. My peace I give to you. I do not give to you as the world gives. Your heart must not be troubled or fearful."

The Giveaway

By this all people will know that you are My disciples, if you have love for one another. (John 13:35)

Each year our Sunday school class "adopts" a needy family for Christmas. Class members donate money, and we help a family assigned to us by our local community charity. The members of our adopted family list a few of their needs and a few of their wants.

This year, though, a family in our own church had fallen on difficult times. The husband, Dave, lost his job earlier in the year and hadn't been able to find another one. His wife, Jen, worked part-time, and they had two children. We knew they were having a tough time financially and were facing a bleak Christmas.

Our class decided to anonymously adopt this family for Christmas. Because Dave and Jen weren't in our class, we could freely discuss the issue and collect the money without embarrassing them. We decided to give them a cash gift so they could apply the money to their greatest need.

When the collection period was over, we asked our church secretary, Judy, to give Dave and Jen the gift, telling them it was from an anonymous donor. Judy said when she gave them the envelope Jen's eyes filled with tears. "Please thank them," Jen whispered, smiling through her tears. "We are so grateful."

Jesus tells us that whatever we do in His name—small deeds or large, a cup of cold water or something to eat—we are doing it for Him. And though our gifts may be small, God will be pleased with the heart behind what we give away. Jesus said that a watching world will know that we belong to Him and that we are His disciples by the love we show for one another (see John 13:35).

Not Home for Christmas

*God is my witness, how deeply I miss all of you
with the affection of Christ Jesus. (Phil. 1:8)*

I felt so silly, crying over a familiar Christmas song. But I couldn't help it. Blame it on a tear-jerker arrangement of "I'll be Home for Christmas." As if the young singer's gorgeous baritone voice wasn't enough to melt hearts, moms and dads serving in the military spoke in the background, sending Merry Christmas messages to their families at home. Then kids chimed in with their own greetings.

"Hi Daddy. We're getting ready to open presents. We miss you. Merry Christmas, everybody."

And I lost it. How many kids wouldn't decorate their Christmas tree with Mom or hand Daddy his gifts? The unfairness of it all sent tears dripping into the dinner I was preparing. I wiped my eyes before my sons and husband noticed.

It's OK to be sad for them, I sensed God saying. *But why don't you also pray for them?* So as I dabbed at my eyes, I prayed for the families represented in the song. A moment of what felt like holiday sappiness turned into a time for remembering those who, unlike me, wouldn't have everyone home for Christmas.

Traditionally Christmas is a family time. As we are preparing festive meals, baking cookies, and dusting off our copies of *It's a Wonderful Life*, it's easy to forget those whose husbands, sons, wives, or mothers are halfway around the world serving in the military.

Paul wanted desperately to be with his friends and fellow believers. His loneliness comes through in his letters and written prayers, along with the evidence that he also drew strength from the prayers and support they sent his way. His words can remind us that prayers make a difference, even for those we will never meet.

Blended Christmas

May there be peace within your walls. (Ps. 122:7)

Last Christmas was our first as a blended family. Figuring out holiday visitation for our three kids required a spreadsheet and countless e-mails. According to the schedules Bill and I had arranged with our ex-spouses, Abby would be with us on Christmas Eve but would leave at noon on Christmas. Bill's kids would come home Christmas morning. That gave us only from nine until noon for all of us to be together. Bill and I asked our ex-spouses to switch the schedule, but they wouldn't.

I wanted our three hours to be absolutely perfect, but that didn't happen.

Abby woke during the night with a stomach bug. She and I were up several times. Bill's ex-wife brought Scott and Missy an hour late. They were grouchy. Abby opened gifts with us, then went back to bed. When we sat down to brunch, I was exhausted.

Abby's dad didn't believe my text message that she was sick until he saw her. "You'll feel better when you open gifts at our house," he said. She sighed, hugged me, and left. I wanted her to stay and worried she would throw up in her dad's car (he would yell and make her feel worse).

And so it went.

Blended families have a tough road to travel. The holidays make their lives even more complicated: Who goes to which parent's (or grandparent's) house when? When will the family be together? Will everyone get along?

One way to bring everyone together is to start new traditions, whether it's having an Advent wreath or taking food and toys to families in need. New traditions help strengthen fragile bonds. And, even more so, praying for and encouraging blended families helps strengthen them. Whom can you reach out and help this Christmas and next year?

The Empty Space

*He went away grieving, because he
had many possessions. (Matt. 19:22)*

Last year our two sons, Parker and Tyler, received every gift imaginable for Christmas. Mark and I went overboard and purchased too many gifts, and so did his parents, my parents, and all of our siblings.

On Christmas day the family room was filled with empty boxes, crumpled wrapping paper, dozens of toys, electronics, and other items. The boys were practically in a stupor after the last gift was opened. Parker threw his hands up in frustration, and with all the strength the seven-year-old could muster, he cried, "Is this all there is? Where's my monster truck?"

Needless to say, Mark and I were mortified in front of our families and appalled at the greed and ingratitude we saw in our son.

This year we have decided to do things differently. We gathered gently used clothing and toys we no longer used and took them to our church. Later we helped distribute them to the poor. The boys helped us, so they have a better sense of how much we have and how little others have. We made a decision to limit our Christmas presents to two for each person. We have enlisted our families' cooperation, and they have agreed to reasonable limits on gifts this year.

Mark and I want to teach our children that Christmas isn't all about getting as many gifts as possible. It is about the birth of our Lord and Savior, Jesus Christ.

From the moment we're born, we have a tendency toward greed. Left to our own devices, we would be totally self-absorbed, and our culture is geared to reinforce that selfishness. But God's kingdom is upside down from the world's system. Material goods do not satisfy—only God can fill that empty space inside of us.

Walk through Bethlehem

Glory to God in the highest heaven,
and peace on earth to people He favors! (Luke 2:14)

Last Christmas, I took a walk through Bethlehem.

I was a chaperone for my daughter's third-grade Christian school field trip to a local church. The church had constructed a Bethlehem marketplace to tell the Christmas story.

As we approached the gate, we had to register for Caesar's census and were given shekels to pay our taxes. Roman soldiers were posted to ensure that we were orderly. Pharisees tried to outdo one another in the volume of their prayers. One of our boys pretended to take a huge bite out of a fish hanging in a booth. A merchant offered to let us smell some spices, another merchant offered fig samples, and yet another gave us a basket-weaving lesson. We watched carpenters and bread makers, sheep and camels.

We rounded a corner, and there it was. The main event. The reason we came. The stable with Mary, Joseph, and baby Jesus, an angel, a star, shepherds, wise men, and animals. The children stopped in their tracks. No running. No playing. The adults stopped their talking and laughing. The world stood still as we looked in awe at the beautiful scene before us, remembering and picturing the story of our rescue. The shepherds, rough and dirty, knelt before the baby. The wise men brought gifts fit for a king.

Baby Jesus yawned and stretched, the animals began to "baa," and "O Holy Night" played over the loudspeakers. And because of that Baby born two thousand years ago, my soul felt its worth.

Take a walk yourself through Bethlehem until you see King Jesus. Kneel before Him and revel in Immanuel—"God with us!"

The Longing

*Let's go straight to Bethlehem
and see what has happened. (Luke 2:15)*

The girls tore into their presents with squeals of delight. And after everything was unwrapped, we had our special Christmas morning breakfast. Then everyone enjoyed a little free time before we went to my parents' house to celebrate some more.

That's when I felt it: the Christmas Day ache. Have you ever felt it? After weeks of secrets and excitement, decorating and baking, shopping and planning, a tiny spark of wanting. It wasn't about the presents I got or didn't get. Instead, the glitter of the season, the high expectations set by advertisers, the music, the get-togethers with family and friends all combined to leave me with "the longing."

This year I let the longing lead me to worship the Baby in the manger, just as the shepherds did so long ago. In Luke 2:15, after the angels made their stunning appearance and shared the glorious news of the birth, the shepherds said to themselves: "Let's go . . . and see." After they found Jesus and worshipped Him, they went into the village and told everyone what they had seen.

And so, like the shepherds, He bids me: Go and see. Go and tell. This time I will go to the manger and see; then I will go and tell of the best Christmas Gift of all. "And all who heard . . . were amazed" (Luke 2:18).

Real love isn't found gift-wrapped with a bow. Real joy isn't found in stuff from a store. Real peace isn't found in the glitter and sparkle of the season. All of these things leave us wanting. Instead, our pangs of longing, our ache for real love, peace, and joy are satisfied only in Jesus. Let your Christmas longings bring you to the Baby in the manger. Go and see. Then go and tell.

While We Wait

I will wait for the LORD, who is hiding His face from the house of Jacob. I will wait for Him. (Isa. 8:17)

"Honey, what's wrong?" Scott asked when he saw Jennifer crying.

"I'm just frustrated that we can't seem to get pregnant. We've been trying for such a long time, but God still hasn't answered our prayers." Jennifer wiped her eyes. "It's just not fair! One of the women at work says if she gets pregnant, she'll have an abortion. But I'd give anything to have a baby. I feel like God isn't listening."

Scott held Jennifer and said, "You know I want a baby just as much as you do, right?"

"I know," Jennifer said. "But should we even bother to keep praying about it? It's been four years now and still no baby."

"The Bible says we need to be patient," Scott said, "to wait on God's timing and to trust Him. Let's keep praying, knowing that God hears our prayers even when we feel like He's not listening. God may want to grow our family through adoption. Why don't we ask Him?"

Jennifer nodded. "You're right. God may answer our prayers in a different way than we expected."

Sometimes God answers prayers almost before the request has left our lips. But other times we may feel He is ignoring them. Or maybe His answer is *no*, or we don't hear Him, or we just don't feel He's responding. But don't ever stop praying. God does listen to all of our prayers and answers them in His own time and in His own way.

Sometimes the answer to your prayer may look different from what you were expecting. But God knows our hearts, and He knows what each of us needs in our lives so we can fulfill His purpose for us and impact others for His kingdom.

What Can You Do?

*This is the message you have heard from the beginning:
We should love one another. (1 John 3:11)*

My cell phone chimed with my best friend's special ring tone, and before I could say anything, I heard the anguish in Lisa's voice. "Sarah," Lisa sobbed, "Sean's been hit by a car, and the doctors don't know if he's going to make it. I'm at the hospital. Can you please come?"

"I'll be right there. I'm going to be praying for all of you," I said.

"Sarah, I've got to go. The doctor is coming." She hung up the phone before I could reply. A parent's worst nightmare, and it was happening to my best friend and her beautiful little boy. I grabbed my purse and keys and ran out of the house.

Twenty minutes later I arrived at the hospital. When I saw Lisa, her response made it clear—Sean was already gone. The tears began pouring down my cheeks. *God, why did You allow this? Please help me know how I can minister to Lisa and her family.*

We live in a fallen world where bad things happen. But our God is the One who created the heavens and the earth. He created you and me. He knows every breath we'll ever take. He also created us to love one another and to minister to people when they are hurting.

Hebrews 13:1 sums up how God wants us to treat those in need: "Let brotherly love continue." It could be something simple like making a phone call to someone who is lonely or something much more difficult like helping a friend through a divorce or the death of a loved one. No matter what kind of circumstances we find ourselves in, we can show God's neverending love to others simply by praying and asking God, *What can I do? How should I pray for them?*

What If?

I have told you these things so that in Me you may have peace.
You will have suffering in this world. Be courageous!
I have conquered the world. (John 16:33)

Have you ever had a fear so deep that it nearly consumed every waking moment? I've had many, and even though my fears aren't always rational, they still take their toll on both my mind and body.

Having a panic attack is a different experience for each individual. For me it includes shortness of breath, a feeling of not being in my body, and having thoughts of losing control. These attacks have robbed me of many precious moments, and although I haven't overcome them completely, I am learning to trust God more.

My most recent anxiety was due to the fact that I was anticipating a three-hour drive to visit my family. I kept reminding myself that it was only three hours and I'd driven it dozens of times over the past four years. But still the nagging thoughts plagued me. *What if the car breaks down? What if I start panicking and can't take care of the kids? What if, what if, what if . . . ?* I gave myself a mental shake and prayed that God would help me trust in Him.

Before I got in the car, I prayed, *Father, please give me peace about this trip. I know You are always with me whether I feel Your presence or not. Help me guard my mind from negative thinking and to focus on You and Your amazing love for me.*

Persistent anxiety and frequent panic attacks can be frustrating problems, but believers have hope. God knows your needs. If you trust Him, you can know that God is most definitely big enough and strong enough to handle anything you might be facing.

Kindness of a Stranger

A Samaritan on his journey came up to him, and when he saw the man, he had compassion. (Luke 10:33)

I was thirty-nine weeks pregnant with our first child. A friend had offered to lend me her fancy car seat to use in my husband's car. Knowing I would be too tired and busy to make the trek to her house after the baby was born, I decided to make a "quick" trip to get the seat.

But the trip wasn't quick. I had an accident. I turned too quickly in front of an oncoming car, misjudging a blind hill. I drove off the road; my left front tire exploded.

This was before cell phones were so common. I was on a two-lane country road about three miles from my friend's home. I stood in the road, tearfully examining the wrecked tire, wondering what to do. Several cars passed by until finally a woman stopped to help me. And because God is a loving Father, my rescuer that day was a labor and delivery nurse at a local hospital. Her own children were with her in the car. She drove me to my friend's house where I called my husband.

I was so shaken that I only got her first name. Many times over the years I have attempted to search her out, but I've been unable to find her. She was a good Samaritan, showing God's kindness and taking time out of her day to take care of a stranger. And while I don't recommend getting in a car with someone you don't know, I'll never forget how Jesus reminded me that day that He is always looking after me.

Make kindness a daily habit. Reach out with encouraging words, a helping hand, a listening ear. We may never know until we get to heaven how an act of kindness done here on earth will reverberate into eternity.

Trustworthy and True

Nothing will be impossible with God. (Luke 1:37)

Ever since we decided to put our house on the market, I had spent all my spare time making it look like a family of five didn't live there. All the personal touches were gone, all the family photos were taken down, all the baby gear was put away. However, I was doubtful that any of this would work toward getting an offer. I had little hope that we would be able to attract a buyer quickly.

My husband had received an appealing job offer from a business in another state, and after much prayer and deliberation, we felt God was opening a door for us and affirming this move. But I wasn't sure how we would sell our house. I didn't know how we would manage two payments if it didn't sell quickly. I loaded the kids in the van and headed to the park so the agent could show the house to our first interested buyer.

While pushing the baby on the swing, my cell phone rang. My jaw dropped when the agent said the client was ready to make an offer on the house and they would draw up the paperwork immediately. Instantly, my heart lifted up a prayer: *Lord, You are so trustworthy. I should have known that You would make a way for us—beyond what I could ask for. You are so good to care about the details of my life. Thank You for taking care of us.*

When circumstances would have us believe our situation is hopeless, God shows us otherwise. He is in the business of overcoming the impossible. God made a way for salvation by providing His one and only Son. How much more can we trust Him in little things because we know He has taken care of our biggest need—the need for a Savior.

A Difference Maker

I know your works—your love, faithfulness, service, and endurance. (Rev. 2:19)

I have never known a more servant-hearted person than Shirley. She has served the Lord, her church, and her family in ways uncounted and often unobserved. She does the laundry for our church's preschool area, from doll clothes to baby bibs, from towels used to wipe off the wet sliding board to smocks worn in the newborn nursery. She helps with Vacation Bible School and children's church. She served on our pastor search committee. She has rocked babies and wiped preschoolers' noses. She never forgets to send birthday and anniversary cards. She holds people up in prayer and is the first to hug you when you are hurting.

One of the most beautiful things I've seen Shirley do is a ministry to the children of a nearby apartment complex. Every week she and a few other volunteers meet the children in the apartment's clubhouse after school. For the next two hours, Shirley gives the children a snack, reads them a Bible story, and helps them with a craft. They sing songs and play games, all while learning about Jesus. The children are from low-income families, and some can't speak English very well, but their little faces light up when they see Shirley every Thursday.

We all want to leave a legacy of faith and to have kingdom impact while we are here. Ask the Lord how you can do that. He has special ways He has gifted you to make that impact on your community and your world. One on one, life on life, we can make a difference for eternity. By serving others, we bring honor and glory to the Lord. So do all you can. Pray. Love. Volunteer. Give. Be the hands and feet of Jesus.

About Walk Thru

the Bible

For more than three decades, Walk Thru the Bible has been dedicated to igniting a passion for God's Word worldwide through live events, devotional magazines, and resources designed for both small groups and individual use. Known for innovative methods and high-quality resources, we serve the whole body of Christ across denominational, cultural, and national lines.

Walk Thru the Bible communicates the truths of God's Word in a way that makes the Bible readily accessible to anyone. We are committed to developing user-friendly resources that are Bible centered, of excellent quality, life changing for individuals, and catalytic for churches, ministries, and movements; and we are committed to maintaining our global reach through strategic partnerships while adhering to the highest levels of integrity in all we do.

Walk Thru the Bible partners with the local church worldwide to fulfill its mission, helping people "walk thru" the Bible with greater clarity and understanding. Live events and small group curricula are taught in over 45 languages by more than 30,000 instructors in more than 100 countries, and more than 100 million devotionals have been packaged into daily magazines, books, and other publications that reach over 5 million people each year.

Walk Thru the Bible
www.walkthru.org
1-800-361-6131

Notes

Notes

Notes

Notes

Notes

Notes

Notes

Notes

Notes